GLENVIEW PUBLIC LIBRARY

W9-ABO-283

Poor Condition ✓
Marks/Stains ✓
GVK Date 2-22-18

I'M
WITH
THE BAND
♥

I'M WITH THE BAND

♥

Confessions of a Groupie

Pamela Des Barres

Glenview Public Library
1930 Glenview Road
Glenview, Illinois

BEECH TREE BOOKS
WILLIAM MORROW
New York

Copyright © 1987 by Pamela Des Barres
Permissions, constituting a continuation of the copyright page, are listed on
pages 303–304.

All rights reserved. No part of this book may be reproduced or utilized in
any form or by any means, electronic or mechanical, including photo-
copying, recording or by any information storage and retrieval system, without permission in writing from the Publisher. Inquiries should be addressed
to Permissions Department, Beech Tree Books, William Morrow and Company, Inc., 105 Madison Ave., New York, N.Y. 10016.

Library of Congress Cataloging-in-Publication Data

Des Barres, Pamela.
   I'm with the band.
   1. Des Barres, Pamela. 2. Groupies—United States—
Biography. 3. Title.
ML429.D86A3   1987   784.5′4′00924 [B]   87-1570
ISBN 0-688-06602-X

Printed in the United States of America

5 6 7 8 9 10

BOOK DESIGN BY RICHARD ORIOLO

BTB

The word "book" is said to derive from boka, or beech.
The beech tree has been the patron tree of writers since ancient times and
represents the flowering of literature and knowledge.

To my husband,
Michael Des Barres, who loves me for who
I am and who
I was

ACKNOWLEDGMENTS

Heartfelt thank yous to my sweet mom for having the love and patience of a saint, and for not squelching my soul; and to my dear departed daddy for inspiring me always to dig for the gold.

Intense appreciation goes out to C. Thomas (my Cleveland High School creative writing teacher), Don Van Vliet, Vito Paulekas, Bob Dylan, The Fab Four, the late Gram Parsons, the late Brandon de Wilde, Frank and Gail Zappa, and Chuck Wein —for altering my priorities.

Adoration abounds for my divine girlfriends who hold me up and calm me down: Melanie Griffith, Joyce Hyser, Catherine James, Denise Kaye, Rona Levitan, Mercy, Sheri Rivera, Iva Turner, and the ever-present Mrs. Zappa.

Merci beaucoup to my darling Patti D'Arbanville for the perfect title.

Special love to Michele Myer.

Beyond space and time—Danny Goldberg.

Thank you, Stephen Davis, for the encouragement; and thanks to Ron Bernstein, Bill Dana, Ben Edmonds, and Mel Berger.

A massive and abundant thankyouthankyouthankyou to Jim Landis and Jane Meara for "being here now."

XXX
OOO

CONTENTS

I'M
WITH
THE BAND

♥

1

♥

LET ME PUT IT IN,
IT FEELS ALL RIGHT

I get shivers whenever I see those old black-and-white films of Elvis getting shorn for Uncle Sam. When he rubs his hand over the stubs of his former blue-black mane, I get a twinge in my temples. In the glorious year of 1960, I was at the Reseda Theater with my parents, and I saw the famous army footage before the onslaught of *Psycho*. I don't know which was more horrifying. I hung on to my daddy's neck and inhaled the comforting familiarity of his drugstore aftershave and peeked through my fingers as Norman Bates did his dirty work, and the army barber did his. I tried to believe that Elvis was doing his duty as an AMERICAN, but even at eleven years old, I realized his raunch had been considerably diminished. I tacked my five-and-dime calendar onto the dining-room wall and drew big X's as each day passed, knowing he would let his hair grow long when he came home from Germany. Being an adored only child, my mom let me keep the eyesore on the wall for two years. I was always allowed to carry out my fantasies to the tingling end, and I somehow survived several bouts of temporary omnipotence.

All my girlfriends had siblings they had to share with, and since I had two rooms of my own, my house was where everyone wanted to bring their Barbie dolls. I ruled the neighborhood until I entered Northridge Junior High. It turned out to be the real world, and was I surprised! My lack of breasts took precedence over my grades, and actual real-live boys loomed before me, loping around, too tall for their own good. I wanted to make my parents happy and get an A in Home Economics, but boys and rock and roll had altered my priorities.

I was always in awe of my big, gorgeous daddy. He looked just like Clark Gable, and disappeared on weekends to dig for gold way down deep in Mexico. He had always wanted to strike it rich, so right before I was born, he and my mom left Pond Creek, Kentucky, heading for gold country, which allowed me to come into the world as a California native. We lived right off Sunset and Vine, in a dinky little hut on Selma Avenue, and after a series of unilluminating vacuum-salesman–type jobs, my daddy made his way farther west into the wild shrubbery of the San Fernando Valley suburbs, to seek his meager fortune bottling Budweiser. He splurged out and bought his very own cream-colored Cadillac that he paid for in seventy-two monthly installments, and we lived in the same split-level for twelve years, so I felt very secure. I had two parents, a dog, a cat, a parakeet named Buttons, and three good meals a day. In my early years, my sweet mom made sure that my wild daddy came across as a tame, devoted father-figure, but no matter how much she buffered and suffered, it couldn't alter the fact that he was from the Old South, and I was from the New West.

* * *

Two incidents occurred when I was fourteen that had a profound effect on my life. The first was when my dad relented and let me remove the wisps of hair from my very thin legs (he *did not*, however, let me place the Lady Schick *above* the knee), and I had a moment of independence alone in the pink-tiled bathroom that will never be equalled for as long as I live, squirting a pool of Jergens into my palm and slathering it all over my hairless, shining Barbie-doll calves. Compared to getting my period, the first shave initiated me into the elementary stage of womanhood with a much more exciting sense of adventure . . . going forth into the world with no hair on my calves—Life, Liberty, and the Pursuit of Happiness! The second incident involved a stolen car, a bad boy, and the song "He's a Rebel." Dennis MacCorkell was the slump-shouldered, shuffling, cigarette-dangling, pit-faced bad boy found in most junior high schools in 1962. He would shout to me whenever we passed in the hall, "Hey! No Underwear!!" I took it as an endearment and blushed appropriately. He had the same seat in his homeroom that I had in Biology I, and one Friday morning I found "No Underwear" carved into the table. I hoped it was a secret message of adoration, even though he was going steady with a tough Chicano girl named Jackie. Over the weekend, Dennis and two other bad boys from another school stole a car and smashed it to pieces and they all went straight to Teen Angel heaven. Jackie came directly to school so we could all see her suffer. She was wearing a black tulle veil, and her friends held her up all day as she staggered from class to class. She broke down during Nutrition, and every girl in school secretly wished that Dennis MacCorkell had been her boyfriend. "He's a Rebel" became associated with Dennis, and rebellion turned into infamy in my teenage mind. Twenty years later, my mom was cleaning out her drawers and came across a little box with a dead rose tucked inside, and a slip of paper cut out of my 1962 yearbook: "Hey, No Underwear, good luck with the boys, Dennis MacCorkell."

Nobody ever forgot Dennis MacCorkell at Northridge Junior High.

"He's a rebel, and he'll never ever be any good, he's a rebel and he never ever does what he should . . . and just because he doesn't do what everybody else does, that's no reason why I can't give him all my love."

I began to associate the Top 10 with events and boys of the moment. My transistor became an appendage, the goopy-haired heroes crooning in my ear became all the boys who ignored me during "I Pledge Allegiance to the Flag." Lyrics were taken seriously. I walked in the rain, crying, listening to "Crying in the Rain" by the perfect-haired Everly Brothers, imagining that I had just broken up with Phil "Caveman" Caruso, the Italian hunk in my Creative Writing class. When Vance Branco didn't show up for my backyard luau, I joined Leslie Gore for the chorus, "It's my party and I'll cry if I want to, cry if I want to, DIE if I want to . . ." I stood by the screen door in a real honest-to-God grass skirt that my daddy brought back from Okinawa, fiddling with my fake lei while all of my guests twisted the night away . . . "You would cry too, if it happened to you."

Although I bought Bobby Vee records and wanted to put my head on Paul Anka's shoulder, I counted the minutes and seconds until Dion DiMucci, suave and greasy, wearing a shiny sharkskin suit, came gliding into my living room via *American Bandstand*, admitted by Uncle Dick Clark.

> **May 9, 1962, Dear Diary . . . DION!!! Oh Help!!! I'm so excited, I think I'll just DIE!!! I was runnin' around, chokin' and cryin' and yellin' and screamin'. wow wow cute cute CUTE!! you woulda died how he said "dum didla dum didla dum didla dum." I was rolling over inside, I was cryin', I love him so much . . .**

I would sit cross-legged on the floor in front of our big blond box, dribbling tears of teen love into my Pop Tart while my mom looked on, shaking her head in amazement the way moms do. I had a shrine to Dion on my dresser, and I wore a locket around my neck with his picture clipped from *16* magazine and swooned over his slippery, sexy cool. It broke my heart when he married Sue Butterfield. I guess he was just pissed off at her when he wrote "Runaround Sue."

* * *

I was truly boy crazy. My first boyfriend happened in the eighth grade. Darrell Arena was a half-semester behind me, but he made up for it with a shiny, hairless, muscular chest that I gazed at while we swam in his big Canoga Park swimming pool. The most we ever did was kiss without tongues up in his maple bunk bed.

May 28 . . . When he put his musclie arm around me, I died!! I hope it's not dumb to put your arm around a boy when he has his arm around you. Wow, he has a build and a half. If I don't see him tomorrow, I'll croak

Darrell rode show horses, and his mom would pick me up in the family Buick so I could be present when he trotted by in his sateen horse-show outfit and pointy-toed boots with spurs. He would smile down at me from lofty horsey heights, and I was in giddyup awe of my very own boyfriend. I wore his big baseball jacket to school, and took deep whiffs of it constantly. After so much dreaming about being near male flesh, just to breathe the male scent brought me to a near faint.

The summer of '62 was about to heat up to a rolling boil. Rock and roll became flesh and bones when the Rainbow Rockers started to rehearse in the garage directly across the street from my house. Jamieson Avenue became a danger zone. I didn't think anymore about Darrell Arena, or any of the other ordinary schoolboys at Northridge Junior High who were barely starting to shave. Breathing, sweating MEN, with shiny black pompadours and guitars, were playing rock and roll right outside my bedroom window!! Never having heard a band tune up before, I was jolted awake one July morning by disjointed twanging and an amplified voice: "Test . . . testing . . . one . . . two . . . one . . . two . . ." I ran out to the front yard and leaned against the chain link fence in disbelief. A neon-green sunflaked '58 lowered Bonneville gleamed hotly across the street, and a black-haired beauty was pulling a candy-apple-red guitar out of the trunk. Three guys were already gracing the garage, setting up drums, tuning guitars, and a magnificent tall creature was crooning into a microphone: "I had a girl, Donna was her name, since I met her, I'll never be the same." Neither would the neighborhood. It didn't take me long to make their acquaintance. In fact, all the girls on the block became an immediate and constant audience.

July 13 . . . They played, and me, Iva and Linda listened. Robby sure is a doll, I talked to him a lot, he's 18 and his shirt was way way open wow! I left at 11 at nite and Robby said "goodbye my love." I sure hope they make the big time!!

The lead singer, Dino, worked out with weights, and by the end of the day, stripped down to his peg legs, driblets of sweat struggling down his biceps, clutching the mike like it was Brenda Lee, he groaned about his lover leaving him while I leaned against the screen door in a legitimate swoon. He was twenty years old and beyond my teen reach, but a couple of weeks later, I got my first wet kiss from Robby. He was the lead-guitar player. It was on the way back from Pacific Ocean Park, where my girlfriends and I had spent the entire day with the Rainbow Rockers, clutching and grabbing on them, round and round, up and down, on the rickety roller coaster, squealing with newfound pubescent frenzy. Just to get my hands on a thigh or a shoulder and squeeze hard was worth ten thousand trips on the scariest ride in the universe.

We crammed into the backseat of the Bonneville, the sea breeze pouring in the windows, and took off for the Valley, eating cotton candy and caramel apples. I could smell Robby's manly manliness; it wafted over me and I collapsed into his English Leather lapels with the giggles. I'll never forget this: He cupped my chin in his hand and pulled my face up to his lips, opened up my mouth with his tongue and slid it right in! What an amazing sensation! It was so wet, and he moved his lips all over, and his tongue poked around inside my mouth like it was trying to locate something. When I had to come up for air, we were in front of my house on Jamieson Avenue, and I felt like I had taken a trip around the world. I flew into the house, threw the door open, and my mom was standing there, kind of tapping her foot because I was a few minutes late. Breathlessly excited, I said, "MOM!! Have you ever been French-kissed!!?" She demanded all the details and proceeded to ground me for an entire week, adding that I could NEVER BE ALONE WITH ROBBY AGAIN!! What transpired is a historical piece of typical teen torment. I stormed into the kitchen, got a massive butcher knife, lay down on the floor, and, clutching my snapshot of Robby and sobbing hysterically, announced that I was going to stab myself in the heart.

Tell Robby I love him
And I couldn't go on
Knowing he's across the street
That our love is gone

Tell Robby I miss him
Tho' he won't miss me
The tears I cry each night
Just bring misery

My life will be ending now
I know it won't be right
I am just a fool to him
I cry each day and night

This bottle that's in my hand
Will stop my hurting heart
From beating without use
Since we had to part

Tell Robby I love him
And I couldn't go on
Knowing he will love someone else
That our love is gone

I gave up on the butcher-knife idea pretty fast.

RESOLUTIONS FOR 1964

1. Don't hang on boys
2. Be serious when it's called for

3. Try harder on my complexion
4. Get better grades
5. Concentrate on my figure looking better
6. Don't rat my hair so much
7. Try to be more feminine
8. Be cute every day
9. Don't use vulgar language
10. Let nails stay long and polished
11. Pluck eyebrows every four days
12. Shave legs and underarms every week
13. Deodorant every day
14. Brush teeth twice a day
15. Don't waste money on trash
16. Don't ruin boys [What could I have possibly meant by THAT??]

It was a rough life, wasn't it?

I had a disturbing lack of mammary glands when I started high school. It was soooo important to entice the ogling high school boys with at least some semblance of cleavage. The lack of a C cup, or even a B cup, was one of those unfortunate things that I had to live with. I remember a matching pair of particularly silky yellow scarves that I wadded up very carefully to stuff into one of my many "slightly padded" Maidenforms. I had to make sure the shape was exactly the same in each cup; the placing of the scarves in each gaping slot was crucial because it had to look like I was bulging with cleavage. I was once called "the stacked girl down the street," and felt a combination of pride and guilt that I still find hard to comprehend, kind of a falsie pride! I hated Gym because you were required to shower and it was a difficult task to hide my stuffed bra under that skimpy school towel! A couple of the older girls must have seen my scarves trailing behind me, because when we passed in the halls, they would punch my chest and yell, "Falsie!" It must have pissed them off that the boys believed I had a bosom bigger than theirs. I can't really blame them.

There was a girl at Cleveland High that I'll never forget, Nicki Petalis. I once saw a cute guy ask her to look down at her feet to find out if she could see them. She cast her doe eyes downward and giggled, "What do you know, I *can't* see them!!" There was a majestic mammary mountain in her way. I console myself with the fact that Nicki's envious proportions are probably swaying at waist level by now, but to this day I look down at my feet and wish I couldn't see them.

C-C-C-L-E-V-E-L-A-N-D, CLEVELAND CLEVELAND YAYYY!!!

Despite the fact that I had small titties, I was nuts about my high school. I had a crush on the head yell leader, Frankie DiBiase, and hoped against hope that I could become a cheerleader and toss the pompons all around his skinny body.

January 11, 1964 . . . I sure do love my golden idol, F.D. Man, don't ask me why, but every time I think of him I get chills, and that adrenalin runs through my body . . . ooooh! OK enough of this, my heart is dying chunk by chunk.

I often got crushes on the wrong people. This yell leader was much too squeaky clean for me, and deep down I knew I'd never get him. I was already on the verge of weirdness, and these types went for the perfectly bouffanted cover girls with little hair bows that matched their little shoe bows, and even if I found the bows that matched, they somehow always came out looking crooked.

Frankie DiBiase actually did invite me to his pool one afternoon, and I panicked. I said could I please come tomorrow, and spent that afternoon cruising Reseda Boulevard looking for a bathing suit that would accommodate my scarves. I finally decided that the scarves would constantly drip and might feel like small boulders when sopping wet, so I spent the entire evening sewing puffy pads into a little pink-checked two-piece. I had only been in the pool for three minutes when I realized that Frankie's gaze was penetrating my bosom. I just knew the puffy pads hadn't fooled him, so when he tried to put his arms around me and squeeze my shoulders together to peek down into nonexistent cleavage, I wriggled away and announced I was going home. After that, whenever we passed in the halls he had a knowing smirk on his face. I was chagrined, but the idea of running for cheerleader never entered my mind again.

I still wore the school colors, got B's, and was trying to figure out what kind of boy was right for me when I got a fatal dose of Beatlemania. The Fab Four entered the atmosphere at exactly the right wide-open moment for Pam Miller of Reseda, California, to become a complete and total blithering, idiotic Beatlemaniac. Paul McCartney personified the perfect MAN, and once again the dumbbells at Cleveland High who didn't ask me to dance at sock hops faded into oblivion. I had been searching for some new idols anyway. The Beachboys and Jan and Dean weren't my teen cup of tea, and Dion had disappeared after getting weird on national TV. There was a rumor going around Reseda that Bobby Rydell had gone and married the massive-titted Mouseketeer Annette Funicello, and besides, his records were getting lamer and lamer anyway; and Paul Anka had gone right into the middle of the road and stayed there.

February 10 . . . Hello Diary, Paul, you are gear. Really Fab. Say chum, why are you so marvelous, luv? The most bloomin' idiot on earth is me, cause I'm wild over you chap.

The country of England, which hadn't existed for me until now, became Mecca, and every day I sent Paul a retardedly corny poem written on an aerogram and sealed with a kiss.

March 2 . . . It's 2:21 A M at Paul's house. He's sleeping. I'm glad. I wish I could see him sleeping, I really do. I wish I could be *with him* sleeping. (just kidding) I hope he read my poem before he closed his beautiful brown eyes.

Even though I dreamed about what was between Paul's perfect milky-white thighs, I had not yet conjured up dimensions. I collected

Beatle bubble-gum cards, and one of them was a shot of Paul playing his bass, sitting on a bed in a hotel with his legs apart. You could actually see the shape of his balls being crushed by the tightness of his trousers, and I carried that card around with me in a little gold box with cotton covering it like it was a precious jewel. I peeked into it reverently, once a day, and lifted the cotton gently, holding my breath as I stared between his legs at the eighth wonder of the world. Every other day on my Beatles station, KRLA, Dave Hull the Hullabalooer would announce whether or not Paul was engaged to marry the creepy freckle-faced bow-wow, Jane Asher. It drove me crazy; it's all I thought about.

> *I stare at his face upon my wall*
> *I know I love him best of all*
> *His gorgeous eyes just knock me down*
> *I sware I think he should wear a crown*
> *The way he moves when he sings a song*
> *Let's hope he doesn't marry before long*

March 20 . . . He's NOT, He's NOT!!! Brian Epstein sent a cablegram to Columbia Records to announce; Paul's getting married is completely and ridiculously untrue . . . Brian Epstein. YAY!!!! There's no queen for my king YET!

I lost some good friends who were growing up and going steady and planning their lives after high school. They left me behind with my Beatles lunch box and bobbing-head dolls, practicing my Liverpudlian accent. And guess what? They're probably still in Reseda with a gaggle of goony kids to kowtow to, being forced to listen to Motley Crue by their very own burgeoning teenagers, and it serves them right.

We gravitated to one another, the Beatlesweeties, and hung around in packs of four, one for each Beatle. Kathy Willis was my George-friend; her dad knew somebody who worked at the Hollywood Bowl and was going to get us good seats for the Beatles concert on August 23. We got our tickets before anybody else, and bought gilt frames to put them in and hung them on our bedroom walls. I paid homage to my ticket nightly. My entire room was covered with Beatle paraphernalia, I wrote with a Beatle pen, slept on a Beatle pillowcase, and breathed with Beatle lungs. Stevie was my Ringofriend, and no one understood the poor thing.

> Oh, Pammy, I feel like the world is caving in on me!! Everyone is trying to take me Ringo away from me. Help me Pam, oh please help me!! I need encouragement *so* bad. I've got to meet Ringo or my whole life will be completely empty. Oh, I'm suffering so. He's my love and I love him. Oh, God, please don't let me Ringo be taken away!

We wrote Beatle letters to each other constantly, whining and moaning, and expressing the deepdeepdeep desire to meet the Beatle of our choice. But Howhowhow???

Linda was my Johnfriend. We spent weekends at my Aunt Edna's house so we could be on neutral ground, pretending it was hallowed Beatle ground. We were two girls in a constant state of Beatle skits. I played John and myself, and she played Paul and herself. We could switch personalities with the flick of an accent. We took each other to parties and concerts, we ate dinner in gorgeous restaurants on Aunt Edna's patio, and professed undying love with semiperfect working-class Liverpudlian accents. At night, we played all four people at the same time, when we would lie entwined in each other's arms, pressing our four sets of lips together in an eternal expression of Beatle Love.

We wrote Beatle love stories for each other, and I could hardly wait to get to school to get my hands on the next installment of my continuing Paulsaga. I had six stories going at once, but my favorite was written by my old friend Iva. Ooooh, it was soooo titillating! She actually got us in the sack.

> Paul fell across you, pushing you into the soft bed. His tender lips kissed yours passionately. You felt so good, so right, to be this close to Paul. He whispered into your ear, pausing to kiss your cheek or your neck, "Luv, oh Pam, you know as well as I do what

comes next. . . ." You drew his lips to yours, ending his sentence.
You knew what he would say and you didn't want to hear it.
Nothing can go wrong . . . love is never bad. Paul's hands swept
over you, his lips touched your neck again and again. "Paul . . .
Paul," you whispered against his hair, his body was so close. As
he held you, somehow he pulled back the sheets on the bed. They
were a blue and red candy-stripe. He laid you gently down and
bent to kiss you. "I'm sleeping in the den, luv . . ." he said shakily.
Then he walked out and closed the door. (A few hours later . . .)
Stumbling through the dark living room, to the bedroom, Paul
quietly opened the door. There you lay. Your blonde hair tossed
carelessly, but beauteously over the pillow, your pink lips still
wearing the smile they had as you fell asleep. Paul thought he
had never seen anything quite so luscious . . . or so tempting.

Sigh.

My dad bought me a reel-to-reel tape recorder and I made up a
lot of adorable little plays, acting out all the different parts, in which
Jane Asher dies many grisly, horrifying deaths. The Pam Miller
character was always around to pick up Paul's pieces.

To his nibs, I sang a different tune:

Dear Paul, Your fans will always love you. Personally, I will
never stop. Since hearing about your engagement to Jane Asher,
I'll have to love you in another way, all of my own.

Paul McCartney of Beatle fame
Has chosen another to share his name
Many girls will cry each night
Saying "this marriage just cannot be right"
Even though all of his fans are blue
It's to her he whispers "I love you"

His face is like an angels, so they say
And it's hers to gaze upon night and day
He is hers to have and hold
Til' their lives are ending
Til they both grow old

Sure, there are people who will say he's wrong
But let's just hope that his love is strong

If he listens to us, where will he be?
He will be without children to bounce on his knee
He'll miss out on the purpose of life
To live, to love, have a child and a wife

If we really loved him, how happy we'd be
That he's found such happiness and ecstasy
She is his chosen flame
To share with him the McCartney name

It's enough to make you throw up.

I developed a series of rituals that I had to perform every night, or I would never meet Paul: 1) Write "I Love Paul" at the top of my diary in my most perfect handwriting; 2) Listen to a Beatles record before sleep. No other sound could assault my eardrums after the *sacred* sound. If the dog barked, I had to climb out of bed and start over; 3) Put a Sweet Tart under my tongue as my head hit the pillow, and let it dissolve as I pictured myself in his arms. In addition to these rituals, I had to write HIS name down every time I farted, and I carried the list around with me until it reached well into the thousands before I became embarrassed and hid it underneath the clothes hamper.

Friday, May 8 1964 . . . I Love Paul. I'm in love with his body and everything that's on it. I love you, I love you, I love you, my precious precious Paully Waully Paul Paul!! Oh, my bee bee, my own lover.
May 10 . . . I Love Paul. Sad News! He's with PigFace in The Virgin Islands and I thought they had broken up. That's not all! Ringo is with Maureen Cox and George is with Patti Boyd. No parental consent. No chaperones.
May 21 . . . I Love Paul. If Walter Winchell doesn't leave Paul alone, he can go to Hell. He seems to *want* to hurt the girls. He says Paul and Jane are buying a house together, and Ringo is buying Maureen a ring. You're so OLD, W.W., but your mind is so childish and ignorant.
June 3 . . . My seats at the Bowl, Oh My God!! I'm about 20 feet from the stage . . . fifth row!!! There's an actual day this year that is called August 23rd! It comes in 83 days!!

June 24 . . . Paul McCartney is the man I love. If he got the chance I know he would love me. I just know it. I love every muscle and fiber and ligament in his thigh. I know that sounds odd, but that's the way I feel.

July 19 . . . It's only 33 days until my eyes will stare into Paul's eyes. Instead of him being a flat surface, he'll be soft and warm.

August 2 . . . It's been a Hard Day's Night and The Beatles are the greatest actors alive. First off, Paul is MY lover, he was such a doll. George was SEX, John was very mental and Ringo is truly a beautiful man. In 21 ravishing days, Oh My God!!

August 23 . . . Day Of All!! Tonight I saw Paul. I actually looked at his lean slender body and unique too-long legs. I saw his dimples and pearly white teeth. I saw his wavy, yet straight lengthy hair, I saw his doe-like eyes . . . and they saw me. Maybe it's fate that brought him to our sunny shores . . . for I am here too.

I intended to meet Paul during his stay in Los Angeles. Stevie, Kathy, Linda, and I conned Kathy's dad into shlepping us to Bel Air, where we encountered several hundred clones of ourselves milling around hungrily. The perfectly manicured lawns were covered with teenage girls and a few die-hard Beatle Boys with their bangs almost reaching their eyebrows. We took our place among the multitude temporarily while we devised a plan that would get us closer to our idols. I was paying close attention to people who didn't look like Beatles fans—could they be Bel Air residents? I pointed this idea out to the others, who busily scanned the crowd for likely looking candidates. A freckle-faced boy about our age was riding a bicycle in our direction, and he looked at all of us with curious, detached interest. *Not* one of us, I surmised, and set out to make his acquaintance. We were about to make his day. Ronny Lewis, age fifteen, was the son of Jerry Lewis, and I was not impressed. At one time, when Jerry was skinny, I thought he was a funny guy, but when I realized he would never change his hairdo, I figured he was stuck in time and not going anywhere. They love him in France, God bless him. We flocked around Ronny, pressuring him with compliments and cajoling him with funny anecdotes. We had to get past the Beatle Barricade and onto someone's personal property so we could prowl the Bel Air hills and FIND THE BEATLES!!!

Ronny was bowled over by the blatancy of our desire, and sneaked us through his mansion into the backyard, where we planned on scaling the wall and plummeting to the depths of the Bel Air brush. By this time we were all hysterical, sqealing piglets, and there was no way he could avoid getting caught up in our frothy fervor. He agreed to head the search party. We roamed around, getting stuck with prickly stickers, telling each other what wonderful things were about to happen. When Ringo laid eyes on Stevie, Maureen Cox would surely fall by the wayside, and when Paul got a load of ME, well, words couldn't be found to describe the possibilities. Sweat-stained and dirty, we all trudged for hours through the bushes and brambles, our hearts pounding Beatle blood. I was the first to see the array of cops lined up in front of what was obviously THE BEATLE HOUSE!! How could we possibly break through this massive battalion? Ronny saw the string of billy clubs and decided to head back home; we thanked him abundantly and threw our minds into the problem at hand. Hiding across the street in the bushes, we watched the goings-on, waiting for clues . . . waiting, waiting, waiting. When it got dark, we decided to head across the street, one by one, crawling on our bellies like reptiles. There was only one way to go, through the garden around the side to the rear of the house, and we all made it! After dusting off we checked out our surroundings, and found out there was still an extremely tall chain link fence between us and the backyard. It was truly impossible to climb over, with barbed wire circling the tippy-top should anyone attempt to be so bold. We collapsed with exhaustion, hoping for accents to float on the wind while we waited out the night. I prayed hard for Paul to glance out his window. I just knew he would see a light shimmering behind the chain link because Pam Miller of Reseda, California, was aglow with incandescent Beatle Love that would never die. I finally slept, cramped and cold, and dreamed of my mother pacing the floor all night, worrying about her ditsy daughter on the loose in Bel Air Beatle Land.

After freezing all night, we sat sweating all morning, watching the pool with unblinking eyes, waiting for John, Paul, George, or Ringo to take a dip. What we finally saw was a roadie, Neil Aspinall, swim back and forth a few times, and a couple of windows open and close. The roadie must have seen us peering in at him, because a few minutes later we were hauled off by unamused boys in blue, shoved into police cars, driven promptly out of Bel Air, and asked very unpolitely never to return. On the way down the hill, a limousine passed by, and I saw John Lennon for an instant. He was wearing his John Lennon cap and he looked right at me. If I close my eyes this minute, I can still see the look he had on his face; it was full of sorrow and contempt. The other girls were pooling tears in their eyes and didn't notice, but that look on John Lennon's face stopped my heart and I never said a word.

The Beatles left town, and I didn't meet them. It was a dastardly pill to swallow, but life went on. The look on John's face made me grow up a little, and I worked hard in school and decided to get a part-time job.

September 23 . . . I guess I shouldn't worry about getting a job, but it's playing with my mind constantly, nagging and laughing and sneering . . . "I told you so."

I wonder *who* or *what* was doing the sneering. When I couldn't find a job, I figured that having a real relationship would help me to mature. Every boy in pants became a potential candidate, and I became a member of the Teen Center on Victory Boulevard, hoping that the perfect cutie would cross my path. I did the jerk, the frug, the slauson, and the swim, all the while checking out the merchandise. I kept on loving Paul McCartney, but I needed some physical contact.

October 17, 1964 . . . We left home in gay moods for another big night at the center. I dressed in my red sailor blouse, and put on my two fake pony-tails to be sure!! I walked in and

absent-mindedly looked around for a dance partner. Greg Over-
lin, of whom I hadn't seen in years asked me to dance a few
times, as did Richie "Sal." (he looks like Sal Mineo) Out on the
small patio, I did the jerk with Wade. None of them impressed
me. I felt eyes on me, and looked up to see the most perfect
boy ever! He had the most perfect curly pompadour and perfect
long curly eyelashes. He looked so bitchen' in his white coat
and black continentals, and he danced so bitchen' too. His name
was Bob Martine. I smiled at him and his leg brushed mine. I
asked him if he could give us a ride home and he gestured with
his thumb "I'm hitching, is that OK with you guys?" Linda and
I exchanged glances. I was game, but I was sure my mother
wouldn't be. He smelled of Jade East and I was swooning.
Suddenly I had this great urge to touch his stomach. I began
to unbutton his shirt, and he liked it! I could certainly be myself
with him, that was for sure. He seemed experienced, but not
too experienced, I mean he wasn't trying to prove anything. A
friend of Bob's agreed to take us home, and we piled into the
old car and were off! When we reached my house, I sat there
on Bob's lap, not budging, he put his hand up to my cheek,
and turned my face to him and kissed me goodnight. Tomorrow
holds promise in it's grasp. I'm not sure of my love for Bob. I
don't know him very well, but I want to.

I fell in green-teen love that fateful night.

Bob and I started going steady the next day, but my passion for
Paul had not diminished: "It's a wonderful feeling being loved by
somebody other than your parents and friends. Bob loves me. When
Paul loves me I will be in unadulterated heaven . . . if the dear Lord
permits."

Mr. Martine finally won me over because he was there in person,
and Paul was with Pigface across the vast ocean. Bob was a bit of a
bad boy, which I found enticingly dangerous, and since he was from
New York, he spoke exotic Brooklynese, newnewnew to my pedantic
Valley ears. It thrilled me that he got in trouble for dragging on Van
Nuys Boulevard, and the fact that he had failed the entire eleventh
grade really sent me reeling. The concept of a Rebel Without a
Cause had always seemed so out-of-bounds romantic, and I carried

a photo of Jimmy Dean in my turquoise imitation-leather wallet at all times. Bob smoked, and even popped reds on occasion, which I found totally shocking. He fought with his hot-tempered Italian dad constantly, and cursed a purple streak whenever he felt like it.

> November 3 . . . Bob called . . . He's so bad, my bad little boy. He was picked up for *Grand Theft* 3 times. He's done lots of other bad things, but he's getting to be a better boy. and he's mine, *mine*, MINE!!!

He even hinted that he had gone all the way, not just once, but several times, and this worried me, because my VIRGINITY was a sacred subject.

> November 15 . . . He screwed ten girls, but swears he'll never touch me . . . ever . . . We can talk about sex and it's a clean word when we discuss it.

Ha ha . . . We spent endless hours on the phone, spewing sticky, sweet teen endearments, and my homework suffered. We spent all our spare time with each other, holding hands and exploring the idea of life together forever. Along with this idea, of course (*despite* his former claims), came his desire to put his hands all over my budding body. I still wore falsies, and in order to keep his hands away from my bewitching fraudulence, I promised to let him get to third base. (I somehow convinced him to save the holy vision of my breasts until our wedding night.) Meanwhile, the world of forbidden flesh loomed large in my immediate future. I learned what *real* making out was all about. With our eyes closed and our faces mashed together, we reached saliva nirvana, panting and moaning in backseats and on front porches. My mom was highly concerned, but she knew I had a virginity thing and wasn't about to let go of it just yet. She liked Bob; he was a sweet boy with a bad rep. My dad worked nights at Budweiser, and sometimes Bob and I had to stop in midsquelch when the Fleetwood high beams lit up the porch and outlined us, grappling and groping.

December 18 . . . I've never been so turned on in my life, and yet so completely relaxed, proud and clear-minded. Bob respects me very much, so I never have to worry.

I wrote a letter to my Beatlefriend Linda about my joyous relationship: "Dear Linda, I just realized a very wonderful and beautiful thing. That yearning, wanting and needing in Bob's heart is churning for me! He's experiencing his *very first* true love, and he loves it so much. He loves it so much that he has amazing control over his young body that craves only one thing. There's a conflict, but I'm proud to say that good overrules evil, and love overrules sex." What a bunch of dog-doo. Little did I know, my honey-boy was easing me into taking hold of his Private Part, and teaching me what to do with it. With a wink, he told me size was the thing and he had a Big Italian One, the envy of all his friends. I had felt it against various parts of my body many times, but I knew if I was going to hold on to this dangerous punk, I was going to have to hold on to his THING also. One of his *older* friends had a trailer, and Bob took me there one balmy evening to introduce me to the pleasures of S-E-X. He knew I had every intention of hanging on to my hymen, so he went slow. The first time, I felt it through his underpants. The second time, he took it out, and I closed my eyes real tight and tentatively grabbed on, petrified of damaging it, like it was a newborn. It was soft and hard at the same time, and not at all what I had expected. My virginal image was that of a cross between a sleepy pink baby worm and a vengeful billy club with one crazed eye. The third time, I looked, and it became my friend.

December 29 . . . Bob and I counted all the way up to good old number *69* tonight, if you know what I mean! I think I know what an orgasm is. I was aflame with desire.

HAPPINESS—JANUARY 1, 1965

Happiness is being 16
Happiness is Cleveland High

Happiness is knowing you are loved

Happiness is a cuddly doll to sleep with

Happiness is Johnny Mathis (?)

Happiness is a blue mohair empire

Happiness is a kiss

Happiness is hoping to have a clear complexion

Happiness is getting a dark tan

Happiness is an orange

Happiness is Freedom

Happiness is a cooler on a hot day

Happiness is an electric blanket

Happiness is dreaming about entering "Miss Teen USA"

Happiness is bowling

Happiness is E.S.P.

Happiness is The Beatles

Happiness is my love for Paul

Happiness is Ringo, the one and only drummer boy Beatle, The spine that sends chills up mine. Ringo of the jeweled fingers and golden drummer hands (whew!)

Happiness is baby Julian Lennon

Happiness was August 23

Happiness is knowing you are loved so deeply by your boyfriend who is so bitchen'

My bitchen' boyfriend was about to be taken away from me. His parents sold their house and were moving back to New York, taking their own personal Juvenile Delinquent with them. My heart was bleeding.

January 7, 1965 . . . 6 days from now I will be a very lonely girl. I'll be lying on this same bed, using this same pen to write in this same diary. I'll look up at the clock out of habit, but I won't really see the time. Minutes and hours will mean nothing for I will be waiting for each day to pass. Each day which will be one useless drudge until my honey-boy comes home to me. He said "Dollin', you're so perfect. God put every little piece of you together just right." I'm crying, and the teardrops will be in this diary for all time.

"Unchained Melody" was OUR song, and it played constantly in my hi-fi mind: "Oh, my love, my darling, I hunger for your touch, a long lonely time . . . and time goes by so slowly, and time can mean so much. Are you still mine????" He went off to New York, and I resumed Beatlemania with my JohnPaulGeorgeRingofriends. I wrote to Bob almost every day, we made tapes for each other, and he got to call me once a week. Part of his greaser charm was that he couldn't read or write very well, so he dictated all this love-angst to his cousin and sent it off to me by the pile. I sniffed the air for Jade East on my way to the mailbox, and tore into the reams of mush with rabid relish. He proposed to me through the mail:

February 18, 1965 . . . Our children will be beautiful. They'll have wavy black hair and big blue eyes. They will be twins, a boy and a girl; James Paul Martine and Jamie Paula Martine.

Poor Bob, I was about to name his kids after Paul McCartney. I saw *A Hard Day's Night* a few more times, perfected my Liverpudlian, wrote stories for Stevie about the swell life she and Ringo were going to have, and actually worked on improving my grades, all the while dreaming of my honey-boy in New York. "Oowah, oowah, cool cool Kitty, tell us about the boy from New York City."

Despite my self-inflicted ban on other boys, there was a guy at Cleveland who looked nothing like my slick, pompadoured greasy boy in New York, nor did he even vaguely resemble the perfect, ideal high school man. He wore worldly corduroy trousers and suede workboots, while Kip Tyler, the president of Cleveland High, tried to entrance us all with his blue-and-white letterman sweater and perfectly pressed flattop. Victor Haydon was always running from the vice-principal because his hair was way too long, and something about him inspired me. I still don't know what attracted Victor to me. It must have been my barely budding antiestablishment ideas, which manifested when I gradually stopped teasing my hair into a coiffed flip like Cindy Bowling and all the other hopeful high achievers. Victor began to hang around me during Nutrition, blowing my innocent mind with radical departures from the truth as I knew it. He thought it was absurd to try to "fit in" to a society that was chasing its own tail and going nowhere fast. This was big news to me, folks, and I pondered it profusely. He told me about this folk singer named Bob Dylan and lent me a couple of his albums. I soon found out that the answer to any and all questions was blowing in the wind. Victor believed in the Rolling Stones with a vengeance, and since I thought Victor Haydon was blazing a new trail, I followed in his giant footsteps to the local record store to check out Mick Jagger. This incident coincided with my brand-new pubescent longings for something hot, and my desire to be considered a daring young thinker of dramatic new thoughts.

My Beatlefriends were aghast. They thought Victor was a holier-than-thou snot who was out to erase them from the planet, and they believed I had forsaken Paul for the grotesque, filthy, big-lipped animal, Mick Jagger.

5–9–65 . . . Dear Pam, I suppose you are wondering why Linda, Stevie and I acted the way we did after school yesterday. The main reason is because you are a phony person. You had better watch out before you become completely friendless. Why on earth could you even start to like Mick over Paul? You think you are an individualist. But an individualist isn't one who wears strange clothes. Pam, you try to be strange, but you aren't. You are just being a loser. Nobody likes you when you act the way you do. Personally, I'd much rather go around with my crowd than with moody Victor who chops everybody down just because he knows he isn't popular. Just remember you won't be a teenager all your life, and when you get in your twenties you will regret your actions. I thought I knew you real well, you were always so enthusiastic about the Beatles and now you're a Rolling Stones fan. I don't see how you could pick them over The Beatles unless . . . you were being a phony all that time. The Stones are dirty and sloppy and they repugnate me. When I think back to how you used to sign your name "Paul n Pam," I can't believe you're the same

girl. I don't hate you, but frankly, I don't like you much. . . .
Kathy 'n' Stevie.

K.&.S . . . I have very sensible answers to your ridiculous questions. Paul and Mick cannot be compared. They are two opposite
types with two opposite types of love connected with them. I have
not taken the Stones *over* The Beatles. I have just let them become
a part of my life too. Is that so wrong? The Beatles can never be
topped, but the Stones will never be topped either. Oh, you don't
understand. They play two different types of music. *They cannot
be compared.* It makes me literally sick how you think you know
so much about the "sloppy" Stones, that you feel you can call
them "dirty." Just because they don't all wear the same suits and
comb their hair the same way. You know nothing of Victor, and
if you did, your opinion would change. Well, maybe not, he
doesn't get along very well with people who's minds are rather
narrow. He can also spot a phony, and if I were a phony, he
would have told me long ago. I don't think I'm one bit strange. I
go to my closet and pick out things that *I* think look good together.
I don't stand there and say "Oh, I think I'll look strange today."
I do what I like and say what I like, and I don't hate you either. I
don't hate anybody. . . . Pamela.

I left Pam in the dust and became Pamela, leaving all the Beatlesweeties gasping for breath.

The girls had no idea to what extent I had glommed on to the
dirty, sloppy Stones. My brief sexual encounters with Bob had opened
up new vistas of turgid, twisting thoughts, and Mick Jagger *personified*
a penis. I took my new records and my glossy steaming photographs
into my rock and roll room, where I scaled new heights of tortuous
teen abandon, wriggling in my seat with newfound throbbing ecstasy.
The second song on the second side of the second album changed
my life. The first time I heard it, I had an orgasmic experience: "Let
me put it in, it feels all right."

I would sit by my hi-fi, playing that line over and over until I
reached my pulsation point . . . "Let me put it in," "Let me put it
in," "Let me put it in" . . . When I played it for my Georgefriend,
Kathy, she said, "Let me put what in where?" I rushed home from

school every day to throb along with Mick while he sang: "I'm a king bee, baby, let me come inside." I began imagining what it would be like to get my hands on him. With my precious Paul, I never really got past the hoping stage, but now I dared to imagine Mick with his widewale corduroy trousers down around his ankles.

My new best friend, Victor, had a real-life rock and roll cousin who lived in a trailer in the desert, with the outrageous name of Captain Beefheart. Vic titillated me with this information more than once before inviting me to see his group, the Magic Band, perform at the Teen Fair at the Hollywood Palladium. I was so thrilled I could hardly contain myself. I put on my newly acquired big, baggy corduroy jacket, my first-in-Reseda Sonny and Cher blue-jean bell-bottoms, and jumped into Vic's Hudson Hornet, ready to steam in to Hollywood like it was the brave new world. Don Vliet, a.k.a. Captain Beefheart, was a wildly intimidating crazy genius who was so far ahead of his time, people are still trying to catch up with him. He was just a wee bit out of place at the Fourth Annual Teen Fair, where the big thing was samples of Knudsens new fruit-flavored yogurt. Teenagers littered the floor with little plastic spoons, while I looked upon the man who was going to alter my life for all time. The first look into his spacy blue eyes (I knew they looked straight through, into the *real* me) told me that my life was just beginning. He was gruff and shaggy, but his gaze penetrated the depths of my emerging individuality, pulled it out, and hurled it on humanity. "You, too, can make people think you are a disgusting weirdo, and create havoc by just walking down the street!!" Beefheart told me that my baggy corduroy jacket was "a gas," and said, "Haven't we met before . . . are you sure . . . ?" I knew I was on the right track, and I intended to plunge ahead into unknown realms of hipness.

I wrote irregularly and infrequently to my boyfriend, Bob, who became increasingly dubious about James Paul and Jamie Paula Martine ever coming into being. I'm sure he conjured up many indelicate encounters between me and half of Cleveland High. He was about three thousand miles away from the truth.

I had escalated beyond recognition in my own estimation.

Beefheart was also a major Stones fan, and suggested that we all go see them at the Long Beach Arena. The thought of seeing Mick LIVE sent me into a swoon, but I kept it under wraps because I wanted to be cool with Beefheart and his Magic Band. Victor and I waited in that long line, amid throngs of teeming teens, from the middle of the night until eleven in the morning to get our Stones tickets. I thought all of us must be the hippest bunch of people on God's earth.

April 26, 1965 . . . Vic asked me to be the local president of Beefhearts fan club! Out of a million girls, he picked me! He tells me that he is super human and in the fourth dimension. Who Knows? No matter how much he keeps asking me, I'M NOT GOING TO TAKE MARIJUANA!! He was reading Sigmund Freud today.
May 3 . . . I hung around all day with Vixon and Tomato . . . We had so much fun at Nutrition. These are my people.
May 7 . . . I feel like I'm a part of Beefhearts group, a big part. They all think I'm a crazy little chick, hep and with it. Don said "If only they were all like you."

I was arriving.

The month of waiting for the Stones' arrival increased my wanton desire to feel *those* gigantic lips on mine. I started writing porno things in my diary for the first time: "Someday I will touch and feel him, I know it. Mick, my dear, dear PENIS!" I brazenly created in pink and red oil colors my concept of what his balls might look like. I turned it in to Mr. Gifford as a modern-art project and got an A.

They came to Hollywood on May 11, 1965, the same day I was thrown out of school for "looking absurd." I can still see my mom trying to explain to the lumpy old-maid VP about the new look in teen fashion. Victor was proud of me, and I figured I looked just right for the Rolling Stones. Vic and I hurtled ourselves to RCA, hoping they might be there recording and, incredibly, they were! We waited around, panting, until they came out, and as if I were in a zomboid trance, I followed Mick into the parking lot. As he got into the rented station wagon, he turned and asked me to help him out of the parking space. I was so enthralled that he had spoken to me, and just being in his presence turned me into such a jibbering, slack-jawed dildo-brain, that I had him bumping into two different cars before he made it out of there. I'm afraid I didn't make a very good first impression. Dazed, I walked right into Keith as he ambled to the car. Even in my bewildered condition, I swore he gave me a sexy look. I wrote in my diary: "He looked me over . . . sexy . . . whew!!" And what did he see? A skinny shivering wreck of a teenager, truly petrified during her daring rock and roll deed. They asked us for directions to the Ambassador Hotel and Victor stood there gaping. Mick leaned out the window and said, "No, I'm serious." So we escorted them up Wilshire Boulevard with "Satisfaction" blaring on the radio as I gazed into the rearview mirror at my steaming photograph in the steaming flesh.

They waved good-bye when we reached the hotel, and our hopes of being invited in were dramatically dashed. We parked and went to call Beefheart, who had met Charlie in England, and he said he would meet us in the lobby. Instead of waiting for him, we decided to cruise the Stones' rooms. They were staying in a series of pink bungalows with hordes of girls standing watch. One of them was Flo, a wiry black girl with a switchblade prominently displayed on a leather cord around her neck. She told us that Keith had given it to her so she could keep the fans from bothering him. She led us to believe that she was one of the chosen who *did* have access to the pink rooms by proudly telling us that the Stones called her "The Grand Canyon." She did a bump and grind to make sure we didn't miss the point.

I stayed clear of Flo and went around the back of the bungalows to peek in the window at beautiful Brian, who was cavorting with two scantily clad ladies of Spanish descent. While I watched, some teenybops banged on the front door, begging him to come out and give them an autograph. He threw open the door in his underwear, holding a broom as some kind of weapon, and shouted, "IF YOU DON'T GET THE HELL OUT OF HERE, I'LL DRAG YOU IN

HERE AND *FUCK* YOU!!!" They ran squealing into the moon-light, and he came over to the window where I was gnawing my knuckles and pulled down the shade. For a few minutes I stood there, listening to scintillating sounds that I couldn't really fathom, and cranked up the courage to knock on Mick's door. "And Mick opened the door. He had no clothes covering his body and a soft light drifted down over his bare chest and legs. He stood at the door a moment in his naked splendor, and then decided he'd better close the door." I guess he just wanted to give some fan a thrill. That's just about the way it happened, only I neglected to tell my diary that I let out a shriek and ran out into the same moonlight as the other daring girls had. Needless to say, that's *not* how it had always hap-pened in my dreams, and I sat down on the lawn and cried over my failure to sweep him off his feet.

Beefheart soon arrived and we spent hours with Charlie and Bill, listening to Muddy Waters while I thought of Mick, two bungalows down, with a soft light drifting down over his bare chest.

The next night was the long-awaited concert at the Long Beach Arena. I might have thrown my bra onstage with some of the other crazed girls, but I was sitting next to Beefheart, and besides, I still hadn't reached the point where it was cool to have small tits, so my bra still held fraudulence. Mick was so sexy. I had never seen anybody move like that; it was downright scuzzy, driving the girls in the audience to poke and prod at their private parts. One half-nude girl climbed down the drapes and hung on to Mick's corduroy-clad leg until two guards pried her off and tossed her back into the wailing crowd. The music was hot and raunchy, my heart was beating below my waist, and my hands were itching to hold something warm. I was a sticky, sweaty teenage girl, squirming my way into womanhood. They only played for about half an hour in those days, so the lights came on much too soon and we were herded out into the night, clutching our Rolling Stones programs and damp, wrinkled ticket stubs, wanting more more more!!

Back at the hotel, I once again attempted to make contact with Mick. I went to the back of his bungalow, behind the bushes, and peered into the window, afraid of what I might see. At first I thought the shade was pulled down because I was gazing at impenetrable whiteness, but as I slowly looked up to the dimpled grinning face of Mick, I realized I was staring straight into his underwear. It's a miracle he didn't tell me to fuck off, since I had annoyed him twice, but he said, "It's time to go home, pretty little girl."

"He thinks I'm pretty!!!!"

Nobody at Cleveland High would believe I had met the Stones, and I didn't really care. I had given up trying to impress people who didn't impress me. What a relief. I owed so much of my newfound attitude to Captain Beefheart that when he invited me out to his backyard to watch the clouds that resembled nuns flying overhead, I gladly followed him. He took my hand and beads of sweat formed on his upper lip like pearls of wisdom. He asked if I would like to feel something warm, and he guided my hand back and forth, back and forth, while we watched the swaying habits gliding overhead. It was our only intimate encounter.

Victor and I decided we needed jobs to support our all-consuming record addiction, so we worked together at a tiny factory in Van Nuys dipping Batman boots and Robin gloves into little bottles of paint. One evening after an exhausting day at work, as I was peeling emerald green off my fingers, Bob called to let me know his parents had changed their minds about living in New York and he would be coming back in two weeks! My emotions were totally mixed. He assumed he would be cradled on my large, cleaving, heaving bosom, and I had recently removed a layer of padding from my brassiere, creating a seminatural look. I hardly resembled the drippy-eyed, doting honey-girl he had left behind on the front porch. What would he think of my "Cher" pants?? I worried myself ill waiting for his knock at my door.

Because of our splendid past, I felt I owed it to Bob to re-create our relationship. I'm sad to say it didn't work. He didn't understand Victor and his artistic tendencies; in fact, to my incredible embarrassment he attempted to beat him up on two separate occasions. This made me look unpeaceful, and I just couldn't take the chance of blowing my new cool. That I had once considered this macho greaser anything but a passing acquaintance made Victor look at me very, very suspiciously. His raised eyebrows helped me to take action. I told Bob as gently as I could that I had changed while he was away, and he begged me to go back to being the girl he had fallen in love with. He then promised to change along with me, and the next day he went out and bought some cord bell-bottoms that were way too short; he combed his precious pompadour down over his ears, and it stuck out on both sides like Bozo. I ached with compassion and cringed quietly.

October 8 . . . I can't figure myself out. I guess I should be happy that he *tries* to understand me. He fails most of the time, although he doesn't know it. School was screwed.

November 26 . . . I went to Hollywood. Bob is pretty sad, but I think he'll get over it. He was crying again. I got my Dylan tickets. 3rd row.

December 23 . . . Bob and I fought all week and I can't be tied down anymore, he just doesn't get it and it breaks my heart. Merry Krimble, as John Lennon would say.

December 31 . . . almost 1966!! It's only obvious how confused and what a wreck I am. Does every young person go through big fire to reach a little brook? All I know is that if my friends can make it, so can I. I hear my dad laughing in the living-room. I remember that every year, laying in bed, listening to dad laugh. I miss Bob. My mind is churning and I can't stop thinking. Where would I be without thought? Bob Dylan captures what's *really* going on.

> *Come senators and congressmen throughout the land*
> *And don't critisise what you can't understand*
> *Your sons and your daughters are beyond your command*
> *The old world is rapidly fading*
> *So get out of the new one if you can't lend a hand*
> *For the times they are a changin'*

2

♥

THE TIME TO HESITATE
IS THROUGH . . .

What a field day for the heat
A thousand people in the street
Singing songs and carrying signs
Mostly saying "Hooray for our side"
We've got to stop, hey what's that sound
Everybody look what's goin' down . . .

One of L.A.'s prime bands, the Buffalo Springfield, told us all about the riot on the Sunset Strip. The funny thing is, I didn't see a single one of them sitting cross-legged in the middle of Sunset, and believe me, I would have noticed Neil Young or Stephen Stills waving a sign to the right or left of me. What a sight it was! Traffic backed up for miles, horns blaring, high beams extending into headlight heaven.

Pandora's Box, the ultimate rock club of the moment, was being torn down to make way for a wider road and a three-way turn signal, and WE, the patrons of the purple palace, were not going to stand for it. In fact, we sat down on Sunset Boulevard and wouldn't budge.

I found something to believe in, and was so proud of being on a mission to enlighten the world. I felt like I *belonged*, united with a thousand other kids, protesting what THEY were doing to US. At last I was surrounded by my own kind. I watched as Gorgeous Hollywood Boys overturned a bus, and I cheered on the offenders from my warm spot on the Sunset Boulevard blacktop. I gazed at Sonny and Cher, arms wrapped around each other, wearing matching polka-dot bell-bottoms and fake-fur vests, and realized we were all one perfect hip force with one big huge beating heart. I held hands with strangers and tried to recapture the moment before it had even passed.

The LAPD arrived in full force, clubs swinging and sirens blaring, but at least we had our moment in the moonlight. We made headlines the next morning, and I surveyed the endless pages of protesters, praying to catch a glimpse of myself among the defenders of teenage rights.

After I made that first trek into Hollywood to see Captain Beefheart at the Teen Fair, I was like a ravenous rat heading for the cheese. Everything seemed to gleam and glow and the Sunset Strip loomed in the foreground like a promise of greatness. Cleveland High became just a place to graduate from and the boys in Reseda were squalling infants, dribbling into their bibs. *All* the boys in Hollywood had long hair and important eyes. They walked cool and talked cool, and my brain was clamoring to grasp any eloquent morsel of information bestowed upon me by one of these amazing creatures.

> December 25 . . . Hello. I'd like to say something. Dig this. You might say I'm rather lost in this big mixed-up place we call life. I try to understand the people I love, and it's hard for me. I know they're great and wonderful people trying to become what others call "nonconformists." I want to be one of them. I *am* one of them. All we are trying to do, is become individuals, not one chaotic mess of human being. And we meet in Hollywood.

After Pandora's Box closed down, we started hanging out at a coffee shop on the Strip called Ben Frank's, conveniently located

between Ciro's and the Trip. The first person I met at the new inner
sanctum was Rodney Bingenheimer. He had his bangs cut just like
Davy Jones because he was Davy's stand-in on *The Monkees*. He
dangled this tidbit in the faces of ga-ga girls, thrilling them with his
latest claim to Strip fame. Within ten minutes he had me in the
back of a Volkswagen in the parking lot, his hands placed firmly on
my tits. I felt like such an inexperienced jerk for prying his fingers
off, but it didn't seem to faze him. I'm sure he had already squeezed
a few that evening.

> February 12 . . . Hollywood Time! It wasn't all too great and
> excellent. The best of all. So many love orgies. Everybody loves
> everybody! I was with Rodney and he doesn't kiss *too* well.
> Yum for my tum. He gave me some groovy pics of Dylan. And
> I met this *groovy* guy who knows The Byrds!!

The second person I met was Kim Fowley. He towered over me
with a wide, toothful grin, stick-thin, unconquered and uncon-
querable. He told me he would rather be married to me for forty-
seven years than to fuck me for forty-seven minutes. I believed this
to be the most profound statement ever uttered; my mind mattered
more than my body. My head reeled with new concepts and I thanked
God for leading me to the only correct spot on the planet for me:
In front of the double glass doors at Ben Frank's. What had I done
until this moment?

The first local group I was dying to meet was the Byrds. I was too
young to get into Ciro's, so I hung around the blatant backstage
door, which was right on Sunset, and waited for them to appear.
They had just put out their first single, "Mr. Tambourine Man,"
and brought Bob Dylan into the minds of millions of new seekers
of profundity. I had been listening to his lyrics for months like they
had been spoken from the burning bush. They were scorched into
my mind like a rancher's brand . . .

> *To let me dance beneath the diamond sky,*
> *With one hand waving free*

Silhouetted by the sea,
Circled by the circus sands
Where all memory and fate
Are driven deep beneath the waves
Let me forget about today until tomorrow.

Back to the Byrds. I fell in love with Chris Hillman the instant I laid eyes on him. He was the bass player, very introspective, deep-deepdeep and contemplative. No matter how many questions I could come up with to plague him, he only answered with one or two words. I knew the world that he gazed out on with his light-blue eyes was fraught with much deeper meaning than the one I was forced to look at from within the confines of my sixteen-year-old brain.

I latched onto the Byrds as I had the Beatles, only this time they were local and I could obsess in person. I asked anyone who would listen for their addresses and sat outside their houses looking and listening for signs of life. All five of them lived in Laurel Canyon, God's golden backyard. Most of California's rock and roll gods and goddesses lived somewhere in the glorious canyon, and I spent hours just roaming around, peeking into windows. I had to locate an ancient map to find Magnolia Street; it was at the tip-top of a high hill, at the end of a dirt pathway, with only one house overlooking the entire universe. It belonged to Chris Hillman. I started going there every day after school, sitting on the ledge, looking out over all of L.A., and on the clearest days I could see the ocean sparkling. A couple of times he roared up the hill in his Porsche, and I *know* he caught sight of me, perched on his rock fence, worshiping at the altar of his existence.

He lived in this fairy-tale pad right out of Walt Disney's wildest dreams, surrounded by eucalyptus trees and wildflowers so fragrant, to breathe was ecstasy.

March 20, 1966 . . . My love's dwelling-place reeks of the seven dwarves and prancing gnomes and elves. I expect Dopey or Sleepy to peek out of the multi-colored windows, and whistle their way to work down the old cracked steps. He came out of the drive-way with some lil' chickie. I hope he didn't see me, what a hunk he is. I really love him you know. I know I sound like a fan, but this time it's different, I promise.

When he went away on the road, I would sleep all night in his hammock and dream of him in his tight jeans and suede fringed moccasins, and delight in being just a stained-glass window away from his worldly possessions. I would lie there in the warm dark, all alone with the tall trees and night noises, trying to figure out a way to make him notice me. I conjured up some phony ID and was one of the many girls leaning up against the stage at the Whiskey a Go Go and the Trip while he solemnly plucked his bass.

April 6 . . . Chris messed up a song because of me, I know it. He was watching me very avidly and he made a wrong chord . . . I'm not digging his young, virile, stocky body *too* much . . . SLURP!

April 26 . . . Operation Chris has now gone into effect. I am preparing for the future. I must have a smaller waist and bigger hips, longer nails and prettier hair. I must grow spiritually. I must obtain Mr. Hillman.

May 12 . . . I'm in love with a 21 year old man who loves others. Is that a joke? I'll be seeing him tomorrow with my youth glaring up at him. Is that a joke? Pretending to care less about him as I watch Mike or David, painfully hoping that perhaps HE will take notice. Is that a joke? Pain and anguish. It's all a joke. It is painful to the point of lonesome glistening tears making their way down my pink and flushed cheeks. Who will have the last name "Hillman"?

I made one attempt to take him a huge bag of grapes that my dad brought back from Mexico, but the plan collapsed when the bag ripped open and I skidded halfway down the hill on seedless green grapes from Ensenada, landing on my face. I scrambled back up, leaving the squashed grapes behind, rolling in profusion toward his front porch. When I arrived home, my mom thought I was having a nervous breakdown. Collapsing in the doorway, I sat in a shivering heap without the strength to stand up and walk, tears and snot mingling with sticky grape juice on my cheeks. I had to think of another way to enter his life.

I pretended my car broke down and went to the house next door to Chris's and asked an ancient old crone if I could use her phone. I struck up an unlikely friendship with the old dame, Mrs. Motzo, and she was thrilled with my frequent visits: I was equally thrilled with her garden, which gave me a splendid view of Mr. Hillman's living-room window. I became *so* adoring of her garden that she gave me dozens of seedlings and cuttings, which I passed on to my unsuspecting mother. Mrs. Motzo's Siamese cat had a litter of perfect seal-point babies, and I cajoled her into giving me the cutest one, with the far-fetched idea that I would lay it on Chris. The little purring thing lived in my car for a couple of days while I worked up the courage to make the presentation. I waited until dusk, and clutched the kitty like it could help me overcome the mad pitter-pounding in my head. I was rabid with nerves, but I had thought so many times about this moment, blind determination led me up the dirt pathway.

> May 1 . . . He was sitting with his knees bunched up to his chin, engrossed in the yee-ha music, and when he saw me, he got up and let me in. He took the kitten in his arms, I wished it could have been me. He had on a T-shirt, jeans and bare feet, but he put on his funny wrap-around shoes because he was going to a session, which he said was going to be "a drag." He offered me some pot, but I said no thanks. He probably thinks I'm a twerp. He couldn't take the kitty because he's about to go on tour, so he took me and the kitty back to my car in his Porsche . . . *I was in his Porsche!!* It was the most perfect time in my entire life. . . . There must be a couple pages of silence . . .

I left two blank pages and continued on with my life. Chris went off to many small cities in the U.S.A. and I kept going to Hollywood, making all kinds of instant friends and spending the occasional night in the hammock on his front porch.

Rodney Bingenheimer invited me to a birthday party for a fifty-four-year-old artist named Vito, and I jumped at the chance to attend. I had heard a lot of tainted stories about Vito and his band of merry maniacs, and had seen them around town, dancing with total abandon, adorning clubs and concert halls, blowing minds before the phrase existed.

My heart was beating madly as we ascended his steep, shadowy stairs, rickety and promising. I was fascinated by the paraphernalia on the stairwell walls: tatty old doilies, fading pornographic photos tacked up with bits of lace and yarn, tattered silk flowers and curling antique postcards, all kinds of old hats, puppets hanging upside down with lopsided grins and scary faces. Amid all this zaniness were several bright and shining photographs of the most angelic blond child ever born. When we reached the top and peeked through the glinting glass beads, we saw Vito reclining on a rose-colored velvet couch, surrounded by lavishly decorated people of all ages and races who seemed to be paying him homage. He had long, graying, uncombed hair and a ragtag beard that looked like it had been dipped in a bottle of glitter; he was wearing only a lace loincloth, and his chest had been painted like a peacock feather. He appeared to be directing a singular puppet show on top of the coffee table. A nude cherub was magically prancing around the tabletop, laughing and bowing and delighting in being the center of attention as Vito tapped out the rhythm for his dance. It was only when the little puppet turned around to face me that I realized he was a little boy, the same little angel boy in the heavenly pictures I saw on my way up the stairs.

As the dance came to an end, while everyone was cheering and applauding, Rodney led me by the hand and presented me to Vito like a prize. I couldn't help but like him on the spot; he had an obvious hint of the devil in his twinkly eyes and his face crinkled into a sexy old grin as he said, "Welcome, my little turkey pie." The little boy jumped off the table right on top of a festive cat-eyed lady next to Vito, dug his little fist into her handmade doily blouse, pulled out her right tit, and began to nurse. I had never seen a baby nursing, let alone a three-year-old boy who could walk and talk and sing and dance!!! I was amazed.

My tongue was tied in knots as I gazed around the room at the colorful clutter that Vito, his wife, Szou (pronounced Sue), and their son, Godot, called home. The ethereal lighting made everything look pink; all the wild-eyed people looked flushed and rouged and ready to wreak havoc. The walls were alive and about to topple down, they were so laden down with outrageous items. Old dolls' heads with unblinking eyes tacked up alongside antique undergarments gave the place a little character. Cockeyed caricatures painted in brilliant colors stared down at me from all four walls. On closer inspection, I realized they resembled most of the people in the room and were signed "Karl Franzoni." I noticed an intensely unappealing guy in hand-painted red tights tweaking all the girls' bottoms, and when he turned around to get his fingers on yet another, I saw that his tacky satin cape had a huge *F* emblazoned on the back. I figured the *F* was for Franzoni; I was wrong. When he saw me looking at him, he stuck out this incredibly long tongue that seemed to unroll across the room, and he called out, "Come meet Captain Fuck!" I didn't make a mad dash to greet him, so he came toward me, grinning hugely, with a tooth missing in front and a wild kink of frizzed-out hair around a gleaming bald spot, like a halo of used Brillo pads. His lizard's tongue leaped out at my right cheek and licked off my blush-on. From that moment on, he pursued me like a rabid dog, but that didn't stop him from pursuing every other female within sniffing distance.

Szou and Vito's charming pad was directly above their very own antiquey-type store where they sold whatever they felt like selling. Szou was the forerunner of thrift-store fashion, and there were always plenty of falling-apart velvet dresses and forties teddies available for a pittance. Whatever she got tired of wearing, she put a price tag on. She also concocted her own creations out of doilies and rags, which cost a bit more but were the ultimate in antique chic.

In the back of the store, behind the pre-post-trendy garments, Vito had stashed a single mattress inside a man-sized mousehole. If a girl didn't watch out, he would reach through those musty rustling taffeta drapes, grab a slim ankle, and let her in on his secret. A few of the girls I knew wound up behind those dusty drapes and described in detail his enormous proportions. By a miracle I escaped this fate.

Under the store was Vito's studio, a huge basement where his incredible statues lined the walls with stunned expressions on their faces. He gave sculpting lessons on Tuesday nights, and dance lessons to free your spirit on Thursday nights. I knew I was on the threshold of freeing my spirit, so I took my place among the maniacs and joined forces with the freaks. My mom thought she had made some humongous error in bringing me up; in a few short months I had become an embarrassing bohemian, exposing wantonly the tits that had been kept so ridiculously under wraps. I was freefreefree, loosening any phony ties that might bind.

The next time I saw Vito was at the eulogy for the pagan saint of the postbop, prepop culture, Lenny Bruce, who had obliterated himself one shiny, startling day up Sunset Plaza Drive. Me and my friend Sherri donned our most daring velvet frocks and hitchhiked out past many, many spanking-new shopping malls to the West Valley. We were on our way to celebrate the short life of a guy we didn't know too much about, except for the indisputable fact that he'd been very, *very* HIP.

Two or three hundred people turned up at his grave site, and we all paraded to a KDAY DJ's patio to listen while Phil Spector recalled Lenny's greatness. Sitting cross-legged on the grass, my black velvet skirt slit all the way up, I solemnly paid silent attention, occasionally stealing a glance at the swing set, where Frank Zappa sat on the slide, wearing short flowered bell-bottoms and big flowered sneakers. A few other people spoke of Lenny's greatness, one of whom was Dennis Hopper, who was staring a searing hole right through me. I recognized him as one of Buzz's hostile bunch, puncturing Jim Stark's whitewalls in *Rebel Without a Cause*. He said that Lenny wouldn't have wanted us to be miserable, so we started dancing and having fun, and I didn't get home until after dark.

I had some profound revelation that death shouldn't be mourned as I bounced down the street carrying balloons, but I didn't know the extent of Lenny's greatness, so maybe I was feeling overly idealistic. Something got into me that day, some kind of stand-up-straight pride about being a blond American girl, so ripe, I was about to pop off the tree.

I was listening to KDAY a few days later, hoping to hear the new Stones single, when the DJ, Tom Clay, made a startling announcement: "For five days I've been trying to locate a blond, blue-eyed girl who attended Lenny Bruce's eulogy at my house last Saturday. She was wearing a long black skirt, slit up the side, and a red-velvet blouse. If anyone out there knows how to get in touch with this girl, have her call the station. I have some great news for her concerning a movie project . . ." I sat there in my rock and roll room, trying to figure out if what I had just heard was in my imagination, or had it come across the airwaves through my funky teenage speakers? When I phoned KDAY, Tom Clay was so thrilled to hear from me that we had our conversation right on the air! He told me this fairy-tale news: Terry Southern, the tall, disheveled British gentleman who was with Dennis Hopper at the eulogy, was dying to meet me. His new book was going to be made into a movie, and he thought I was the spitting image of his title character, Candy.

I had never read the book, but I knew it was soft-core, sex-ridden stuff, and I was delighted to be thought of in those terms by the author. It made me realize that I was really coming of sexual age, even though I still had not participated in the ACT itself. (Bob Martine and I had certainly discovered the thrills of oral ardor, however, and under his Italian tutelage I had become a truly proficient pupil.)

I met with Mr. Southern at MGM Studios on another bright and shiny day, clutching my recently read copy of *Candy*, wearing a short frilly item acquired for the occasion, feeling totally like a tantalizing Hollywood starlet. I was alive and alert, and on edge with excitement as I met him on the gigantic steps of the gigantic studio. He was the epitome of elegant debauchery as he elegantly kissed my hand and said, "Hello, Candy." I tried to demonstrate my innocent allure as he ushered me through the majestic golden gates by asking him what the letters *MGM* stood for. "Mystery, Golden Mystery, my dear girl . . ." I believed it for a long time. As we walked through the lot, I tried to imagine where they caged that glorious lion that could roar on cue, and I wondered if I might run into a major motion-picture star, and if I could contain my excitement enough to continue to be alluring.

We went into a massive sound stage, and right in front of my already wide eyes stood Tony Curtis, in all his gooey, black-haired splendor. He had been one of my drive-in movie idols from pre-pubescence, when chlorine sparkled in my ponytail and the whole world was in Taras Bulba Technicolor, so, needless to say, I was a goner. Mr. Southern introduced me as his new star and Tony Curtis made small talk with me in his "Yonda lies da castle of my fodda" accent. I was a double-goner. We watched for a while as he made a fool out of himself with Anna Maria Alberghetti, romping through a B-feature light comedy/romance. We left between takes, and as he waved good-bye to me, his hair-goo gleamed in the spotlight.

My fifteen minutes of fleeting fame came to an end when Terry Southern's funds fell through and I was brought down to earth with a thud. The only thing I got out of the experience (besides a heavy acting bug) was several calls from Dennis Hopper begging for a tryst, but he scared me with his devilish demeanor and those pop-eyes that seemed to poke at me across the expanse of lawn at Lenny Bruce's eulogy that sunny Saturday.

I graduated high school in a white-lace drop-waist dress and candy-apple-red flats alongside two Miss Americas wearing fabric pumps that were dyed to match their handbags. Bob Martine was one of the onlookers as I grabbed my diploma and split the scene. I was now free to go to Hollywood any night of the week, and I did. My mom and dad wanted to know what I was going to do with my life. Didn't they know I was among those in the throes of a revolution? Couldn't they see the invisible peace sign tattooed on my forehead?

I needed some information that couldn't be found in an encyclopedia, so I turned to the Ouija board. When Iva and I put our fingers on the pointer, it went wild. Our first encounter was with a fellow named G.S. He told me he was my personal guide, and loved me dearly and forever. He reeled off the people who were "the chosen ones," "the special ones," and "the evil ones." I, of course, along with a few people like Chris Hillman and Mick Jagger, was "above chosen." Good old G.S. got "inside" people, and he spent a good deal of time hanging around inside Chris.

> **August 14, 1966 . . . We have a mission to accomplish, as G.S. puts it, "Tear down the gates of hate." People *hate* too much, and we are living in a world of plastic. Until now, we weren't even noticed, but NOW (as the spirits predicted) the riots on the Sunset Strip have started. I marched with Randy during the peace demonstration yesterday. Unbelievable! I just listened to Randy, Rat and Animal on CBS radio tonight. It's great, we're being heard!! The revolution has begun.**

I had a constant ball in Hollywood in the guise of the Great Mission. I met Rickaewy (prounounced "Ricky") Applebaum at Vito's dance class, and saw right away that G.S. had entered the body and mind of this frizzy-haired, angelic, poetic, wild boy; I could see it in his eyes, which penetrated my ego and hurtled it into space. He passed me a note that said, "You possess my soul, and all I'm asking from you is a leaf."

I was so happy I wept.

> **October 8 . . . He sat down next to me and asked why I was sad.**
>   **R. Did you lose the one you love?**
>   **P. (smiles)**
>   **R. Can't you find him?**
>   **P. No, I can't.**
>   **R. Well, I love you, and you don't even need a road-map.**

I took Rickaewy to Reseda to spend the weekend in the spare room, and when my mom saw that he had half a beard on one side and half a moustache on the other, the evaporated milk curdled in her coffee. She tried so hard to be nice because he was a human being, but her eyes pleaded with me in agony. I told her he was a misunderstood poet and we were in love, but two weeks later it was all over, even though Vito had sanctioned the relationship as "very groovy." My mom heaved one of many major sighs of relief.

I made a bunch of new girlfriends by just gliding down the Strip, smiling overtly at all passersby, most of whom would smile back at me with that knowing "sixties" look. Some would walk with me down the crowded boulevard, spewing their newfound wisdom into my newly opened ears, and I would expound to them, and we would nod in perfect agreement. It was such a relief to know you weren't alone with those humongous unprecedented ideas.

One of the girls who wound up right beside me was Beverly, the most ravishing beauty ever born. She had everything that I longed for in the way of stunningness; her breasts were the perfect size and shape and they swayed with her every step, her eyelashes were long, her eyes were round and green, her honey-colored hair was thick and hung like gold to the middle of her back: She was the first girl I was ever attracted to and the concept was astonishing. I imagined kissing her and tasting the honey that was surely in her mouth, just about ready to dribble down her perfectly pointed chin, down between her perfectly pointed titties. She was gaspingly gorgeous, a combination of baby-doll innocence and hard-core tragedy, and she fluctuated between the two with uncertain irregularity. She was haunted by some sorrowful thing that followed her around like the Grim Reaper, and I tried desperately to keep the thing at bay.

We dared to do things together that we wouldn't have done alone, and we stood back defiantly, waiting for a reaction. One night, after a baby-powder session, which was a ritual we performed at least once a week, we decided to surprise one of the cute guys we met on the Strip. We sat naked in the middle of her feather bed and proceeded to cover each other from head to toe with an entire can of Johnson's baby powder, administered with oversized powder puffs with joyous aplomb and shrieks of delight. It was like a pillow fight with powder puffs at a pajama party for two. We usually cuddled up and fell asleep after this ritual, or sometimes we'd get all dolled up and go dancing, but we had one of those harebrained "I Love Lucy" schemes in mind on this particular warm night at two A.M.

White as sheets, we ran to the gray VW that she called "Friths-bottom" and started driving out to this guy's house in North Hollywood. Halfway through Laurel Canyon, we realized that we were being followed by half a dozen men, who were probably jacking off under their steering wheels. I felt like titillating them literally, so I pressed my powdered tits against the window as one car pulled up alongside us. When I realized this guy was half crazed and about to climb out of his moving car, I shouted for Beverly to turn up one of the tiny twisting streets to escape from all these guys who thought they were riding in a porno parade. We hid in a rustic garage, imagining horny men cruising the canyon until dawn, looking for the naked ghost girls, and laughed our asses off. When we arrived at our destination, we woke Mr. Adorable from a deep sleep, and the look on his face when he opened the door was worth ten thousand words. Our barks were infinitely more blatant than our bites, so all he got besides a few powdery kisses was a very large eyeful.

Beverly and I became a team—we even got married; she was the groom because she was tougher than me, and she looked better in pants. She wore a baggy suit, drew on a little moustache, stuffed her goldilocks into a fedora, and we walked down an imaginary aisle. I wore a white satin teddy and satin spikes, and cried when she put her grandmother's wedding band on my finger. We never consummated our marriage. I, for one, was too shy to bring it up, and I never knew if she felt intimate toward me, although we were very romantic on a Romeo-Juliet level of adoration. I was in awe of her beauty and the graceful way she could go from one extreme to another and back again before I managed to make it to the second extreme. When I gathered up the courage to make an attempt to enter her gaping pit of grief, she slammed the door so hard it gave me a stomachache. Because she wanted to spare me the details of her despair, I often felt left out in the cold, hard daylight, while she floated around in a warm, gray agony that I could never comprehend. She wrote in gray ink and had tattered black lace covering her windows, and she collected frogs, mostly those horrible stuffed little guys from Mexico that played poker or pool with their little frog lips pulled back in a grimace of fraudulent humanity.

Her Valley mother gave up on Beverly long before I met her, but Beverly sat in her candlelit room burning human hairs and fingernails to provoke the one she loved into giving her the time of day. Yet there was a little streak of joy in her that gravitated to me, and her perfect dimples pierced her alabaster cheeks, giving me chill-bumps whenever we had powder parties and whenever we went dancing, and the time we walked down the aisle together in our antique wedding attire.

Vito's exquisite little puppet child, Godot, fell through a skylight during a wacky photo session on the roof and died at age three and a half. I was beside myself with sorrow, but Vito and Szou insisted on continuing with our plans for the evening. We went out dancing, and when people asked where little Godot was, Vito said, "He died today." It was weird, really weird, but I tried to feel like I did at Lenny Bruce's eulogy as I danced the night away, stealing glances at Vito and Szou while they screamed and sweated, hurling their grief into the four corners of the room. Szou found out she was pregnant a week later. We all waited for Godot to come back, but Szou had a girl and named her Groovee Nipple.

Vito's troupe danced all over town and were never asked to pay a cover charge. We ran into other girls we liked and carried on flamboyant fellowships that lasted as long as we let them. One night at the Galaxy, a little club next to the Whiskey a Go Go, they announced a new house band, the Iron Butterfly, and I merged with their music like it was beating through my bloodstream. I eventually merged with all the members of the group except the bass player— he just wasn't my type.

I showed my affection for the opposite sex in those days by giving them head, and I was very popular indeed. I tried not to think of myself as being cheap or easy or any of those other terms that were used to describe loose, free, peace-loving girls; I just wanted to show my appreciation for their music, for their taste in clothes, for their heads, hands, and hearts. I found myself in many broom closets and backseats with my head buried in many pairs of satin trousers, but I held on to my virginity like it contained the secrets of Tutankhamen. I kept the padlock on until I was nearing twenty, and the guy I finally chose to do the breaking and entering was, unfortunately, Mr. Wrong.

The main miracle in the Iron Butterfly was Daryl, the lead singer. He wore shiny pink and white with his scrawny chest exposed under the bright lights where he saturated his satin with sweat, which was a major part of his damp appeal. He loved being adored and he adored himself above all; there was a mirror directly opposite the stage, across the dance floor, and it was difficult to attract his attention away from his own splendid reflection. "Look at me, Daryl, give me a sign that you know I'm right under you, my flushed cheeks upturned, waiting to catch your highly prized beads of sweat. . . ." On occasion I would give him a tweak in the crotch area and his gaze would settle on me like I was being christened.

I was of two minds about my behavior, but I could not, would not, stop myself.

November 6, 1967 . . . Does God disagree with the things I am doing? If he will put up with me, I'll straighten myself out. Perhaps if I had been born in Idaho none of these things would be burdening my head . . . but I'm in L.A. and here I'll stay. Too late now. What makes me walk up to the stage and boldly touch Daryl's private parts? What am I trying to prove to whom?

I had an insane crush on Daryl, but he had a batty beauty that he dedicated songs to named Della. She looked like Olivia Hussey as Juliet, and together she and Daryl stuck out like a throbbing thumb. He wore his hair in a dark, shiny pageboy, and she tended to it with care and devotion.

As an entertainer, Daryl had no competition; he was in constant motion and would rub his dick against the microphone pole when he got excited, which was most of the time, and we all swooned like we had as preteens when Bobby Vee winked at the camera on *Amer-*

ican Bandstand. (Of course, we were safe in our black-and-white living rooms then; now we were teetering on the brink of psychedelic madness.) Darling Daryl's stage outfits were grandly outlandish, kind of a cross between Charo and Tom Jones with a tinge of Mick Jagger thrown in for credibility: hot-pink crop-top, belly button hanging out, and the widest, shiniest pleated bell-bottoms ever seen on a man; or a skin-tight one-piece turquoise jumpsuit, which he would unzip, taunting his public with his pubic hair. He paraded around the stage, teasing the adoring Daryl devotees as he humped the air, all the while admiring himself flagrantly. He was in ecstasy up there and he just asked for it (begged and pleaded for it!).

I had a desperate need to show him how much I appreciated his stage persona and songwriting abilities, although I didn't want to interfere in his relationship with the divine Della. Since I requested nothing from him, he gladly placed himself in my hands on many different occasions in many different locations. I loved feeling his forbidden flesh and smelling his sweet skin; I could close my eyes and imagine him shimmering onstage, and for those few moments I gave him back some of the intense pleasure he had given me so many times. And I still felt like he was doing me a favor.

Haight-Ashbury wafted south and I longed to stand on that very corner, breathe the unwashed hippie air, see all the dirty bare feet, and even if it was only for a weekend, I wanted to live in a commune and eat brown rice off communal dishes, maybe meet some pretty hippie boy and discover the true meaning of life.

I didn't want to go alone, especially since my '59 Chevy convertible bit the dust, so I invited my one remaining Beatle friend, Linda, to make the trip with me. I was hoping she might want to expand her horizons about four hundred miles and accompany me to San Francisco. As it turned out, she moved into the first commune we entered and became "housemother," which means she did all the cooking and cleaning. Very communal.

We got a ride up there with a few other L.A. explorers and went directly to Haight-Ashbury to see what was going on. As excited as

I was about being in a new environment and being where the concept of peace and love had reoriginated, I was dismayed with the hippie look. The girls had straight stringy hair with lots of split ends, and had their bodies covered up with long sacky peasant dresses and shawls. Makeup was a no-no, but the natural look was much too natural for me; I had my lipstick tube on my person at all times. The boys looked a little better; they all wore jeans so at least you could see the shape of their bottoms. The girls got away with murder, hiding a multitude of sins under a multitude of yardage, but the feeling of "we are one" pervaded and I blended in with the mass consciousness as though I had been born at the Free Clinic.

Linda and I walked back and forth and up and down the streets and let it be known that we were looking for a commune. Everyone seemed to panhandle from everyone else, so we asked a bespectacled, pimply blond guy for some spare change just to see how it felt. It was our cosmic luck that we chose this particular guy, because he asked us to come to his commune, Kerista House, and share dinner with "the family." The way I imagined communal living was a far cry from what greeted me after our journey across the bridge into Oakland. In the living room were about six or seven funky sheetless mattresses and a couple of ripped-up chairs, and people were lolling around, dressed in those hand-painted Indian bedspreads that should have been on the bare beds. Tacked up on the peeling walls were numerous curling posters for the Avalon Ballroom and the Fillmore, announcing such major acts as the Quicksilver Messenger Service and the Strawberry Alarm Clock. The girls gave us serene know-it-all smiles and the guys looked us up and down just like regular guys in L.A. always did, which was disconcerting; I thought there might be another level of communication in the land of peace and love. The towels in the bathroom looked like Salvation Army rejects and had obviously been the target for all the Kerista House feet. I tried to avoid looking at the little piles of pubic hair adorning the once-white sink, and concentrated on the true meaning of communal living. These people had deeper things on their minds than Mr. Clean and Spic and Span.

After our meal of sticky brown rice and smelly old vegetables, which I consumed with a joyous show of good vibes, I itched to get back to Haight-Ashbury to enjoy the night life. Linda chose to stay behind and become one with the pimply guy and the rest of the family. She had recently been traumatized when her air-force father burst out of the closet, where he had been lurking for many years behind his collegiate crew cut. He totally shattered his large family's foregone conclusion that Daddy would love Mommy forever. Linda wanted to believe that it was OK for him to be gay, since we were all one anyway, but she was having trouble convincing herself. At this moment, all she wanted was to feel like she belonged somewhere, and to create another family to merge with. By staying at Kerista House, she was flipping her father the big bird.

Haight-Ashbury smelled like a redwood-sized incense stick as I made my way through the wild conglomeration of peaceful humanity. The air was so sticky-sweet that I knew if I happened to touch anyone or anything, I would stick to it like bubble gum on the bottom of my high-heeled sandal. There was lots of pot going around, but I still believed it led to heroin, so I declined as if I were high enough already. I probably got high on the air anyway—I felt like I was walking on it.

When I reached the Psychedelic Supermarket, which was blaring the Grateful Dead into unwashed ears and sending out a spectrum of colors for dilated eyes, a perfectly stunning specimen asked me for some spare change. I didn't have any, but I made a show of looking for some, hoping he would linger long enough to become entranced by me. As I dug around in the bottom of my hand-embroidered purse, made by Szou, I noticed he was wearing a top hat and had one of those big white Eskimo dogs on a homemade paisley leash. He was kind to me even though I couldn't accommodate him, and I watched as he scored a few coins from another girl. I didn't act surprised when he came back to ask me if I would like to get a doughnut.

As we walked around the corner, he bent my ear as though he had been alone on a desert island for two years. His name was

Bummer Bob because he was the first person in San Fransisco to call panhandling "bumming"; his dog was called Snowfox, and was the best friend a man ever had. His eyes were pale but piercing, an intense blue, and he stared hard as he spoke of his lonely life, but he liked to be alone because no one had ever understood him. He was a poet, a *misunderstood* poet, but that was OK too because someday they would all know his name; but he would still wind up alone, so it didn't really matter anyway. We ate doughnuts in the darkest doughnut shop in the world, and he read his poetry from a tattered book by candlelight with such ferocity, I thought he might cry. I don't remember what any of it was about, but I thought it was scary and beautiful. He read it like I were a huge audience, and seemed surprised when he reached the end and I was the only one applauding. We walked over to Golden Gate Park and made out fervently. I imagined he was Keats or Byron, a doomed beauty from another realm, and I was the only one on earth who understood him.

Years later I saw him on TV being interviewed by Truman Capote; he was Bobby Beausoleil, Charles Manson's cupid-faced killer. He chopped off Gary Hinman's ear and taunted him with it, then tortured and killed him and some other unfortunate guy. He had no remorse at all, and even said he would do it again. His eyes had turned into hard, flat, matte black buttons, like somebody had thrown darts into them, and I tried to remember what his poetry had been about. I could only recall a beautiful, strange boy who was all alone with his poems and an elegant top hat, and I wondered what happened to Snowfox, the best friend a man ever had.

The next glorious day held a monumental event, the first Human-Be-In at Golden Gate Park. (Whoever dreamed up that name for the event was a total genius and should have his or her name written somewhere to commemorate his or her moment of brilliance!) It was like an enormous picnic, only everyone was together instead of on separate blankets with separate identities. The sky was the bluest, the trees were the greenest, babies in tie-dye were toddling around with gooped-up bananas in their little fists, dogs were running loose and free, everyone was smiling and glad to be alive on the planet. It was a true resurgence of love and it must have been felt as far away as the isle of Capri. I was floating around in the Garden of Eden, thrilled to be a human being at the Human-Be-In, knowing the world could be saved if we loved one another. I was draped in flowers, bestowed upon me by my brothers and sisters. I was a laughing, loving, living, breathing Princess of Peace . . .

Saturday, January 14, 1967 . . . I loved and laughed with 15,000 people, including Allen Ginsberg, Lawrence Ferlinghetti, Tim Leary, Michael McLure, and the wonderful San Francisco pop bands. I loved "The Quicksilver Messenger Service." I was quite attracted to Gary, the lead singer, and was fortunate enough to tell him he was beautiful.

When it came right down to it, rock and roll groups were my life. I slept that night on a stinky, smelly mattress at Kerista House with two other people I'd never met, and had the best sleep of my life. Linda had turned into housemom overnight, and when I asked, "Are you sure you'll be happy here?" she staunchly defended her new station in life. We hugged and I told her I would be back soon and we could share hot apple pie at the Doggie Diner, which was directly across the street. She was beaming as I bid farewell, but in a tremendously spacy way. Maybe she had taken acid.

At home, in my warm, cozy, clean childhood bed, with all four Beatles grinning down at me from all four walls, I thought of Linda and tried to imagine her picking pubic hair from gritty tiles and poking through garbage cans for wilted green beans, and I was glad to be snug as a bourgeois bug in a rug.

I tromped around the Strip, becoming a regular with all the other regulars, getting more daring and having more fun. An elegant old man, Bob Stone, head violinist with Toscanini, who was a fixture on Sunset, proclaimed me "the Queen of the Hips and the Rocks." He wanted to be the King, but was about fifty years too late, which he constantly regretted. He called titties "headlights," and bottoms "bumpers," and we called him "What's Happening Bob," because he always wanted to know. Whenever I was hungry, he would buy me a burger at Ben Frank's or Canter's and try to talk me into giving him a tumble. The horrible night I found out Chris Hillman had gotten married, I fainted into the glass doors of Canter's and almost cracked my head open. Bob was there to console me while I sobbed into my strawberry cream pie. I got crushes on lots of different boys, but Chris had captivated a chunk of my heart for eternity.

June 8 . . . I'm in rather a serene mood, I want some excitement, something thrilling, a change—radical and swift, beautiful and new. I'm not certain whether I want it to be lasting or brief.

It turned out to be brief and lasting.

A new club called Bido Lido's opened up at the other end of Sunset, in a basement up an alleyway under an old office building, and I was thrilled because I always loved a new club. Beverly and I dressed up as man and wife one sultry evening and decided to check out the brand new band, the Doors. Excitedly, we steered ourselves down the steep white steps, pressing against the wall in dramatic fashion when someone attempted to pass us on their way up. (I got to rub up against Sky Saxon of the Seeds on his way up the stairs for fresh air.) The club was packed to capacity, so Beverly and I connived our way to the top of the only booth to see what the big fuss was about.

A bunch of pretty ordinary guys came onstage and proceeded to go into a pretty ordinary number when a guy in black leather slithered on and filled the place so completely that everyone else might as well have been in the La Brea tar pits. I sat bolt upright and gasped at the glorious sight—someone new and local to drool and dribble over! It was a historical moment. He clutched the microphone like it was a crucial part of his body and he moaned like he really meant it. He moved with the unnatural grace of someone out of control, grounded only by the fact that his feet happened to be on the floor. On top of all this, he looked like a Greek god gone wrong, with masses of dark-brown curls and a face that sweaty dreams are made of. And he sang with a strong baritone groan, punctuated with snarls and sweetness and indecent desire. I blacked out.

From that night on, I was part of the Doors' audience, standing in front, listening to Jim Morrison put into words all those deep, dark feelings of angst that we thought were unspeakable. The girls understood his rebel poetry and imagined all that animal magnetism under the sheets. "The men don't know, but the little girls understand."

May 20 . . . You surge to the stage, moving around and around like a human tide coming in, and the lights go out. You're screaming and breathing and waiting in the warm dark, knowing that Jim Morrison is about to plant himself right above you.

That was the first night I saw him dive into the audience. It was a swan dive, the kind I was trying to do at the YWCA in the summer of '56, only Jim Morrison didn't hold his nose. He just let go of himself and careened into the black hole, knowing the masses would hold him up. HE came to US, like no one had done before, and no one would do again.

The Iron Butterfly's bass player sunlighted at a hospital during the day, doing menial tasks, and one afternoon he came upon a clear liquid, used to inject into ladies in labor, commonly called a saddle-block. He had an occasion to sniff it and found that it instantly altered his consciousness to the extent that he lifted several quarts of it that very day. I happened to be at the Butterfly house that very day, hoping to find Daryl in a receptive mood, when Jerry arrived with a load of this stuff, called Trimar. At this point in my life I was a drug virgin; I hadn't tainted my lungs or liver yet and didn't have any imminent plans to do so. Daryl and Jerry were pouring it onto whatever piece of cloth was available, inhaling deeply, and collapsing like Jell-O in a giggling heap. A few minutes later they were seminormal and would sniff again, going into ecstatic paroxysms that dissolved into beatific grins. In between takes I wanted a description of the feeling it gave and Daryl shoved a soaked wad of cloth into my nose. I fell spinning down the rabbit hole with all the walls breathing and twenty wah-wah pedals twanging in my brain. Of course, at that point I got my own sodden wad. I believed that the clearness of the liquid denied the fact that it could possibly be a harmful drug. The going rate for Trimar on the street was ten dollars for a teensy-tinsy vial, and I had a quart bottle in my newly acquired '62 Olds glove compartment at all times. I had yet to smoke pot or take pills or acid, but I spent many hours in the zone with my crystal-clear killer drug. (Even when I found out that it was used in zoos to knock out gorillas and elephants, I refused to believe it could also knock out my brain cells.)

I met a girl at the Cheetah who lived above the Country Canyon Store, smack-dab in the heart of Laurel Canyon, and we became instant friends. I would sit and gaze out her huge picture window that overlooked the roof of the store and Kirkwood Avenue (where you turned to go up to Chris Hillman's house), contemplate my future, and daydream about being someone's rock and roll wife. Sandy worked at some straight job, so I would spend the night and wake up around noon to a quiet, empty house and pretend I lived there with Donovan (if I was in a mellow mood) or Jim Morrison (if I was feeling brilliant and daring). On nights when Beverly and I had spent many wild hours of Sunset Strip fun, we would both sleep over, then wake up the next day and gaze out the window together.

We hardly ever wore any clothes when we were alone, and a horrific incident took place at Sandy's canyon sanctuary one afternoon. Beverly and I were stark-raving in front of the enormous picture window, dancing to "Turn, Turn, Turn" by the Byrds without a single care in the world. As we collapsed to the floor, out of breath, we heard a pounding at the door and dashed to cover ourselves with Sandy's fake-fur couch cover. Two gruff voices demanded entrance, insisting on having a piece of what they saw being flaunted in the picture window. When we refused them, one guy tried to break down the door while the other started on the windows. I frantically chased around the house trying to shut and lock the open windows before Mr. Obnoxious got to them. When we screeched for the police at the top of our voices and grabbed for the phone to scream rape, their pig-headed commotion ceased and we assumed the goons had come to their senses and fled the canyon. After we calmed down, the whole thing seemed hilarious and we had a big laugh. I was still giggling on my way into the bathroom, and as I sat down on the pot to pee, I looked up and saw one of the lascivious old farts squinting in at me, his stubble damp with dribble. I let out another piercing squeal, Beverly ran in shouting that the police had just arrived, and with a bug-eyed grin he was gone. It seemed like I was always in the danger zone without knowing how I got there.

I had been hanging around the canyon house for a couple of weeks, when I awakened one day to the glorious sound of the Doors seeping in under the windowshade in the womb room where I was still sleeping at two in the afternoon. I knew they had recorded an album, but it hadn't been released yet! Who had a copy? Who-who-who within a hundred yards of my presence had a copy? Preparing myself for a blast of the perpetual sunlight, I emerged from my blankets to seek out the owner of the record. I was thrilled to realize that the music was coming from the green shack-house to my left and down a few dozen precarious steps. In Laurel Canyon, that meant right next door. I threw on a little purple dress and started down the steps to make the acquaintance of the ultrahip neighbor who had a prereleased copy of the Doors' first album.

I decided to peek in a window first so I wouldn't catch this hip person in the middle of an act of intimacy brought on by the sensual moans of Jim Morrrison. I tiptoed onto the rickety porch, looked into the kitchen, and clapped my hand over my mouth to capture the scream that threatened to shatter the staggering moment. Jim Morrison in the FLESH, wearing nothing but his black leather pants, was digging around in the fridge, humming along with "The End"; "Mother, I want to . . ." Oh my God!!! I pinched myself, peeked again for the sheer joy of it, and scrambled back up the stairs to decide what to do next. He moves, he breathes, he lives next door!!!!

By the time Sandy got home from work, I was a puddle on her kitchen floor and had reached the place where Carlos Casteneda only dreams about. In one of my semilucid moments, I told her about her infamous, soon-to-be-famous neighbor and she suggested I knock on his door and introduce myself like a good neighbor should. In my bonzo condition, I said, "Why didn't I think of that?" I don't know how long it took me to get down the steps; the gongs were always bonging away in my brain, so I couldn't hear the birds twittering or cars going by, much less the ticking of my cheap Timex.

When I came to my extremely sensual senses, I was in the middle of a perfect backbend on Jim Morrison's tatty Oriental rug, my purple velvet minidress completely over my head, his redheaded girlfriend glaring down at me. I expected Rod Serling to appear in the doorway to narrate this ultimate in "uh-oh" moments.

Trying to regain a drop of composure, I stood up out of my backbend and offered the redhead a spot of Trimar, avoiding the lizard king who hovered in the corner whispering "Get it on" under his breath. She told me I had better leave and I didn't even remember arriving! Bowing and scraping, I backed out the door and ran back up the stairs, berating myself profusely for being such an idiot. I should have known he didn't live alone (not that it would have made one bit of difference in my cockeyed condition). My ears had just stopped ringing when there was a noisy commotion down in the green house; we heard a shrill voice screaming "Don't you dare go up there!" and then Jim was at the door, smiling sheepishly, a glint in his eye. He was very interested in my quart of Trimar, accepted my handkerchief, and inhaled deeply. Social amenities were out the window for the next few hours. We sniffed the stuff, lolling around the floor, laughing at everything, until the bottle was dry. The good thing about Trimar was that you got no hangover from it, no headache or any kind of comedown, but you definitely wanted more. By this time it was the middle of the night and I was unable to obtain a second bottle, so Jim said a pleasant good-night and thanked Sandy and me for the wonderful hospitality. I was disappointed that he had made no attempt to lay a hand on me, but I had hopes for the future, the very near future as a matter of fact.

The very next night, the Doors were playing the Hullabaloo Club at Sunset and Vine (formerly the Moulin Rouge with the big forties lady's face peeling off the front of the building, her red neon lips still flickering) and I made sure to have a bottle of Trimar for the event. I had recently learned about sound checks, and knew to be at the club between four and six o'clock, when the band checked the monitors and instruments for the evening's entertainment. I went around to the back and perched blatantly on the steps to the backstage door, wearing a handmade black-and-white–striped bell-bottom set, carrying my precious, pathetic muskrat jacket and an orange-juice jar full of Trimar. I could hear the rest of the band tuning up inside and desperately hoped that Jim would arrive, sans redhead, scoop me up, take me BACKSTAGE, and kiss my lips off. And that's exactly what happened.

I had a couple of hankies in my homemade matching black-and-white bag, and during our make-out session we indulged wildly in the mind-damaging drug. I had never kissed anyone while high before and it was a revelation! I melted in his mouth like honey, my whole body became sticky liquid, and his fingers on my face pushed holes through my cheeks like they were on fire and left gaping holes where more honey gushed out. I sat very still in a gooey puddle while he went onstage to check his groans, and when he came back I was coming to my senses. He took me by the hand and we climbed a rickety ladder up to a dingy, dark loft where a bunch of old lighting equipment was rusting away, and taking my muskrat jacket, he laid it out on the wooden planks like a damsel was in distress. What a face he had! One of God's greatest gifts to rock and roll was that guy's face. And there he was right above me, his lips parted and his eyes closed, going in and out of focus as I inhaled my hanky. We rolled around up there for a timeless time until a familiar sound crept into our senses. Jim recognized it before I did and was making his way down the ladder as I sat up and heard the first few bars of "Light My Fire." Was the sound check still going on? I pulled my clothes on, following Jim, and as he reached the microphone I looked down to see the place full of wriggling, squirming audience! I was ONSTAGE with the Doors, my mouth hanging wide open, dragging my tatty coat, my half-bottle of Trimar, and my soppy hankies, too shocked to move. A kind roadie put his arm around me and escorted me to the wings, where I waited for Jim to collect me after the show, which to my delight he did.

He drove my Oldsmobile all around Hollywood and I sat next to him, cuddling up like I had his ring around my neck, and we talked about Trimar. He said it might be "hurting our heads" and gave me a lecture on drug abuse, telling me the persona he put forward was an elaborate act, and he really wanted to be noticed as a poet. On our way to Tiny Naylor's on La Brea, he pulled the car over, grabbed the bottle of Trimar, and threw it out the window into a yard full of overgrown ivy. "Now we won't be tempted." We had date-nut bread and fresh orange juice while the sun came up, then cruised the silent Strip to a little hotel where he was staying during his feud with the redhead.

May 31 . . . After some heavy necking, he climbed from behind the wheel and said, "I really want to see you again, darling, come here and see me or call any time." I called and he had checked out. What a drag.

That was the only time I had my hands on Jim Morrison; he turned out to be very much a one-woman man. As far as I know, he spent the rest of his life with the redhead, whose name was also Pamela, and the relationship was of the stormy nature, but I guess he loved her madly and vice versa. I didn't dare return to the green house after she ordered me out, so I had to be content with waking up in a hot sweat, that glorious face hovering over me in my damp dreams. He did a good deed for me without even knowing it; he helped me ditch the Trimar. I figured he had reason to toss it in the ivy; I'm sure he had a lot more experience with drugs than I did, and even though I went back to scrounge in the ivy for it, I didn't sniff it anymore. I followed his advice, and every time I heard him sing "Light My Fire" I was certain he had changed the words to:

> *"The time to hesitate is through*
> *No time to wallow in the mire*
> *Trimar, we can only lose*
> *And our love become a funeral pyre . . ."*

A little less than a year later, my newest best girlfriend, Miss Lucy, and I were desperate enough for a good time to check out Ohio's version of the Archies, the Ohio Express, at the Whiskey a Go Go. They were gallantly attempting to entertain the jaded fun-seekers when Jim Morrison staggered in. I wrote a massive entry in my journal at three A.M. (I had changed from *diary* to *journal* by this time; it sounded more mature.)

April 27, 1968 . . . Insanity. I've never seen true insanity until now. I've never sat beside it and heard it speak in senseless empty words, trying to communicate with the outside world until now. I suppose I encountered it briefly as I stood beneath him so many times on stage as he moaned and pleaded with us. The night of the trimar, when he told me his entire scene was an act, I should have looked deeper into the words. He *is* the act! My God!! Now when I listen to his records, groaning and screaming, my stomach churns and I clutch at myself, imagining what he might be doing this very minute. How perfectly he has reached his insanity! Can insanity be perfect, I wonder? He took a full bottle of beer and threw it into Miss Lucy's face tonight, and when she screamed, "That wasn't very nice!" he looked up painfully and said "I know." Why did he do it? What's the reason he spits on people, beats on them, throws up on them? What can be going on in his head? I'm fascinated while others are repulsed. How wonderful to do what your body tells you to do. Animals don't care where they pee or throw up. If it weren't for his money and friends, he would lay in the gutter at night. They had to turn the sound and lights off at The Whiskey tonight because he climbed on stage with the very upset Ohio Express and shoved the microphone down his pants! People aren't ready for him, but they watch *because* it's him. If Joe Blow was making an ass out of himself up there, everyone would split instead of waiting patiently for him to grab his penis. (wishing *they* could) He's such a one-of-a-kind freak, so beautiful . . . I've never seen a more exquisite face. I wish I could communicate with him again, to hear him say something other than "Get it on," "suck my mama," or "alright . . . yeah."

"In the no-pop-star-is-perfect-department: Jim Morrison managed to wreck two cars in one week. He managed not to wreck himself or anyone else. Careful choice of targets?"

I just clipped this out of a magazine. They failed to mention that after he wrecked the cars he just left them in the streets and wandered into the abyss. Life would never be boring with him. It seems such a short time ago that we were running down the stairs together, and he said "I was always going to marry a virgin." (That's when I *was* one) He had some sensible moments then, even though he read all he could about incest and sadism and always fought with his girlfriend; at least he could communicate with the people around him. Captain Beefheart asked the drummer, John Densmore, why he didn't get Jim to meditate, and he said first he would have to get him to communicate! The group seems to have given up worrying about him. What can they do?

When we were sitting at his table tonight I had my eyes closed and was listening to the music when I heard him mumble "I'm going to take over . . . out of sight," and then he reached over and slapped my face real hard and yelled "Get it On!!!" All I wanted at that moment was for him to beat the hell out of me . . .

Did I really? I guess I was in some kind of teenage masochistic mood that night.

He prodded and provoked, tested and tormented everyone around him to see if he could get an honest reaction. At least that's the way it appeared to me, an eighteen-year-old bystander, basking momentarily in his glamorous, tawdry glow.

The last time I saw him was right before he left for Paris. I had decided to try commercials on for size, and was walking down La

Cienega after trying to pitch Adorn hair spray to Middle America when I heard someone yell, "Hey, slow down!" Jim was on the other side of the street, driving a big American convertible full of guys, and he turned left into the Benihana parking lot, stopping me dead in my tracks. He was bearded and heavy but had a twinkle in his eye and seemed on top of the world. He told me how nice it was to see me again and how pretty I looked. He took my hand and kissed it, winking at his friends like I was a real dish; then he backed into the honking traffic and careened down the street.

3

♥

HAVE YOU EVER BEEN EXPERIENCED?

*T*he Iron Butterfly was steaming into the chorus of "I Was Taught to Ignore Evil Temptation" (I should have dedicated that one to myself!) when I spotted a large reel-to-reel tape recorder gleaming underneath one of the tacky tables from across the dance floor. Someone as fanatical as myself had carted the massive thing into the Galaxy just to capture these ecstatic, unforgettable moments for all time, and I had to find out who it was so I could congratulate him or her on having such immaculate taste. When the song was over, I watched as a small doll-girl with saucer eyes and raven ringlets planted herself in front of the tape recorder and started fiddling with the dials. She looked sort of familiar, so I flitted across the dance floor, anticipating a brand-new friendship. I still saw a lot of Beverly, but she had allowed her sad side to overpower whatever *joie de vivre* I was able to inspire, so I was slowly seeking a divorce. She had discovered the numbing joy of downers and I had to take second place to Seconal, and sometimes third if she found a partner willing to dabble in her coveted crime. I dabbled with her momentarily, just to be in the realm of her senses, but I made a dangerous fool out of myself in front of the Whiskey a Go Go over a dangerous fool who wasn't worth all my weepy, downed-out dramatics.

New girls were just as exciting to me as new boys (well, almost), so I approached this adorable big-eyed girl with high hopes and asked her to dance with me to the brand-new Butterfly song, which I thought was called "In the Garden of Eden," but which was really "In-A-Gadda-Da-Vida." (Eventually it would become the Iron Butterfly's only hit.) For the next few days she and I presented our entire identities to each other, wrapped up like giant presents with big shiny bows. Her name was Sparky, and she looked familiar because we had graduated from Northridge Junior High and Cleveland High together! Even though we had walked on opposite sides of the campus, we both worshiped the same yell leader, Frank DiBiase. You remember him as the skinny little twerp who wanted the entire school to know that I wore yellow silk scarves in the top of my pink-checked two-piece.

Sparky and I called each other "Doll" because of the women's-prison movies that we watched and mimicked together. There was one incredibly horrific B feature called *Caged!* where the steel-eyed ominous matron gets a twanging fork in the tit, heaved with relish by a psycho case who should have been in a straightjacket. Just as the hard-assed matron is laying down the law to our doe-eyed heroine in the cafeteria, this loon on her left leans forward and sticks it right into the old dame's heaving bosom. A joyous riot ensues as the old dame dies a slow death.

We also enjoyed the forties moll movies and sometimes dressed

Teen atop Caddy

♥

The necklace said "Dion 4-ever"

♥

MARGARET MILLER

MARGARET MILLER

Twisting the night away with Daddy

♥

Bitchen' Bob and
The Beatles

MARGARET MILLER

Making out with Bob Martine
in front of the ever-present
faces of Paul McCartney

MARGARET MILLE

Pre-Beefheart

MARGARET MILLER

Post-Beefheart

EARL LEAF

Entering unknown realms of hipness
at the Lenny Bruce eulogy

Flower child

TOM WILKES

BARRY PEAKE

Sugar-Pie Honey-Bunch

A *memorable scene from The Massage Parlor*

JULIAN WASSER

Burrito Heaven: (from left, top row) "Sneeky" Pete Kleinow, Christine, Gram Parsons, me, Chris Hillman, Miss Mercy, Brandon de Wilde; (from left, bottom row) Chris Ethridge, Cynderella, Miss Sandra

like those stacked-heeled dolls and called each other "Butch" or "Cleo," pretending all the boys we encountered were men. Divulging secrets constantly, we were best friends within a couple of weeks. When I daydream about Sparky and me in those early days, I conjure up Sandra Dee lying on her perfect creamy tummy, wriggling on a frilly pink-eyelet bedspread. Her demure nightie has been adeptly angled to cover strategic thigh area, and she squeals with demure delight to her giggly girlfriend about some tall, blond Troy Donahue American.

One of our earliest and most unforgettable evenings began on a brightly lit corner in the Valley, where we stood under a lamppost asking likely-looking passersby if they would please go into Thrifty's and come out with a jug of Gallo. The first two must have been Prohibitionists, but the third prospect was kind of Dustin Hoffman-ish, and he did the dirty deed for us without much coaxing. Sparky and I had never been drunk before, so we had no idea how much of the swill would do the trick. Right next to Thrifty's was an all-girls Catholic school, so we shimmied over the fence to break the liquor law with the Lord. I kept saying I didn't feel anything, but I could hardly get the words out, I was cracking up so hard. We must have swigged three quarters of the big green jug, and dribbled the other 25 percent down the front of our matching handmade hankie dresses, before we went out on the corner to hitch into Hollywood, stopping briefly to pee in holy bushes.

We had zero trouble getting rides, but quite often a pervert would be sitting behind the wheel. Praise be to Allah that a decent, regular guy picked us up that drunken night, because we were extremely easy targets with a disadvantage. Sparky must have ingested more booze than I did because I carried on most of the conversation with Mr. Normal. He probably thought he was being quite daring by stopping for two hopped-up, falling-down teenage girls, so I helped his fantasy along a little by telling him we were members of a witches' coven on LSD. He took us all the way to the Strip so he could hear the whole sordid story.

Sparky had long ago succumbed to jibberish, and had already

started drooling, when we pulled up in front of the Whiskey to see the stunning double bill of Steppenwolf and John Mayall's Blues Breakers. We had been members of the audience the night before and were entranced with the bass player (his name escapes me) and baby-faced Mick Taylor, the best guitar player I had ever heard. When I reached over and opened the huge American-car door, Sparky fell into the gutter, her eyeballs spinning. I knew we were in trouble at that moment because I looked straight into the red eyes of a stern-faced Strip cop who was standing on the corner waiting for the likes of me to come along. I made drunken attempts to revive my new best friend who was happily lying in the gutter telling me she loved me, she loved me, before I made a mad-dash escape across the street and into the Union 76 ladies' room. As I careened, bug-eyed, across the Sunset on a red light, I heard Rodney Bingenheimer cheering for me to outrun the two enraged cops. My heart was pounding but I felt safe on top of the commode, knowing that MEN would never enter a LADIES' room, much less open the door to a stall!! I was outraged and appalled when they forcibly removed me from my secure hiding place and *dared* to handcuff me! I heard one of them say to the other, "We can add resisting arrest to the drunk and disorderly." I tried tears and begging forgiveness, but they turned a typical deaf ear to my tragic pleas. By the time we got back to the squad car, quite a crowd had gathered, cheering me and jeering the cops. I felt like a celebrity and took the appropriate bows until they tossed me into the backseat, where Sparky was also handcuffed and in a fit of weepy giggles.

The charming police officers ignored us all the way to the Beverly Hills police station, and Sparky was too far gone to realize what was really happening. She had a stupefied goony look on her face that belied any semblance of rational brain activity, and I'm sure she thought she was in the middle of one of her wacko dreams. When we arrived at the station and a police woman removed the gold-plated cross from around my neck, I called them all blasphemous motherfuckers who would burn in hell for wrenching Jesus away from me in my time of need. It took them a long time to fingerprint us, and I'd love to have a framed eight-by-ten of my mug shot, but when I realized they weren't going to let me call my mother, I pounded the walls of my cell and called them the most heinous things I could conjure up in my condition. I told them that if my mother died with worry and grief, thinking I was dead in a Mulholland ravine, it would be all their fault. They were invisibly unimpressed.

As the night wore on, Sparky threw up on the prickly gray blanket, where she lay mewling in a comatose state, and I slowly regained my sanity, hoping and praying we would be shown mercy. When we reached the same wavelength, we had mammoth hangovers and were scared to death of being jailbirds. After they condescended to let us call our worried moms, we were led to a kindly old judge who put us on three years' probation and gave us a curfew of eleven o'clock for six months. This was unthinkable! Our lives on the street were just beginning, and nothing happened *before* eleven o'clock!!

After we had been dismissed from the courtroom, we begged for a private audience with His Honor to plead for the right to our nights. I was surprised that he allowed us into his chambers, maybe he was having a particularly boring day, but we played the mortified, chagrined good girls to the hilt. Poor Sparky, reeking of regurgitated Gallo, tried dismally to hide her soiled hankies from His Honor, while I brought forth poignant spurting tears. After several threats and warnings, he lowered the sentence to six months' probation and a two-week curfew. After kissing his kind old ass for a few minutes, we were back out in the sunlight on our knees, kissing the green, green grass of Beverly Hills, our heads splitting open and spewing out cheapo rosé.

I took Sparky to Vito's very next outing at the Shrine Auditorium to see L.A.'s local soul band, the Chambers Brothers, and their forty-five-minute rendition of their only hit, "Time." She adored the concept of Vito, but kept her distance from his lascivious, dribbling old tongue, and was very diplomatic about fending off Captain Fuck's proposals. Szou took a fancy to Sparky as well (it was *so* cool to be bisexual!), but Sparky hung on to me like we did it all the time, so

Szou assumed we were a true-blue item and laid off. The dancing was always fun. Vito and Karl brought out the lurking lunacy in everyone, so *nothing* was too weird or too freaky, and we all tried to outdo each other on the dance floor. People would stand and gawk as Vito went into his usual routine of picking one of us up and slinging us across the room, preferably with our dresses up over our heads. I realized that it was no fun to wind up across the room in a heap with several hippies peering at my pubic hair, so I astutely avoided Vito when he came at me with outstretched arms. (He thought we should be *thrilled* at the prospect.) I preferred to roll all over the floor with the girls, tits and panties flying. Vito's private part was Hollywood-famous, and he made sure he prodded anyone who dared to come close enough for inspection. He would beckon pretty girls to come join the troupe, making promises of madness that would surely come true.

After the Shrine, Vito invited a select few to come home with him to observe a tender fondling session. I had never witnessed two women in the heat of passion, so I dragged Sparky along to check it out. When we arrived at the pungent palace, the moans had already started and we pressed through the oglers to Szou and Vito's tiny bedroom, which consisted of a doily-laden four-poster on which two tenderly young girls were tonguing each other to shriek city. It was such an odd occurrence; no one seemed to be getting off sexually by watching the pubescent girls, but everyone was silently observing the scene as if it were part of their necessary training by the head-master, Vito. (Except for Karl, who was making no attempt to control his ecstasy.) One of the girls on the four-poster was only twelve years old, and a few months later Vito was deported to Tahiti for this very situation, and many more just like it.

Miss Lucy, a Puerto Rican bombshell who was a regular around Vito's, didn't seem to be enjoying this particular festivity, and was in the living room trying on Szou's wall hangings. She had a sway-back, so her bottom stuck out like she was asking for it, and she was in the process of swaddling it with a long red-fringe scarf, wrapping it around and around, when Sparky and I emerged from the den of iniquity, having seen quite enough, thank you. "Good evening!" she said with disgust as we found a spot to sit down amid piles of rags and lace pieces that Szou had been combining to create a new garment for some lucky customer. Now, "good evening" didn't really mean good evening, it meant get lost with this lame-o situation, or how disgusting, or forget this shit, but Sparky and I knew just what she meant concerning the porno display and sighed in agreement. I admired Lucy from a distance before this incident; she was a couple of years older and had been on the scene longer, and wasn't afraid to speak her mind right out loud at all times. I felt closer to her after the astute "good evening," and from that night on she teamed up with Sparky and me whenever we went dancing.

I loved being with Lucy; she had *no* inhibitions and helped me to squelch any that I was hanging on to (she thought my virginity was hilarious). She loved both sexes, though she hung out most of the time with very, very sweet boys. The love of her life was a half-Indian multisexual called Mr. Bernardo, who was currently residing in county jail. She bestowed upon me a lock of his very long black hair, forcibly removed from his head in prison, and I carried it around in my wallet long before I met him. "Miss Thing," as she was lovingly called on the streets, came from Puerto Rico via New York City, and was a hot tamale with a blazing temper; although she usually got along with everyone, watch out if anybody got in her way. Sparky and I felt secure holding her hand.

I met a guy with several cameras around his neck at a love-in, and as he recorded history, he took lots of shots of me prancing around half naked, preening for the sun. His name was Allen Daviau, and he wanted to take pictures for my acting portfolio for free!! He hovered around, tagging along behind me for days, capturing my teen essence for eternity. We spent hours in my backyard while I emoted intensely on the patio and cuddled my cat for the camera in a very cutsie way. I wanted to attract many moguls and become the next SOMEBODY.

One morning, Allen called and told me to put on my freakiest ensemble and rush downtown to dance in a film with the Jimi

Hendrix Experience. When I arrived, wearing a teensy blue-velvet
item, I could hear "Foxy Lady" pouring out the windows of this
huge circular hippie pad, painted neon green and hot pink. Three
frizz heads were the center of attention, and as I entered, the frizz
in the middle said, "What're *you* doing later?" I smiled and started
shaking, because Jimi Hendrix was a formidable-looking gentleman.
He had a big psychedelic glaring eyeball on his wacky jacket and his
hair kinked out blatantly in every direction. I could smell sex all
over him; even his pockmarks sizzled. He was black and I was extremely pink (or was it yellow?) and not ready for an encounter with
this formidable man on fire. I tossed my hair in a pretense of *savoir-
faire* and went off to find Allen. He put me on a tall white pedestal
and I wiggled my ass for hours while "Foxy Lady" played repeatedly
and the cameras rolled. Jimi's rake-thin sidemen were right up my
back alley, and I made sleepy eyes with the bass player, Noel Redding, until the end of the day when he asked me to go back to the
hotel with him. I thought Jimi and his jacket would give me the
evil eye, but he just laughed, knowing he was too much for the likes
of little me. Longer, taller blondes loomed large in his legend.

There I was, in what was about to become my favorite position
in the world, hanging on to the hand of an English rock star. We
swam in the pool and kissed each other from head to toe. Noel was
a country boy from Kent, and a very good introduction to English-
ness. He was freshly famous, and very happy to be in America where
girls were ripe for the sticking. He approved of my virginity, but
wanted to be the one to lead me down the porno path to the glories
beyond, and insisted that I save the moment of explosion for him.
He took me to the Hollywood Bowl the next night, where I reveled
in being by his side. I was with the band.

> August 17, 1967 . . . We swam and laughed and had a beautiful
> time, he made exquisite love to me and I to him and he soon
> fell asleep.
> August 18 . . . I went to Devan's for a Jimi Hendrix party, Noel
> didn't show up so I went to the hotel where I bumped into Mitch
> Mitchell (the drummer) and he dragged me into Noel's room,

much to my liking! And there I remained until 5 A.M. He is a lovely man, thick dark hair, pretty, thin, delicate body, dimples, fine hands and a VERY British accent! He gave me his address and I am to "look him up" when I get to London. I really grooved with him.

I somehow held on to my heart when he left town, but couldn't wait for him to come back, and I treasured the naughty notes he sent me from swinging London, carrying them around with me until they were in tatters. One of them said, "I can't wait to taste you again," and it burned a hole through the lining of my pink-velvet purse.

Besides my delicious, insane Hollywood girlfriends, I made some Valley girlfriends who were a couple years younger than me so I could show off some of my newfound incredible hipness. I taught them how to give head on an Oscar Mayer weenie, and turned them on to Love, the Byrds, and the Doors. I told them what it was like to be *backstage* at the Hollywood Bowl, on a bass player's arm.

I met Donovan's conga player, Candy, at the Whiskey, and he invited me out to Malibu Colony to meet Donovan, so I, in turn, invited my teeny teens to come along so they could see firsthand just how hip I really was! We were all grooving in front of the fireplace with Donovan in his long white robes, watching the smoke caress his porcelain skin and curl around his curls, when Wendy, one of the teens, decided to make a call to her mother to tell her how great the movie was. Trembling and crying she returned to the serene scene, busting apart the holy moment between Donovan and his guitar. She must have blown her alibi because she sobbed, "They know everything!! They're sending the POLICE to come get us!!!" She had been beaten down by her mother and had blabbed to beat the band!! We had to get out of there fast, to spare Donovan an intrusion by the boys in blue. The baby girls were sobbing and I was humiliated beyond recognition as we scuttled from the premises amid chaotic, unpeaceful vibrations. I turned around on my way out the door to bid adieu to the prince of pop poetry, but he was running toward the ocean, his white robes flapping in the wind, his arms outstretched, hurling his pot into the salty waters of the sea.

January 1, 1968 . . . Before I know it, I'll be a complete adult. I never liked that word, so maybe I'll never consider myself an adult . . . per say . . . and I must always remember:

Don't count the stars
Or you'll stumble
If someone drops a star
Down you'll tumble . . .

Still desperate to be famous, I scoured the town for an agent, *any* agent who could get me in the right elevators. I took the perky shots that Allen Daviau had turned into glossy eight-by-tens and traipsed up and down the Hollywood streets, calling attention to myself. I left two dozen photos with two dozen agents, and sat home by the phone, waiting for twenty-four calls. I got one. I went in to read a commercial for the agent, and I couldn't act!! What a horrendous discovery! One of the lines in the ad was, "You can twirl in a double-belted kiltie!" I thought I would make it look real, and I twirled into her desk, stammering and blushing. She signed me anyway, and I vowed to take acting lessons and become brilliant. I decided to devote my life to my art, and stop making the Sunset Strip my reason for drawing breath.

February 28 . . . I made a fantastic resolution that I am definitely going to keep. NO MORE STRIP! It's ruining me. Groups aren't important, hippies are just as phony and screwed as execs. I need something to sustain me other than cavorting up and down the dirty streets, begging and dying for a smile and a kind word.

Sparky and I got a job at a big, ugly cheapo discount store, selling candy from a little glass cubicle, and promised each other to keep our lives in order.

We Do Solemnly Sware to:

1. Stop forever taking any kind of drug, including grass and Trimar.
2. Don't rob from the cash register and customers (even a few cents). Don't take candy for ourselves and friends, and don't eat extensively.
3. Stop swearing.
4. Don't depress so easily.
5. Keep no secrets from each other.
6. Keep the Strip pact.
   Signed with love, Linda Sue Parker and Pamela Ann Miller

We sewed our hearts together and tried to put them in the right place.

I was mad for the lead guitar player in a local group called Love, and during a rash moment of weakness in the back of Vito's blue VW van, I let my unrequited crush lead me to the evils of marijuana. All of us girls, Beverly, Sparky, Lucy, and a fabulous earth-mom newcomer, Sandra, and I, were on our way to the Cheetah to see Traffic, featuring the angelic presence of Stevie Winwood. I was raving on to the girls about Bryan MacLean, the redheaded, freckle-faced wonder who decided that he just wanted to "be my friend." Pot often circulated the van, but this time, when Karl passed me the reefer, I said, "Why not!!" and indulged deeply.

Saturday, March 1 . . . Oh, such fun tonight! We went with Vito, dancing to Traffic and rolled all over the auditorium. Beverly, Spark and I ran into John Densmore of The Doors, and for Bev it was sad; he wasn't too nice to her, and she takes these things so hard. All of us girls had a slight orgy in Vito's bus. We have such pretty "bailies" (our secret word for tits.) Stevie Winwood is like a porcelain doll, he's so pretty. I told him so too, and I got a heavenly smile in return. I sobbed over Bryan again. He's so nice to me, but we're just pals. If he only knew what he caused me to do tonight!!

I neglected to document my pot experience in case my journal fell into the wrong hands, but I didn't stop there; it became part of my life to tie one on once in a while, mainly in Vito's bus where it was all one big, silly fantasy sequence anyway. I had deep, dramatic thoughts like everyone else when I smoked, and I wrote my share of poetry, which I hoped might change someone's life someday:

> *I wonder how many grains of sand*
> *Are on every shore of every land*
> *I'd like to count them one by one*
> *Yet I know that cannot be done*
> *I'd like to run on every beach*
> *Yet almost all are out of reach*
> *I'd like to swim in every sea*
> *But only one is close to me*
> *So I'll be content to stay right here*
> *On the shore so very near*
> *And wonder how many grains of sand*
> *Are resting here, within my hand.*

The mind boggles.

The "slight orgy" we had in the bus involved all of us girls taking off our see-through blouses and kissing each other's bailies. Vito kept his eyes glued to the rearview mirror and encouraged the proceedings with gusto. We spotted a couple of marines in uniform at a bus stop and all pressed our tantalizing titties against the windows and watched their faces change color and their eyes bulge out like horny toads. I'm sure it will be something they'll tell in the old folks' home in the year 2010:

> We were minding our own business, waiting for a bus to Fort Dix, when an old blue van pulled up at the light, and a dozen wild hippie women were kissing each other and pressing their bare breasts up to the glass, and calling out, "I bet you'd like to touch us!!" Me and Harry got instant hard-ons inside our uniforms, and had to put our hats over our you-know-whats! No sir, no decade can hold a candle to the sixties.

Sandra was Italian and thought it was great. She should have lived in an exotic villa where she could have had lots of babies, lots of candles at the table, laden down with pasta, and some dashing Zorro to burst through the door at dusk, bringing home the Italian bacon. She was a small, lusty, olive-skinned little hunk, and was the first one of us to get pregnant. When she did, her stomach was proudly displayed, always bare, embellished with painted-on eyes and lips, and with dangly earrings glued to the sides of her nonwaist. Sometimes she would paint a big black star coming out of her navel that matched the one on Lucy's cheekbone. She added a down-to-earth touch that our ever-growing gaggle of wonderful girls needed to keep our toes touching the ground.

Lucy and Sandra shared the vault in the basement of the log cabin that Tom Mix built on the corner of Laurel Canyon and Lookout Mountain Drive, across the street from Houdini's crumbling mansion. I guess the log cabin could have been called a commune, because crazy Karl Franzoni lived in back of Tom Mix's personal bowling alley (under which his beloved horse was buried), behind long black drapes, like the phantom of the porno opera. I only went back there in a dire emergency, like the time he painted my portrait, but I was sure to have two chaperones by my side at all times. The first time I happened upon him down in the tomb, he was naked-nakednaked except for plastic clip-on curlers in his pubic hair and a big pair of pointy stomping boots. He was practicing with the tenpins, and looked like a nuthouse escapee from someone's wildest nightmare.

The girls and I spent a lot of time locked up in the vault, making lists of all the gorgeous boys in bands that we wouldn't kick out of bed. Lucy and Sandra wrote their lists on the wall and crossed them off one by one as they encountered the lucky lads. I kept my list in a little gold loose-leaf notebook in my purse: None of the names had been crossed off yet, and Mick Jagger was number one, written in flaming red.

Directly across from the vault was a large closet where Christine Frka privately resided. She had immigrated from San Pedro with

Sandra but preferred to seclude herself from the sex-crazed goings-on, insisting she was frigid. She was immaculate, tall and extremely thin, with a twisted spine which made her look slightly off-center. I'm sure she had a complex about it, which was why she insisted on a sexless existence. (The only time she told me about sleeping with a certain pop star, she said, "I laid under him for a while and then asked him if he was finished.") She made all her clothes by hand, stitch, stitch, stitch, on speed. She created one full-length patchwork coat with fur of dubious descent on the cuffs and collar that people tried to buy right off her back. She wouldn't sell. She had blinding big green eyes, and would peer at us from behind huge stacks of fabric remnants, her face thick with Merle Norman's lightest light-face goop, as we frolicked around the bowling alley. One day she wanted to come out with us to our favorite thrift store, the Glass Farmhouse where we got all our special effects. It was all the way across town in Silverlake, and all five of us hitchhiked holding hands, even Christine. Well, she wouldn't really *hold* your hand, but she would let you hold hers, always remaining aloof and slightly suspicious.

We became a fivesome, attending all events, parties, concerts, love-ins, clubs, *any* kind of festivity, as a unit. The local girls started to copy our thrilling ensembles, complete with fifty-cent special effects: ribbons around wrists and ankles, tatty silk flowers, pieces of lace in strategic spots, antique panties worn *over* other garments, piano shawls, slinky teddies, hand-embroidered tablecloths, and the occasional silk umbrella. We were causing such a commotion that within weeks we had our very own camp crawlers, but it was always the five of us at the center, holding on to each other, hoping to inspire or annoy onlookers.

Frank Zappa wanted to live in the log cabin, and I guess he had clout with the mad-as-a-hatter landlady, because Karl and the girls were ousted from the basement and forced to seek accommodations elsewhere. It was easy to dig up a pad around town in a day or two for seventy-five a month, no first and last, no cleaning fee, and no questions asked, but it was no fun to leave the log cabin. It was a real and true log cabin, built with actual logs on a ton of acreage, complete with a stream and minilake, caves, hideaways, blossoms of every scent and shape, creating vines to swing on from end to end. There was supposed to be a secret passageway that led to Houdini's castle across the street, and we were still searching. It was truly Disney time, and we had no intention of staying away for very long. Lucy knew Frank from New York; how intimately we never found out because she did nothing but allude. She kept her big red mouth shut about that one, because Frank had a divine wife, Gail (who later became my mentor), and a brand-new baby daughter, Moon Unit.

The Mothers of Invention was a motley assortment of ageless wonders concocted by Frank to spin his perverse yarns into memorable pieces of music. I was in the audience the night Frank introduced virtuosity-rock to a bunch of unsuspecting bozo brains and called it a freak-out. I gazed, amazed, as this goofy-looking goateed genius led his team of Quasimodos through their brilliant paces, punctuated by the hurling of severed baby-doll heads into the crowd of gaping groovers. You either adored him or abhorred him, and I adored him beyond the breaking point. After the show, he wandered around among us in all his motley splendor, and I couldn't resist putting my hands into his long, tangled black hair (after following him around the auditorium for twenty minutes, working up the nerve for this very spontaneous act), and he responded by rolling around the scrungy floor with me, to my joyous amazement. Frank Zappa epitomized all that I believed I was starting to stand for, and I *knew* he must have spotted me among those struggling to be hip and realized I was teetering on that very verge. Of course, I craved more than a roll on the floor with him; I wanted to have a CONVERSATION with him. I tried to pierce his soft, warm brown eyes with my begging-for-a-crumb baby blues, but it was too dark in there and the tumble on the floor was over much too soon for my liking.

So it looked like I was going to get a second chance to prove to Frank that I was worthy of recognition. When Lucy suggested that we all drop in on Frank at the cabin, I was beside myself with anticipation. When we arrived, he was sitting at the piano in the cavernous living room made of actual logs; there was a fire crackling in the huge rock fireplace, and little baby Moon was crawling around the floor, gurgling. I heard clattering in the kitchen and figured Gail must be in there, churning out a fantastic dinner for her brilliant husband. It was beyond idyllic, right out of an ersatz version of *House Beautiful*. He was genuinely thrilled to see Lucy, and picked her up off the ground and hugged her until her back cracked; when he came over to meet her new best friends, we all curtsied for him as though he were a reigning monarch. I got all tongue-tied and cross-eyed when we met, but he didn't seem to notice; actually, he seemed quite enchanted with us. I was secretly depressed that he didn't remember me from our eye-piercing roll on the scuzzy Shrine floor.

Gail came out of the kitchen and I tried not to stare. She asked all of us if we would like a cup of tea; oh, it was so civilized. The whole setup instantly changed my mind about domesticity: You could be a rebel, a profound thinker, and a rock and roll maniac and still eat breakfast, lunch, and dinner, have a baby, and drink a nice cup of tea with your friends. I never liked tea until I met Gail; she was the teapot queen. In fact, she was so queenly that I was afraid to speak to her at first. Being THE WIFE of one of my idols put her in a category that I hadn't yet encountered. She was exactly what I aspired to be, and I was in awe of her for the next several months.

Even though I wanted to do and say the wildest things possible and look totally mind-boggling, I still looked up to, and felt lesser than, an awful lot of people. I would kill and murder to get myself into a certain enviable situation, and then feel like I was the only person in the room who should throw in the tattered towel and go home. I've got to hand it to myself, though; I waded through those feelings of complete and utter inadequacy and gritted my teeth, waiting for the most celebrated celebrity in the room to bust my butt and tell me I was out of my element: "Go back to Reseda, NOW!!" But it never happened and slowly my fraudulent composure started breathing by itself. I acted "as if," until I was.

While Frank probed our brains for interesting info, Christine busied herself tidying the enormous pad. Moon crawled up to her and she slung the baby girl on her scrawny hip and kept tidying. This must have impressed Gail because she offered Christine a full-time live-in position, taking care of Moon, complete with household tasks. This was a very enviable position for an eighteen-year-old wack-job from San Pedro in 1968. This wonderful occurrence, of course, clinched our friendship with the Zappas and we started spending a lot more time at the log cabin, our home sweet home away from home.

I soon realized that the first quiet evening we spent there was a rarity; the house always had a Mother or two in residence, and Frank's manager, Herbie, was in and out all day and night. They were forming their own record label, Bizarre, and floods of secretaries and assorted business types came and went. Many freaks and hopeful happeners appeared at the infamous doorstep and were sometimes invited in for tea. Frank's in-house artist, Calvin, a buzz-haired beauty, sat in different locations in and around the house, sketching outlandish interpretations of each Mother, while my darling Sandra made goo-goo eyes at him one time too many. The result eventually became a protruding hand-painted tummy, which turned out to be a ravingly beautiful baby girl she called Raven.

One evening we appeared at the cabin in full matching regalia: plastic baby bibs and oversized diapers with yellow-duck safety pins, our hair up in pigtails, sucking giant lollipops. Frank flipped and invited us to dance ONSTAGE with the Mothers that night in Orange County, California Suburbanland. I was about to enter show business and I had visions of sugarplums dancing in my head. We had been calling ourselves the Laurel Canyon Ballet Company, but Frank suggested we change our "professional" name to Girls Together Only, or the GTO's. We adored the idea and expanded on it, deciding that the O could stand for anything we wanted it to: Outrageously, Overtly, Outlandishly, Openly, Organically. The potential was obviously endless.

That particular night turned into fiasco city. Before we could even get up onstage, some matronly box-shaped matron dragged me into a little office and pointed to the pink edge of nipple that peeked out from under my bib. She was so appalled she sputtered, her matronly spittle landing on the little duckies parading across the bib. Thank heavens I had it on! She was not about to allow half-naked girls onstage in Orange County, and for the rest of the night we were surrounded by gray guards who were told to make sure we didn't set foot on the stage; all they did was ogle us, salivating. We didn't entertain the audience that night, but the door had been opened and we were about to pour in.

My heart was wide open with ecstasy and madness and I was ready for a real love affair. I fell in true love with Nick St. Nicholas, a fluffy, blond German lunatic with his own language and a delirious way of looking at the world. I met him at the Galaxy, and he took me out a couple of times before it hit me that this could be the guy who could have anything he wanted from me. ANYTHING. I can still smell the thick, gooey incense that floated around his room, following him out into the street, where he attained regal status wearing his creamy satin shirt with mother-of-pearl buttons, the top two carefully undone. I would sit in his twenty-five-watt red-bulb living room while he decked himself out in front of the bathroom mirror, the door slightly ajar so I could admire him admiring himself. My knees trembled when he dabbed himself with Aramis, long before it had its own counter at the May Company. The way the scent blended with the gooey incense made me dizzy with the onslaught of love. He was eight years older than I was, and the years stretched into an eternity when I pondered how much more he knew of the world than I did. I worshiped the blacktop on which he drove his brand-new cream-colored, wildly hip Jaguar XKE. There were times when I would stand in the space where he parked it, gazing at his name plate, damp-eyed and agonized because he hadn't called me for three weeks. I had imagined what "the real thing" felt like, but here it was, poking me in the heart with razor-sharp vengeance, demanding total attention, which is what it got. I ate his name for breakfast, and I couldn't eat lunch or dinner because my stomach ached from wanting him so bad.

The first night I realized what I was in for was after a wildly romantic dinner at Stephanino's, a trendy fish joint at the elegant end of Sunset. Nick took me back to his bachelor pad and took my clothes off, and I plunged right ahead with what I did best. I was fainting inside to get a look at him beneath his finery, to touch him and press my nose against the dabs of Aramis, but I still made sure to stroke the right spots that cause instant ecstasy. I had come up against insistent men before, but my desire to remain uninvaded always won out and I was able to delight them in many other ways. Nick wouldn't stop pleading for entry. He wanted to see the light at the end of the damp tunnel, and the pressure had never been sweeter and more full of sticky endearments.

He fell asleep after a futile struggle, and my left arm was securely fastened under his perfect golden back. I couldn't bear to disturb his peaceful, elegant oblivion just because my arm was full of pins and needles, my hand a numbing lump. I lay there, imagining my life as a one-armed GTO, until he let out a sigh and rolled onto his perfect golden side and I got the chance to scurry away into the dawn like a bereft squirrel. I hitched through the canyon, berating myself for being the ultimate chicken-shit and not measuring up to the supreme test of womanhood. The sun came up on my angst and my perfectly applied eyeliner, which had spread across my cheeks like big blue veins during the heat of halted passion. I was a tortured teenage virgin.

March 13, 1968 . . . I can't believe I saw him. So near me. I touched him and felt his nearness to me and saw the green greenness of his fantastic eyes. Oh, I hope that's not all. I must have him. I must I must. I must admit, I acted in my most obnoxious and possessive manner around him. It always seems to happen. I become outrageously demanding and overly attentive, phony and conspicuous. I gave him everything, except for the one thing he wanted . . . my virginity. And why didn't I? Perhaps I was thinking of today and the many tomorrows that follow. I loved him so much when he slept. I got to touch him everywhere, listen to his heart beating, kiss his hair. I pulled back the covers to look at the curve of his body, the way he folded his hands at his chest. Oh my Nicky! How can he exist without everyone noticing him? Why don't they stop dead in their tracks when he walks by?

Keeping the "Strip pact" proved to be difficult, but I found different things to occupy my nights as I pined over the perfect image of Nick St. Nicholas. I saw a lot of Captain Beefheart and Victor, who had become a member of Don's Magic Band, calling himself "the Mascara Snake." Beverly had a crush on Drumbo, Don's drummer (obviously), so she and I traipsed out to Canoga Park, where Don and the band lived on a run-down ranch. We smoked a lot of pot and Don put on a record called "Come Out So They Can See It." We lounged around the living room while a guy with a really deep voice repeated this phrase overandoverandover until it turned into many different ideas: Come out and expose yourself, come out and slit your wrists, come out and show me your soul, come out and come into a bucket, come out and then go back in again. When the record was over, the needle skipped and skipped, so we listened to that for a while too. I, personally, could find no meaning in it, but I tried. We went outside and stood around in a circle, in a semblance of meditation. I rolled my eyeballs in one direction and then the other, trying to stop them in midspin. It was almost impossible.

I went to see the Byrds play whenever they were local, and my crush on Chris deepened, but he always treated me with a sweet detachment, and besides, he was already on his second wife and I hadn't even had my first affair yet. He probably saw me as a baby who needed burping. I danced with the GTO's and my self-esteem burgeoned, because we created miniriots wherever we went. We saw less and less of Vito because he was pissed off that his fledglings had fled the flock and were doing well without him. I missed the idea of him more than the reality of having to avoid his large, rechargeable Everready.

Sparky and I still worked at "the section," the candy counter at Whitefront where we sat for hours with our toes in the generic

M & M's, writing in our journals, peering through marshmallow bunnies at overweight customers aching for a sugar rush.

April 2 . . . I found a nest of weevils in the toffee peanuts and a nest of ants cowering in the corner. . . . *Some* franchises!

The Whitefront was a big, dismal white elephant, selling mass quantities of various discount items to the very middle of Middle America. They plodded around aimlessly, gathering up handfuls of polyester, dragging their snotty children behind, almost pulling little arms out of sockets. Every fifteen minutes the hideous voice of Jules Shear permeated the atmosphere: "Attention shappah's, we have a fantastic baagan for you in aisle three of the undergaament section!!" Sparky and I tacked up pictures of pop stars all over the section, and in between selling rubbery fruit-flavored Mexican hats and stale rocky-road squares, we gazed raptly at Jimi Hendrix and Jim Morrison.

Once in a while the owners of this unnecessary establishment would bring in a celebrity of sorts to enhance business, and one Sunday morning, the tallest man in the world bent double to set foot on hallowed Whitefront linoleum. We were mesmerized. Little children followed him into the store, and he gave each one of them a huge plastic ring the size of his salami-shaped fingers to wear as a bracelet. He lumbered through the store with his Colonel Tom Parker–Barnum and Bailey–type manager, who began putting him through his paces the instant he reached his designated spot for the day. He placed his foot next to a normal guy's foot, he placed his hand next to a normal guy's hand, he posed for pictures with people who didn't dare let him touch them (just in case he was wearing some Alice-in-Wonderland potion on his skin), and as he did all his tricks, his long, somber face looked as if he were constantly weeping subconscious tears. Sparky and I saw the entire world in this tragic tall man and wanted to show him some tenderness, so we picked out several of our best bonbons and presented them to him with little curtsies, showing him some respect. We shook his hand, did a soft-shoe with him, and had a little laugh. On his way out of the store, he stopped, towering over the candy counter, casting monster shadows across the glass. Handing us two of his plastic ring-cum-bracelets, he said in his big, booming voice, "You were the only people who treated me like a human."

I consumed many cups of English Breakfast tea with Gail Zappa, marveling at her expertise in every subject. She would listen attentively while I expounded about Nicky, Chris, and Noel, and then tell me they should be so lucky to be near me.

I got a postcard from Mr. Redding that needed five cents' postage: "We'll be in L.A. in July. Don't forget, you asked me to *give* you something." That was his way of being romantic and discreet, but I had no such notion of Noel being the first guy to enter my sacred vessel. I swore to myself that if Nick St. Nicholas called me again, I would humbly offer myself to him with grace and dignity, wearing my most lethal black-lace panties.

April 7 . . . I am in such internal agony. I never knew what it was like to love someone so fully, and have them so unconcerned and out of touch with me. In fact, I'm *so* miserable that the complete impact of it has not yet found me. I'm in a type of void; between agony and ecstasy. My great loss, I'm overwhelmed by it! He's resting in the sand now, right next to me as I write this, overcome by sleep and so peaceful and unaware of my presence. Even if he woke up and looked at me, he would still be unaware of my presence. My God, tears won't even come. I suppose this intensity of misery goes beyond tears. Alas, my "protection," "excuse," the thing I clung to is gone and Nicky has it and doesn't care. Oh, Nicky, where are you??

Needless to say, the bed I had slept in the night before was no bed of roses. Sparky's parents had gone on a little holiday and I invited Nicky over, eager to show him how much pent-up love I had saved for him alone. He always put me on edge to the point of sheer exhaustion. I tried so hard to measure up to my idea of what his idea of a groovy chick might be that I was constantly out of breath. Since he was somewhere on Pluto, it was up to me to create paltry conversation and invite response, drawing it out of him bit by bit, like my daddy digging for gold. When he finally realized that I was ready to take the big step, he led me into the bedroom and entered the sacred vessel without much fanfare. I lay there beside him all night, like billions of girls before me, wondering, "Is that all there is?" And the next day he took me to the beach with a bunch of friends like nothing had happened. I could hear the sound of my heart breaking with the waves. He didn't call me for six weeks.

Losing my "well-contained" virginity (that's what Noel Redding called it) sent my pea brain whirling, and I wrote a letter to Sparky about the feelings burbling within me, I created another pact to be broken:

Dear Doll, So much heroin, so much diseases, scum, filth, crabs, clap, needles, fucking, boys not caring, methedrine, people existing only for their penises and needles. God, where are they? With us, and I'm splitting!! God must be trembling and nervous waiting, watching us, wondering if we're going to stumble into something inescapable. We've been so lucky, so blessed not to have fallen into the traps. Ah, I feel relieved already. I'll probably do this several times in my life; step back, observe and evaluate myself . . . sort out faults with NO excuses. I wonder what did it this time? Nicky? No, I think it was last night in that house with Lucy. Seeing my friend surrounded by such continuous scum! Those people *hooked* on heroin . . . crabs crawling on me. I can be so crude and obnoxious, I know it at last and I will be able to conquer it. The moon is in Virgo for the next few days. Amazing evaluation period. I'm in the middle of my most favorable days; 5–9, and today is the seventh. Right in the middle. My main fault is dishonesty. That's how I lost my Nicky. Lately when I think of him, it's gotten so painful, like I'm drowning or sinking in quicksand (or something just as terrible). Why have we found it so urgent lately to parade our bodies in front of ogling spectators? I'd love to be psycho-analyzed. I have a grand idea! Why don't we both go to group therapy?! It's a thought. My mom confessed to me last night that she was worried about my pervertedness.

How sad that a sweet and loving mother should have to worry about such a thing. I Love You, Pammie.

I just couldn't seem to make up my mind. All the ideas I had about how to live my life were knocking heads with Bob Dylan's "You know something's happening but you don't know what it is, do you Mr. Jones?," free love, flower power, and long-haired weirdos who seemed to have the secret of the universe tucked into the back pockets of their bell-bottom jeans. My former self would have been married to Bobby Martine *before* he grew his hair out, twiddling my thumbs until he came home for his TV dinner, after he slaved at some normal-formal menial job. I would be fixing up the baby's room with Disney drapes, and I *wouldn't* be worrying about some blond German bass player who spoke in a heathen language, or if I should trim my pubic hair so it wouldn't show under the shortest skirt ever worn on earth.

May 16 ... I am so confused with my life. Where am I? In between a girl and a boy, in between sane and insane. I scare, offend, shock and dismay most everyone living, but Spark says you can't live to please others, and I know that's right. I'm so rude to the "other breed," but they have a right to their perversions, as do we. How can I become enlightened? I don't want to remain on this level. I'd like to meet Bob Dylan or John Lennon or some other prophet I really admire, and have a conversation.

Half of me was thrilled to be helping to pull in the new era, and the other half wanted to be wrapped in swaddling clothes, sucking my thumb in a safe, predictable place, dribbling tears into my Pop Tart.

I thought I would get some peace and serenity by attending the beautiful Renaissance Pleasure Faire out in Calabasas. In order to get in, you had to deck yourself out in Elizabethan dress or arrive on horseback. It was magic time, way out in some semblance of woods where you could pretend you were a member of the queen's court, eat a dripping-to-the-elbows butter-drenched artichoke under the trees, or stand by the entrance wearing a see-through piece of Elizabethan lace and wait for the inevitable pop star to enter the gates grandly, draped in velvet. The previous spring, I casually leaned against the tarot-card booth, hoping for a glimpse of the Byrds. (They all arrived, dazzling me one by one. David Crosby, wearing his famous green-suede cape, graced me with an impish grin before passing among the crowd like a pop pope. Chris Hillman acknowledged me with a nod and I was a puddle of artichoke butter seeping into the ground.) This year I was propped up against the satin-jester's-head-on-a-stick booth, complete with jingle bells, waiting for Nick St. Nicholas. "And he arrived, totally regal and above it all, like he was looking down on the peons from a great height, only with compassion. When his sea-green eyes settled upon me, he smiled briefly, enveloped me in his arms, and was gone."

Alone, with the sun beating down on my truetruetrue love for one who didn't love me, I agreed to the first invitation that came my way, which happened to be from Tommy Boyce and Bobby Hart (the two guys who wrote the Monkees' songs and even had a couple of hits of their own). Bobby had a movie camera and wanted me to straddle a big white horse, completely nude, while he filmed me galloping through the flowered fields with my hair flying and my teenage tits bouncing up and down (probably in slow motion). They plied me with handmade trinkets from the fair and plenty of pot until I agreed to the escapade. It was then that they introduced me to my pony partner, an eleven-year-old boy. The GTOs hung around with an eleven-year-old beauty, Bart Baker, and though I had never been intimate with him, a couple of the girls confessed to heavy petting with the beautiful blond prepubescent. We took Bart shopping with us and dressed him up and loved having him around, so I didn't mind having this gorgeous little boy, Sean, hanging on to my waist as we trotted through the daisy-filled field. The air was warm and sweet and I was high as a kite, so when Bobby instructed us to get down off the horse and frolic as the camera rolled, I was happy to accommodate him. I always considered the camera my friend, and as I said, I was floating on air and thrilled to be alive.

Sean and I played ring-around-the-rosy and collapsed into the flowers. He was a frail beauty, who in three years would be a Romeo; his cheeks were flushed and his eyes were shining. Bobby, playing director, told Sean to kiss me, so he gave me a light kiss on the mouth and pulled away, blushing. Bobby then instructed me to teach Sean to kiss. Cradling him in my arms, I opened his sweet lips with my tongue and everything around us disappeared. After the kiss, Sean stood up, stammering; I pulled my little piece of lace back on and the game was over. As we walked back to the fair, Sean was watching me with wonder, and when he asked for my phone number, I gave it to him, never dreaming that he would call me every night for the next six weeks. Bobby took me aside and told me that Sean's mom was a famous blond actress and would flip if she suspected me of any hanky-panky, and one night as Sean and I discussed his history homework, his mom got on the phone and told me I wouldn't be hearing from Sean again. And I didn't.

Nick St. Nicholas became engaged to a little blond beauty, Randy Jo, and it was raining, raining in my heart. Even though the date had been set, he surfaced in my life every few weeks and took me to his bed. I humbly crawled in, and as time went on I started lighting up like a firecracker. I thought about sex all the time and didn't want to seek out another lover, because the new heart that had grown between my legs was beating only for this exquisite moron.

> June 1 . . . I fucked Nicky last night. It excites me to death to write the word "fuck" concerning Nicky and myself. I've used that word a million times without realizing its meaning. I wish people didn't use it as a swear word. Ahhh, I climbed all over him and on him and under him, I clutched at him and moaned. I get weak and light-headed at the thought. It's such a huge relief to lose *every* inhibition and lose my mind to my body. When he fell asleep, I could hardly move without choking or reaching into the air for nothing. On the way out, I stopped to kiss his bass. I'm so in love, I don't even realize what I'm doing.

"Get your motor running . . ."

I saw him with Randy Jo one bitter night, cuddling on a street corner, and I made up my mind never to see him again. Even in the dark, I could see him look at her the way I saw him look at me in my steamy dreams every night. After collapsing into a runny pool of serious pain, I vowed to put my energy into my girlfriends, the GTO's, and my acting classes. Through a haze of anguish I realized I was still a nineteen-year-old girl enthralled with the mystery of life. Sparky got bored in the candy section and wrote me a letter about this very sentiment at the very moment I needed reinforcement:

My Dear Doll, You and I have always had that vitality for living that so very many let drop because of self-pity, we realize we are still whole, sane, healthy, youthful chicks whom millions of deprived people would give their arms to be like! We're so lucky that we love life and love living. Can you imagine how horrible it would be if you wanted to walk in front of a moving car just because you were sad about Nicky? Or if I committed suicide because Daryl was rude to me? I'm so glad we can laugh. God is so wonderful, he gave us the most beautiful gift ever, ourselves. I love you, Sparky.

Some dildo with a double first name shot Robert Kennedy, and any vague political interest I might have conjured up disappeared with his toothy grin. I stopped thinking about being a good citizen, and for five minutes I entertained the notion of moving to Europe. I bought a little flag and put it at half-mast in the candy section, and was dismayed that they wouldn't close the doors on a national day of mourning.

June 4 . . . America . . . America . . . Kennedy was shot through the head after he won his primary. He's severely critical, God knows what's going to happen. Hugh Hefner's party was a sad affair. Joey Bishop kissed my forehead. *So What!!* How can I care about that after what has happened to such a beautiful man!

June 5 . . . Well, he's paralyzed now, and his future is extremely ominous. How odd, yesterday we had hopes for a new and better world because of this man, and now the world mourns as he dies. If he were in office, I would become a better citizen and so would everyone else. God help us in our time of need. June 6 . . . He died DIED. Two days ago he gave the world the peace sign and now he lays dead. I'm going to carry this with me until I die. The sting of a distorted country.

June 7 . . . Nothing is fun. How dare I dance and run and jump when Bobby Kennedy will never again breathe the air? This has dug into me and put a scar on my heart.

Slowly, the planet began to spin again after I lost Nick St. Nicholas and Bobby Kennedy. I put on my dancing shoes, sequined my cheeks, and scoured the streets for some fun. Lucy took Sandra, Christine, Sparky, and me to visit Tiny Tim at the Sunset Marquis. She knew him from the streets of New York, and since this was his first trip to Hollywood, she wanted to welcome him with bells on. We arrived and heard the shower running along with his trilling falsetto, and had to wait outside the door for him to emerge while Lucy told side-splitting anecdotes about "Mr. Tim." The water stopped and we pounded on the door. "Ooooohhhhh, who could it be at my door . . . ?" We started giggling and he called out, "Who is it, who is it, whoooooo is it????" Lucy announced herself, and after a bit of shuffling behind the door, we heard the water start up again. "Just a minute, Looooocy, I have to take a shower!" He had just taken a shower!! Lucy told us that he took about ten showers a day, and couldn't bear to be sweaty. We waited around for shower number two to end, then the door opened and a vision in white greeted us. Mr. Tim had on a white suit with face and hands to match, he reeked of baby powder, his black hair was in ringlets gone awry, and he was wearing just a touch of lip gloss and rosy-red cheeks. He held a bottle of sickly sweet perfume in his long white hand, dabbing behind his ears with alarming frequency while fluttering the free hand over his heart in an overwhelmed pitter-pat gesture, rolling his eyes wildly. It looked like he was trying to take in the scene and get a hold of himself, but might faint instead. Lucy pushed him down onto the couch and started fanning him. "This happens all the time, he's very shy around women." He was flabbergasted and scared out of his wits, and, drawing long, shuddering breaths, he peeked at us from between his fingers while we tried to blend into the wallpaper. After we had been there about half an hour, and he had taken another shower, Mr. Tim loosened up a little, went over to the fridge, and asked if we would like to play hockey. To our surprise, he opened the freezer and removed several hockey pucks wrapped in wax paper. Carefully, he opened each puck and set it on the tiny kitchen floor, and pulled a hockey stick from behind the counter and took aim. After he knocked them back and forth, we each took a turn with the stick and had a wonderful time. He took another shower from the exertion, and came out of the bathroom powdering his nose with a huge puff full of baby powder. "I have a secret," he said, and led us to a small kitchen drawer where he lifted up the silverware to reveal many, many candy bars. "My manager thinks I'm getting chubby, but I'm just pleasingly plump." We were very moved that he trusted us with his secret, and promised him we wouldn't tell a soul. I guess enough years have passed so that I'm not betraying his confidence. We had to leave for a meeting with Mr. Zappa and he bid us adieu, kissing us ever-so-lightly on the cheek. "Good-bye Miss Lucy, Miss Sandra, Miss Sparky, Miss Christine, and Miss Pamela." We had been titled.

Me: July 21, 1968.

Pamela Miller. Age 19 ¾. 5'4" in height. Blonde (most of the time) Blue eyes (that don't see very well without spectacles) 116 in weight (about 6 pounds too many) Budding actress, afraid to go on stage, too busy to study, no confidence, too lazy to acquire it.

Dreams of fame, lovely clothes. 92 exquisite men to love me, beautiful wooden houses in Laurel Canyon, Porsches, Pop-stars.

I am now in my very own group, the GTO's, with my idol, Frank Zappa at the helm.

Weeps privately and alone quite often . . . because of Nick St. Nicholas (love? . . . love!) lost dreams, superficial things. And why am I so rude to the poor people who don't know any better? (do I?)

Wondering what life has in store for me, just about ready to plunge into it. (bellyflop?) Am I late? I feel I haven't lived much—and what have I been doing if not living? When shall I begin? Now! My God, I began living when I was born. (I don't believe in the theory that you begin to die when you're born. How can it be that you "live" for nine months and die for seventy years?) What can I do except live within the boundaries of my mind? How grand to escape, tho' I'm not as confined as most, all bottled up in their cliches and prejudice. At least I've broken some molds.

Pamela Ann Miller, 19 ¾, blonde hair, blue eyes, 116 pounds: ready, willing and able to LIVE LIFE TO THE FULLEST! TAKE ME I'M YOURS!!!

4

♥

SWEETHEART OF THE RODEO

My life was splashing in front of me like sensational headlines as I groped my way toward the spot onstage that I had occupied only in rehearsals. I was about to present myself to a throng of grasping, gyrating fun-seekers, and this time, instead of jostling for a place among them, I was going to hurl myself at their faces and ENTERTAIN them. Even though I had prepared for this moment all my life, it still came as a surprise to the shy part of me still lurking around the edges. It was pitch black and I could see the glowing exit sign beckoning, but the stage was creaking as the rest of the GTO's tiptoed to their spots, and despite my desire to disappear through the floorboards, I wouldn't dream of damaging the girls. We had rehearsed the show to smithereens, but I was visibly trembling under my feathers and sequins as the spotlight altered my pupils. I hurtled back in time to my first ballet recital in 1956 (also at the Shrine Auditorium!). When the lights came up on me as a little kid, I stood stick-still as all the other little tutued wonders got into position. I was supposed to hop around in a little circle on one toe, a finger to my lips in a sweet little "ssh" gesture, but I stood there in horror, gaping at the audience until they gaped back at me because I wasn't doing what all the other little tutus were doing. This brought me back to the planet and I burst into a perfect pirouette. My mom said her heart stood still.

A few Mothers of Invention were our backup group, and the charming melody of "The Captain's Fat Theresa Shoes" snapped me to attention as all the hours of rehearsal worked a miracle. We sang about a pair of huge ladies' shoes that Captain Beefheart wore, and the fun-seekers loved us!

> *The T of his T-strap stands for tippie-toes*
> *His tippie-toes fit him to a T*
> *Oh C.B. do a tap dance for meee-eee*
> *With your bigga fatta Tippie-Toe-Theresa-Shoes!*

Six months earlier, our conversations with Mr. Zappa had started escalating to constant replays of stunning nonsense. He would beat his knee and encourage us to foam at the mouth with previously unuttered info. He made us feel like we had very important ideas, and praised me for keeping up my diary/journal so faithfully. I started carrying it around with me at all times, and would stop to write whenever inspired:

July 30 . . . Mr. Zappa was in the highest of moods; for the first time he hugged me tight, tight, tight and swung me around in the air. I *love* Mr. Zappa to such an idolizing point. He really started me thinking, inhibitions are the fear to LIVE, love, and just reach out for life and take it in your arms. I find myself just accepting things instead of loving them, so can you imagine the bumpkins who walk through the world buying flower muu-muu's and losing their children? I'm still not THERE yet, though, like Mr. Zappa, Captain Beefheart, Paul McCartney, etc. God, I pray for The GTO's, perhaps we can open a few minds.

Frank and the Mothers were going to play the Whiskey, and glory of glories, he asked us girls to work up our theme song, "Getting to Know You," to perform on Saturday night!! Whenever we wanted to meet someone, we would accost them and croon, "Getting to know you, getting to know all about you, getting to like you, getting to hope you like me . . ."

August 10 . . . Our "coming out" was superb, we did two num-bers and danced for awhile and received A STANDING OVA-TION!! As Rodney says, "You just scream success." And we do! The GTO's are on our way!! Everyone said Mick Jagger was there. Can you imagine?? Mick watching me?? I didn't see him, I wish wish wish I did. I really had a gala time with Victor. For the first time in my *entire* life I finally feel on his level. We communicate 100% better, and I have so much to thank Mr. Zappa for. Such a lovely man, so "where it's at," so concerned and involved in it all. And ME, I'm a part of it!!

Mr. Bernardo disappeared from Miss Lucy one night and we heard the very next day that he had been seen in San Francisco with Mercy Fontentot. Lucy was crushed because Bernardo and Mercy had been on the very first cover of *Rolling Stone* together, which had created some inexplicable bond between them. He dared to flee the audi-torium while we danced our partially nude butts off with a new local group, Three Dog Night. He hadn't even waited for us to take our curtsies, and here we were, two days later, watching Lucy sulk; very heavy tragedy sulking on the rock steps of the log cabin. We always commiserated heartily with each other, and that's what we were doing when the foliage dramatically parted and Bernardo appeared, arm in arm with Mercy Fontentot. Conversation ceased and we were

staring at a plump version of Theda Bara wrapped in layers and layers
of torn rags, an exotic bag girl with black raccoon eye makeup that
dusted down both cheeks and looked like she had twisted two hunks
of coal round and round on her eyelids. Her lipstick was a red seeping
slash and both earlobes had been split down the middle by the weight
of too many dangerous earrings dangling too far down. She was
carrying a beat-up satchel that had once been an alligator, its seams
bursting open, shedding gaudy garments with each step of her black
patent-leather pumps. It looked as if she had come to stay. It was
frightening.

The relationship that Bernardo had with these two amazing girls
went beyond what I could conjure up, with my limited experience
in matters of the heart, because Mercy had indeed come to stay,
and Lucy wasn't about to give him up. They tolerated each other,
and since neither one of them was having s-e-x with Bernardo, it
was slightly less complicated than it sounds. (Bernardo was a BTO,
the male version of a GTO, only the boys "got in there" with each
other on a more serious basis, sometimes disappearing for days behind
closed doors.)

Mercy scared me. She was such a threat to normalcy that I thought
of her as a human facsimile, and would nod in agreement rather
than tell her she ought to put her brain in an industrial-sized washing
machine, wring it out real good, and hang it up to dry. She always
seemed on the verge of saying something very profound and would
catch herself just in time to leave you hanging in suspense until you
realized she had left the room. When I met her she had already
taken a thousand acid trips and her mind was on the endangered-
species list. She was tired of the San Francisco hippie scene and was
looking for something new. Her timing was unravaged and impec-
cable.

One sparkling afternoon, we were sipping tea with Gail in the
spic-and-span kitchen cleaned by Miss Christine, discussing our am-
orous exploits, when Frank walked in and said he wanted to have a
serious talk with us. He had given it a lot of thought, and believed
that the GTO's had real rock and roll potential, fabulous original
ideas, and maybe even some hidden talent that might be tapped,

and why didn't we all capitalize on it??! Why didn't we write a dozen songs while he and the Mothers were on the road, and when he came back, MAYBE we could record them for Frank's new label, Bizarre Records!! MAYBE we could be the very first all-girl rock group and write all our own songs for our very own album, have our very own groupies, and be world famous!! It was too much to fathom, and for a few minutes we sat in silence, staring at each other, until Lucy jumped up and hugged Frank, and then we were all squealing and shrieking, jumping up and down with Gail, beyond thrilled. When Miss Christine wrapped her thin white arms around me, I knew it was a very special moment. During the hubbub, Frank interjected that Mercy would be a much-needed addition to the group because she added an imperative bizarre element that we sorely lacked. We were stuck with her and she started to grow on me like a barnacle.

> August 21 . . . My God!! I have 52,000 goosebumps from read-
> ing Frank's fantastic article in Life magazine. Just to be a part
> of this scene makes me want to scream and cry. To be consid-
> ered a MEMBER. God, I hope The GTO's make it. It almost
> seems destined, all of us chicks with the *exact* same attitude,
> loves and dis-loves. Last night gave us such tremendous hope.
> MZ and GZ [Frank and Gail] think we'll make it. MZ is going to
> send some pix of us to Life magazine, and we have already
> been mentioned in his ten page article in this issue! Our scene
> won't just be singing, but everything The GTO's stand for. It's
> destined!! GZ says, "The country is ready!"

Mr. Z took off to entertain the goofballs, and the six of us turned the basement of the log cabin into our workroom and entered our songwriting phase. We were still making lists of ideas when Miss Mercy danced down the bowling alley with a pretty pixie-haired blond girl who had a big bottom and announced that she should join the GTO's. She was Cynderella, and she had a great idea for a song about an old crone in a place called Eureka Springs who loved the local blacksmith so much that she became the garbage collectress just so she could pick up his trash every day until she died. We were feeling expansive and liked her idea, so we greeted Cynderella with open arms, but decided not to accept any more applications. All available positions had been filled.

Cynderella also added a bizarre element. She was a confirmed fibber and we never knew if her long-winded stories were true or made up as she went along. She had so many different childhoods that if the conversation was lulling, I could ask her about her upbringing and hear a fantastic tale about Russian royalty or a black daddy in Watts who beat her ass every morning after dishing out the cold Cream of Wheat. She had a funny, deep, musical voice, and I liked to hear her talk; besides, she openly admitted to being a liar and it was fun figuring out which concoction might be true. At seventeen she was the youngest GTO, but I guess she could have been thirty.

Our first collaboration concerned all of our experiences in Phys. Ed. in high school, and we entitled this groundbreaking masterpiece "Who's Jim Sox?":

> *How embarrassing it is at only 13*
> *To have to take showers*
> *In front of a dyke gym teacher*
> *Who drools at the sight*
> *Of your pectoral muscles flexing*
> *Smelling of four laps around the track*
> *50 push-ups multiplied by 200 girls*
> *The cracks of backs hitting cement floors*
> *As we strained our bodies into womanhood*
> *Room 323*
> *Stagnant Sox*
> *Sweaty girls*
> *Broken locks*
> *Two by two to the opposite gym*
> *Our nylons rolled under our sox*
> *Today is the day of heavy socializing*
> *Heavy socializing, heavy socializing*
> *Finally getting to The BTO's!!*

Not one of us had written a song before, and our songwriting sessions were more like slumber parties, lasting all night and into the next day. It was a great excuse to talk our brains out, reveal our budding concepts, and divulge fantastic occurrences that had made us what we were at that precise moment. It was group therapy with an eight-week deadline, and we were grinding out the lyrics. Rodney Bingenheimer inspired us to compose a tribute to his historical significance in the music industry. We were amazed with his staying power and the collection of photos of himself with every conceivable rock and roll figure pasted on every square inch of his apartment. It was great to have to take a pee in Rodney's bathroom and peruse his ever-expanding peepot portfolio.

> *We have a friend named Rodney Bingenheimer*
> *He has a dutchboy hair-cut and he's five feet three*
> *He lives down the street from The Hullabalooo*
> *And he doubles for Davy Jones*
> *(He got beaten up by Brian Jones)*
> *He's so amazing you should see his walls*
> *It just screams "Get in there with the pop-stars!"*
> *"Let me in, let me in, I'm with one of the Vanilla Fudge*
> *I know Sonny and Cher*
> *I meditated with George Harrison*
> *The Hollies are my best friends*
> *And I ate lunch with Grace Slick yesterday."*
> *We see you at Music City and down at The Ranch Market*
> *Waiting for pop stars to casually stroll by*
> *Oh, Rodney, if you introduce me to Mick Jagger*
> *I'll let you meet my little sister*
> *And she's only twelve years old!*

Sparky and I had many encounters with black guys on the Strip and we called them cones. It wasn't meant in a derogatory way; we truly admired them for their insistent persistence and the poetic way they had with words. Sometimes Sparky would take her enormous tape recorder to capture this eloquence for eternity:

Wouldn't it be sad if there were no cones?
No, not ice-cream cones
Cones are soul brothers with processed points
At the tips of their foreheads
Some wear lime-green phosphorescent
Imitation leather jackets and pants
Others are fairly normal formal excepting
Those flood ankles on their bright orange slacks
"That's a flashy outfit mini-mama
Hey now, Hey now, Hey now, I could kiss your thigh"
They stand in front of The Wiggy A Go Go
Slapping their chins
We really respect them for their confidence
It's too bad everybody can't be as confident as a cone
(They're great losers)
Do the skate, shing-a-ling, Boog-a-loo
"Come with me, darlin' an' we'll spin some fine platters"
Oh, cones, you send us with your fantastic lines!
"What's your favorite form of recreation, darlin'?
Hey now, Hey now, Hey now, I could kiss your thigh
Say, Snow White, can I give you a ride in my
outa-site metal flake Bonneville?
Hey, darlin', come with me, woman
to my righteous pad in L.A. and we can booze it up
And have some fiiiiine lovin'
Hey now, Hey now, Hey now, I could kiss your thigh."

Bart Baker, the gorgeous little eleven-year-old boy, came to visit us in the basement and we thought he was perfect inspiration for a song about:

LOVE ON AN ELEVEN-YEAR-OLD LEVEL
What does his mother say when we kiss on the doorstep?
(He has to be home by ten)
I wait around til' three o'clock when he gets out of school
He flirts with all the ten year olds
And I'm so jealous I could die

(He just screams Brian Jones!)
Brian Jones! Do you realize this eleven year old kid
looks like Brian Jones?
A kiss on the cheek would be enough
But when he does more . . . wah! wah!
He has captured my heart . . . Bart
I'm ready to settle down
Do you think your parents would let you quit school at 16?
It's only five years. I can wait.
How could you doubt him, even when he lies?
When he says he's out playing ball
He's being a two-timing man
He has captured my heart . . . Bart
Oh, how he wrinkles my dress and tangles my hair!
(Get in there, Bart!)
Sneak out your window and I'll meet you tonight
You'll be back in time for school
When we're together, am I eleven or are you nineteen?
He has captured my heart . . . Bart
You're a heartbreaker, Bart Baker.

Mercy wrote a lovers' triangle opus involving Brian Jones (she wished!), Bernardo, and herself called "I Have a Paintbrush in My Hand to Color a Triangle," and another gem which described her personal philosophy, entitled "The Ghost Chained to the Present, Past, and Future (Shock Treatment)":

I see all the people I want to see
I be all the people I want to be
And find all the treasures I want to find
Along with the images, they're so unkind
Shock treatment, oh let me go-oh
Shock treatment, oh let me go-oh

To show how my wondrous days and enchanting evenings were coming along, here is a sampling of my journal in the summer of '68:

August 4 . . . Shall I start off with "so much has happened"? Well, it has! First of all, dear journal, you are going to be in print for millions to see! The tentative title is "Groupie Papers." We had a very successful meeting, and MZ is finally going to sign us! He has filled our heads with dreams of wonder (fame, money) I think the GTO's can help humanity (not soul-saving or anything, but really help them to see there is another way to exist—it's there and I'm living proof!) I saw Iron Butterfly last night and was thrilled to my underpants to see Daryl. I got the immediate urge to seduce! I watched his body and really had to hold myself back from running on stage and grabbing his lovely penis. . . . Ha, I've matured. I used to do *just* that!! Ha Ha!

August 7 . . . Lucy and I have been discussing "Wear Your Love Like Heaven" [Donovan song] and that's what I do a lot of the time. Jesus is intimidated continuously. He is so great, but has turned into a farce, He is so much more than that. He is a complete way of life, not a five second prayer at the end of a hypocritical day. I think he gets into people's heads to see how other people react to his words being spoken . . . to see if they are listened to or heeded . . . Bob Dylan, John Lennon, Donovan . . . make sense? "Wear Your Love Like Heaven," "All You Need is Love" . . . "with flesh-colored christs that glow in the dark, it's easy to see without looking too far, that not much is really sacred." Who knows?

August 11 . . . HI HI HI! We had a business meeting last night, and The Lindy Opera House is ours to rehearse in any time we want it! I have a crush on little Bart Baker, we wrote a song about him. Mr. Tim just phoned, he is TCBing for us, he is *ever so grand!!* The man from Rowan and Martin called and is coming to see us at The Lindy tomorrow. Amazing! A-MAZ-ING!!

August 15 . . . Where will I be in one year? So much to do and see. Time splits before I get a good look at it! Tomorrow is GTO photos, fun! Thank you, God, for my brain, my arms, my eyes, my ears!! I should be so happy to be the proud owner of an intact body (and sometimes intact brain) I wish I had someone to pour my love into. What a crime, either my love is all bottled up inside me or escaping into the air. Oh, yes, I met Gram Parsons last night and I told him I rolled for him and asked why he quit The Byrds and he said "to do my own thing." I can't wait to see what that is.

August 22 . . . My daddy is driving mom nuts; we're going to
have to move out of our beloved house because he hasn't struck
it rich in the gold mines yet. I feel so bad for her, she loves the
house so much. Oh well, I guess my childhood is being sold
with the house."
August 31 . . . Last night Pink Floyd came over and they received
The GTO's attention instead of our songs getting worked on.
We saw the films of our Whiskey show, and they made me
realize we're going to make it! Sometimes it's a fucking struggle, though. Lucy has to be kicked in the butt to get her to work.
I'm sure John Lennon had to ball out Ringo Starr a few times.
(HOW presumptuous!!!)

Right in the middle of this madness, I started feeling queasy and
sore all over, and a trip to the old family doc told me I had hepatitis!!
I had been running on empty and was too busy to notice! Since
mom and dad were broke due to fool's gold, I was carted off to
County General downtown to throw up in the hallway with those
less fortunate than myself. For two weeks I forgot my name, trapped
in a rebellious body attempting to rid itself of unnecessary invaders.
I spent my twentieth birthday in the drafty, smelly hallway, holding
the flowers I got from the Zappas in my lap. "Dear little Miss Pamela,
Hurry up! We miss you in Laurel Canyon—Lots of love from all
of us at the log cabin. . . . Say now darlin'."

September 10 . . . I'm on another type of horrid diet and all I
get is crap. In this room all I'm surrounded by is a FAT blubbery
old asthma case, a *fat* stick-out haired lady who pees the floor,
an *old* gall-bladder whiny, a hideous old BIG-mouthed repulsive
hernia, and an ancient drawling white-haired lady who can never
get up. All I can think of is Nicky and Noel and getting O-U-T!!

I wrote a few lyrics . . . "Dropping perfumed handkerchiefs . . .
blowing kisses across the room . . . Make us swoon . . . Whispering
sweet nothings . . . Into little pink ears . . . Has it passed with the
years?" Out of sheer boredom, and hopes for posterity, I also made
a list of the GTOs' private lingo:

GTO's	Girls Together Outrageously Occasionally Only Openly Overtly
GS	Get Smart
MZ,FZ/GZ . . .	Mr. Zappa, Frank Zappa/Gail Zappa
Chickweblis . . .	Us, the chicks: a name we call one another
Chickwebli . . .	All of us
Cones	Colored hang-ups
Klondikes	40's gun molls
Bailies (Jack, Bill or Beatle) . . .	titties
JHE	Jimi Hendrix Experience
Rob	Bob Dylan
BCP's	Birth Control Pills
Moche	Anything revolting
T.T.	Tiny Tim
Blackback	Whitefront Discount Store
TCB	Take Care of Business
Bozo-ing	Daydreaming
Melancolony . . .	Melancholy
Heidi	a snot-nosed kid
O.T., O.F. . . .	Obvious toupee, obvious fall
Goddess	Greased-up guy with fluttery eye-lashes and come-hither look

I knew that the Jimi Hendrix Experience was about to hit town and I was chomping at the sick bed to let Noel become number two on my list. I willed myself well, and took my clean bill of health to the palace that the Jimi Hendrix Experience was renting in the hills.

October 2 . . . I CAME! How do you like that? I phoned Noel (nervous and sweating) and he invited me over "anytime"! I dressed quickly and gala and split. We got along fantastic, but he must have thought I wanted to be platonic because after two hours I had to seduce him, and we soon wound up in his room (fire-place, red lights etc.). Lovely romance, we played around for awhile and then he made love to me. AMAZING! I was totally under his control. He put me in a hundred positions and did such stupendous things! It's doubtful that anybody could surpass his proism. It was like being caught in a web, unable to free myself—wanting to get more tangled. What was wrong with Nicky? I don't understand. Noel said, "That, my dear, is what you call a fuck."

The next time I saw Noel he was wildly drunk, and after a bit of salivating down in the game room he disappeared, promising to return in fifteen minutes.

Hello. I'm here at Noel's and was abandoned approx 40 minutes ago. It just screams espionage. I'd leave, but my purse is upstairs, besides we took a cab up here, and Benedict Canyon at night screams danger. How do I get into these predicaments? I guess I'll just wait.

Well, he never returned, and I was forced to poke around for my purse and beat a hasty, embarrassing retreat into the dark and scary night. The hazards of loving these fools and the music they made were numerous and agonizing, and they didn't do too much for the budding ego either. I left him a note, hoping to relieve some of the hurt: "Where did you go? It was quite obvious to me that you didn't want me there anymore, so I went home. I can't recall anything I said or did to bother you, but then again, you were very stoned. It seems to me that everything was a waste, a waste of thinking about you, waiting for you, just a waste of time. I just want you to know that I'll not soon forget you, firstly because you made me temporarily forget this screwed up world we live in, but also helped me to realize that it's *all* we have, and it isn't something I can laugh my way through. I feel like I'm just one more piece of trash in this cluttered waste-basket. Miss Pamela." (Lucky for me I always saved important correspondence!)

The time finally came when we sat in the thunderous cave of a living room, stacks of lyrics in our laps, waiting for an audience with

Frank. He had seen fit to put his confidence into all of us chicks, and I was hope hope hoping we wouldn't let him down. While the Mothers were on tour, we actually accomplished the task that Frank had put before us, but we had no idea if our scribbled prose would even qualify as songs. Along with the previous selections, Sandra had written a deep double-entendre, fraught with meaning for her idol, Bob Dylan, called "Do Me In Once and I'll Cry, Do Me In Twice and I'll Know Better," Cynderella's "The Eureka Springs Garbage Lady," my love song to Nick St. Nicholas, "The Ooo Ooo Man," and one that Sparky and I wrote for all the jack-offs of the world called "The Moche Monster Review":

> *Yonder comes a soft car*
> *Which probably won't take me very far*
> *The organ-grinder behind the wheel*
> *Is hoping he can score a feel*
> *His eyes are bulging at your bod*
> *He thinks you are a free-loving mod*
> *Moche Monster!*

Christine's contribution was a tribute to her parents:

> *I'm a television baby*
> *My father's a knob*
> *And my mother's a tube*
> *When I'm sad my horizontal dips*
> *And my vertical skips*
> *But when I'm glad, my brightness meter*
> *Shouts brightest!*

So we sat holding hands, trying to keep calm until Mr. Z appeared. No matter how often I saw Frank, he was always mystery man to me. His opinion counted above all others, but I found him totally inscrutable. I couldn't even bring myself to call him Frank; I devised names like "Hank" or "MZ," but mostly I called him Mr. Zappa. I believed him to be a humanitarian of the highest order for attempting to alter the world by scaring, repulsing, reviling, and cracking up humanity. He goaded them into a response, raised their eyebrows by telling them there was a freak-out in Kansas, and he was about to read MY lyrics. I could hardly sit still, anticipating the worst and the best in continuous rotation.

He sat in front of us, barefoot and shirtless, reading our efforts: The only sound in the room was the shuffling of blue-lined notebook paper and his occasional chuckle as he perused the pages. "I'm fainting with joy! He loved them! He loved them! He beat his knee over 'Cones' and 'Rodney B.' He looked up after reading them and I *knew* he loved them; he said they were *all* inspiring. Can you believe it? He wants to fix us up with Newmother to help us with the melodies and then maybe we can go into the studio and RECORD them! It's 2 good 2 be true!!"

Newmother was Lowell George. He had only been with the Mothers for a few months (ultimately he was axed because he smoked too much pot; Frank was an avid abstainer. Lowell went on to form his own group, Little Feat), and he jumped into the assignment because he wanted to show Mr. Z a few of his many talents. Lowell had the sexiest face and eyes, but I'm afraid there was a dashing prince locked up inside a greasy-haired chub-ola. He moved and danced like a thin guy, and could have been a knockout lady-killer if he lost several dozen pounds. He was big and cuddly and moon-eyed over me, so we became instant friends. (I always loved to be drooled over.) Frank also put his keyboard player, wacko Don Preston, on the case, and it didn't take long to turn our little ditties into actual melodic songs; hum along with Girls Together Outrageously! We had serious trouble harmonizing, so we all sang together like a grade-school choir, which didn't faze Frank—he thought of us as a living, breathing documentary. We put in a lot of work before the big day when Mr. Z sat in front of us as an audience of one, and after our stirring performance, he gave us a standing ovation.

Frank was involved in a multitude of other projects, one of which was the Plaster Casters of Chicago. He introduced me to the original Caster, Cynthia, over the phone, and since we were both wild over

Noel Redding, we felt a kindred bond for each other through the
two thousand miles of telephone wire. The Plaster Casters were two
girls so desperate to get near their rock idols that they devised an
extremely enticing approach: They would give the idol some sci-
entific head or a handjob, plunge the erect quivering member into
a bucket full of slimy white goo called alginate, yank it out the
moment it got soft (instantly, I would imagine), pour a mixture of
plaster into the gaping hole, and leave it there until it got hard.
While the hardening went on, the idol had the opportunity to ravage
the Casters, which is what usually happened. Afterward, the girls
would peel away the alginate, and lo and behold, the stiff member
of some famous member of some famous rock group would be captured for eternity!! It gave everyone involved such a wonderful thrill;
real-live history in the making. The big drawback to this charming
concept was that the girls had to get intimate with guys they weren't
wigged out over, just to further THE CAUSE. I couldn't have done
it, but I admired Cynthia's fortitude in carrying out these daring
dirty deeds. We started a correspondence and promised to meet soon.
Frank wanted to put her casts on display in a major art museum.
He was, once again, ahead of his time.

Right in the middle of the GTOs' earth-shattering lyric/music
sessions, my parents lost their house in Reseda, and I had to traipse
around the big Valley looking for a cheapo replica. My daddy was
hangdog depressed; he couldn't *believe* that his worn-out pockets
weren't lined with pure gold. He had ridden around on donkeys for
months, sweated rivers into the blazing Mexican sun, forged new
trails deep into the mountains of Guadalajara, only to find that it
would have cost more to build roads to get *to* the gold than the
whole mine was actually worth. He sat in front of the TV, his Rhett
Butler face reflecting "Come on down!" consciousness, staring blankly
at a little Mason jar full of shiny gold pebbles, while Mom packed
up her whole world and I scoured North Hollywood, finally finding
a little dump in our price range.

October 15 . . . Here I sit in the new pad. I finally found a ghetto
in North Hollywood after 92 agonies. It was hideous, I stuffed

seven rooms of things into three and it looks like a 93 year old
woman lives here and never threw anything away. It's an apartment and I hear 50 footsteps upstairs, Oh well, it's onward and
upward with The GTO's. Christine and I went to see Mr. Tim
and he was in the lobby with a mud pack on. *So* charming. He
wanted to play ice-hockey again, but Christine wanted to visit
her new fave-rave, Alice Cooper, at The Landmark.

The Landmark Motel was in the throbbing heart of Hollyweird
on Fountain Avenue, very close to where Jim Morrison threw away
the quart bottle of Trimar. Burgeoning rock celebs always stayed
there; in fact, Janis Joplin was about to poke holes in her veins for
the last time within its seedy walls. Christine was aflutter over Alice,
a skinny, caved-in guy from Arizona whose real name was Vince.
I had never seen her so perfectly put together—her new outfit of
one-half pants leg and one-half skirt was pressed to a stiff sheen; her
clown eye makeup was nearing Emmett Kelly status; and she plucked
imaginary lint from her lapels, expounding nonstop about the virtues
of Alice Cooper. He was virtuous indeed; their blossoming romance
was right out of a twenties movie, all innocence and flushed cheeks.
They held hands and gazed at each other sideways, this tall, skinny
girl we called the Dr. Seuss character of the group, and Vince/Alice,
soon-to-become idol of millions. I don't know if they ever had sex,
but they were clearly in love and made for each other at that precise
moment in time. She gave him an outrageous makeup job and threw
some of his clothes together into an outfit that defies description,
enhancing his scrawny rib cage immensely. I met the rest of his
group and took a shine to the drummer, Neal, and we sipped sodas
by the pool while Alice effused over Christine and his new record
deal on Frank's Bizarre label.

Alice had his very own autobiography, called *Me, Alice,* because
he became so royally famous. He described us very sweetly:

I met The GTO's at Canter's for the first time. The GTO's were
the first organized groupies, and GTO stood for many things: Girls
Together Outrageously, Girls Together Only, Girls Together Occasionally and Girls Together Often. The five or six of them, Miss
Christine, Miss Pamela, Miss Mercy and Miss Lucy, had started

a rock band, but they were more of a mixed-media event than musicians. People just got off on them. They were a trip to be with. . . . Miss Pamela was a smiling open-faced girl who looked like Ginger Rogers. I met Miss Christine, the GTO I was to fall madly in love with, across a bowl of shared matzoh ball soup. She was one of the skinniest girls I ever met; she made me look muscular. When she teased out her frizzy mouse-brown hair, she looked like a used Q-tip. The GTO's were close with Frank Zappa. In 1969, Frank was still a teen hero, he was my teen hero at least, and Zappa really just about supported The GTO's. There wasn't a zanier entourage in existence.

In November 1968, Frank was definately MY hero, and he supported the GTO's in style by giving us thirty-five dollars a week, EACH! I was *so* professional that I bought a briefcase to carry around my lyrics and journals, so I could peruse professionally at any given moment. I decorated it with ribbons and sticky silver stars, and painted "Miss Pamela's property" with alternating shades of hot-pink nail polish just in case someone might wonder who the exciting blond executive with the briefcase was.

Frank signed a complete lunatic street-personality named Wild Man Fischer to his label, to round out the madness. Wild Man sang retarded songs on the street to anyone who walked by, sometimes following them for blocks to complete his repertoire. His unwashed matted hair, filthy feet, spinning pupils, and putrescent gooey teeth sent me across the street many times, and I was secretly appalled to have any kind of link with a human of his caliber. I tried to be nice to Wild Man, and if I had a few of the girls with me, I would stop briefly and applaud his wackiness as he bobbed up and down singing, "Merry go merry go merry go round boop boop boop!! You and I go merry go round!!!" Once he grabbed and pinched me with his grungy, slimy hands, and I let out a shriek, flinging off the lacy garment he had tarnished as he cackled greedily like the Wicked Witch of the West. I was about to be linked with him in yet another way; Frank wanted to show off his ridiculous entourage in its entirety, so he booked us all into the Shrine Auditorium on December 5, a

Christmas show starring Wild Man Fischer, Alice Cooper, the GTOs, and, of course, the Mothers of Invention.

The girls and I plunged into action, sharing rehearsal space at the Lindy Opera House with Alice Cooper. (Wild Man had perfected his show already.) We worked up daffy deliveries of our silly ditties, including a bit with Rodney Bingenheimer playing Santa. We would all take turns climbing up on Rodney's lap to tell him three things we wanted for Christmas, and my first wish was to sleep with Mick Jagger. My second wish coincided with the co-creation of country rock: "I want to fly with the Burrito Brothers!"

My precious Chris Hillman had a new band called the Flying Burrito Brothers with the notorious Gram Parsons from Waycross, Georgia. Gram was totally countrified in a slinky bedroom-eyed way, and Chris had played mandolin with a bluegrass group called the Hillmen, way before the Byrds. Gram did one album with the Byrds called *Sweetheart of the Rodeo*, and then took off with Chris to start the world's first country-rock group, waywayway before the Eagles laid their golden egg. Miss Mercy won a writing contest in a local newspaper with a little piece on Gram:

The first glimpse I got of Gram was at the premiere of "Yellow Submarine," a gala event, and then I went comatose and I was captured and spellbound from here to eternity because he was so real he was unreal. I was with my group, The GTO's, and precious Miss Pamela had grabbed my arm and pointed my eyes to the left aisle, the lights had dimmed, as a tall, lean cat in a sparkling Nudie suit drifted by. He was true glitter-glamour rock. The rhinestone suit sparkled like diamonds, it was submarines all over the suit outlined in rhinestones, and the color was scarlet red. His Nudie belt hung on his hips like a gunslinger. Pamela always raved on about Gram, and I'm the only GTO that listened. She was always in contact with the special earth angels. During a recording session of Permanent Damage, she called Gram and he invited us over to see him. We drove to the outskirts of the San Fernando Valley, to a modern cowboy ranch with wagon wheels paving the drive-way. At this point in his life Gram had swiped Chris Hillman and Mike Clarke after he played with the Byrds on "Sweetheart of The Rodeo." We entered the house and shy

Chris Hillman and the cat in the Nudie suit greeted us with a grocery bag full of grass, and Gram was so down-home dazzling with sensuous Southern hospitality, it just slayed me. These are the first words I recall him speaking to me: As he leaned over his pile of records, and put on an old George Jones album, a tear fell from his eye, and he spoke, "This is George Jones, the king of broken hearts." Imagine crying over a hillbilly with a crew-cut. Gram was on a battlefield to cross country over to rock and vice-versa, unfortunately "Okie From Muskogee" ruled the Palamino juke-box, and although Gram was rich through a tragic inheritance, he never bought his attempt at success. Gram had long hair so the audience called him a faggot and would attend his Pal dates to ridicule him. I don't think they ever listened to "Hickory Wind."

Mercy was the only GTO who would attend Burrito shows with me; the other girls turned up their powdered noses at country music, and Miss Lucy laughed right in my face. Anything Chris did was OK with me. I was front and center at every show, reverting to my former baby, blushing, innocent, goo-goo-girl self whenever "Mr. Hillman" settled his penetrating gaze upon me. I was hoping I had grown up enough for him to take me seriously, but he was still married to his second wife, a British girl, Anya, so I had to settle for penetrating gazes and occasional perfunctory platitudes. Still, I never missed a show, and Burrito music pulsed through my veins. George Jones and Waylon Jennings appeared out of nowhere, and Merle Haggard popped to life like an inflated balloon with cowboy boots on. A whole new redneck world opened up in front of me; songs about trains and bars and jails became my new Top 10, and all I wanted to do was impress Chris with some country knowledge. If I could drop the title of Loretta Lynn's latest effort in one of our piddling conversations between sets, I felt a silent humble victory. I wore less and less makeup and took to frequenting Nudie's, a country-western clothing store, looking for the odd cowboy trinket to countrify my outfit. I asked my mom for her best fried-chicken recipe, just in case Anya dropped into the ocean and Chris realized I was about to become a woman. My mom was agog at my brand-new calico consciousness. She moved through each phase with me, but I think the Burrito phase was an acceptable one. At least outward appearances would suggest that I had normalled-out a little bit.

Gram Parsons befriended me, much to my constant thrill. I considered him to be a heavily misunderstood genius, a gentle, soft-spoken, well-mannered country boy who drowned his and the world's sorrows in little vials of powder and reams of reefer. When he sang about the agonies of love, his heart breaking, tears rolled down his cheeks without his knowledge. The Whiskey a Go Go was unfamiliar with sobbing men in Nudie suits, but I wallowed in his tortured Southern soul, swaying back and forth on the dance floor like a weeping-willow tree.

Rehearsals for the Shrine show went on and on despite traumas within the GTO camp. Christine was torturing Alice Cooper by dropping perfumed handkerchiefs in the pathway of Arthur Brown, who happened to be rehearsing His Crazy World right next door. Miss Lucy and Mercy bickered over Bernardo, so Sparky and Lucy became a twosome, gazing out at the rest of us like invading intruders. They worried about becoming too commercial, while I wanted to be on the cover of any and all available magazines. Sandra moaned over Calvin as her hand-painted tummy grew to enormous proportions, and Cynderella started a liaison with Russ Tamblyn, the leader of the Jets in *West Side Story*, and her heart was in Topanga Canyon. It was HARDHARDHARD work to get us all in the rehearsal room at the same time, and Frank had assigned his veddy British secretary, Pauline, to this insanely arduous task. She was prim and proper and fussed over her flock every second, carrying lyric sheets and schedules, looking up to the spackled ceiling for assistance from above. Mercy, Cynderella, and Christine developed a major chemical dependency and were often late, so our delirious rehearsals lasted deep into the night while poor Pauline sat in a metal folding chair counting out the steps to "The Captain's Fat Theresa Shoes."

When Frank came to see our final rehearsal, he was so impressed he gave us the big news that we could start our album after the Shrine show, and even though we were having internal squabbles, this fabulous news brought us together again. We went out that night, holding hands, and conquered Canter's: Phil Spector bought us burgers and we performed every song for him in between bites.

The night of the show, I was petrified; not only had my mom decided to come, but Chris Hillman and Gram Parsons showed up in our dressing room to wish us good luck. CHRIS HILLMAN in MY dressing room!!! He kissed me on the cheek and I didn't know how to react, it was all tootootoo wonderful. I took deep slugs of air and paced back and forth while Alice Cooper screeched loud, plaintive love-angst for Christine, his painted face peering through an empty window frame. We waited out Wild Man Fischer's insane song called "The Circle"; in between each verse he ran around the stage, he circled the inside of the Shrine, and then he went *outside* and ran around the entire Shrine Auditorium!! The wait was endless. It was finally our turn to take the stage, and on my way down the stairs I saw Nick St. Nicholas, and he smiled his loony smile at me in the dark. I died ten thousand deaths because the third song was called "The Ooo Ooo Man"; I was about to get down on my knees and sing to a fake snowman while two Mothers dropped fake snow from above. It was an obvious love song for Nick St. Nicholas, a tribute to his serene madness, and I hoped his seventeen-year-old fiancée would understand. When it was my turn to climb on Rodney's lap to tell Santa what I wanted for Christmas, I announced, "I want to sleep with Mick Jagger, fly with the Burrito Brothers, and become world famous." Two out of three ain't bad.

A week later, the Jeff Beck Group played the Shrine and all of us girls got divinely dolled up and cheered them on. I played *Truth*, Jeff Beck's current album, so much that the grooves were merging together. After the concert, which left me panting, we went directly backstage and announced to anyone who would listen that the GTO's, Frank Zappa's all-girl group, were in the building and wanted to meet the Jeff Beck Group. We knew no shame and were ready to let our newfound almost-fame do the talking for us. It worked, of course, and we realized that being in our own group would bring numerous extracurricular rewards. The British boys always wanted to meet Mr. Zappa, and Jeff was no exception, so we took him and his keyboard player, Nicky Hopkins, back to the cabin where we all had a fantastic gab-fest. We blabbed about our album and recited some of our lyrics for Nicky and Jeff, and they were rolling on the floor within thirty seconds! When Frank asked if they would like to put some of their virtuosity on our record, Jeff asked, "When do we start?"

We were all in the dimly lit little studio, humming along with Mercy as she belted out "Shock Treatment" optimistically off-key, when the entire Jeff Beck Group sauntered in to add some amazingness to the proceedings. I was very pleased to see that Jeff brought Rod Stewart, whom we all became instantly chummy with, calling him Rodney Rooster because of his choppy stick-up hairdo. Frank put Jeff and Nicky right to work, and they bombarded our meager efforts with brilliant bravura. We sat watching, enthralled and captured, while Rod the Mod hunched forlornly, then paced round and round in circles, then finally left the building. After Jeff's solo on "The Eureka Springs Garbage Lady," we went out to the suburbs of Glendale calling "Rodneeeee, Rodneeeee!" until we found him sitting on the steps of a grade school, peevish and petulant, feeling left out. We ooh'd and ahh'd over him and dragged him back to the studio, where he enhanced "Shock Treatment" with his raspy sandpaper shouting. We all stood around in a circle with headphones on, following Rod Stewart's lead: "Shock Treatment, oh let me go-oo, shock treatment, oh let me go-oo." I couldn't believe my eyes and ears. Frank was smiling away with his baton, the girls were caterwauling as best they could, Rod had his eyes closed and was sweaty and wailing, Nicky and Jeff were rocking out to the music, and I was in the middle of my own recording session!

I wanted to bring in the sexy new year of 1969 with my new unmet friend, Cynthia Plaster Caster of Chicago, Illinois. I had no idea how fucking cold it was in Chicago, so I took a lot of feathers and see-through frocks, sexy spiked heels, and delicate lacy items to impress this yet-to-be-met doll-woman. I don't know what I expected;

someone wilder than myself, certainly a hot dish with tons more sexual experiences, and tons more finesse and "hands on" moments than I could even imagine. I was hoping to get a massive shocking earful of information on how to handle myself in certain sensual situations.

The first shock I received upon arriving was a big splat of snow in my face, and then the major surprise of the year, the Caster Queen, Cynthia herself. She had a sweet, precious face, completely hidden by long, thin black hair, and a chubby huddled body cowering into itself, covered with layers of sweaters and coats, scarves and boots. She grinned up at me with pure sweetness, and underneath the streaming hair and woolen sock hats, her pale white cheeks pinked up at the sight of my skimpy dress and skimpy body. Despite our differences, which were profuse, we got to know each other over those two weeks, and eventually wound up giggling on her canopied bed like two Sandra Dees.

She was painfully shy and I couldn't imagine her with the alginate and plaster, buried in Eric Burdon's crotch area, but I saw the casts for myself, and was wowed by the artistry involved. For Cynthia it was a science, her true calling in life, the thing she was born to do, and Frank was her mentor, just like he was mine. She was a little reluctant to discuss the casting, so I perused her diary: "It molded superbly, we applied some baby-oil to his hair and he only got stuck for five minutes. I had been counting aloud before we thrust Noel into the mold, and when I announced the crucial moment, he became panicky and began to get soft, thus instead of diving mightily straight in, we had to shove it and pound it in, and it twisted like a worm."

She took me to a local club where we saw Fleetwood Mac, and laughed ourselves loony because Mick Fleetwood had a hole in his pants and his balls were popping out. We laid on her frilly bed while it snowed mountains outside, listening to the Jeff Beck Group and dribbling over Rodney Rooster's scratchy bedroom voice. I told her all about the week the GTO's hung out with the Beck Group at the Sunset Marquis, watching soccer on the TV while listening to Rod glorify Britain and commiserating with "Wanky" Waller about his lack of sexual exploits. Cynthia ached to preserve Jeff Beck's member for posterity. Her crack-brained profession belied the fact that her sensitive adamant soul belonged to Noel Redding, however, and she bit her lip with jealousy, hating me a little bit for having slept with him. She had cast the entire Hendrix Experience, and Noel's wormy cast sat next to her night light, in a place of honor. There was a poster on her wall of a group I had yet to hear of—four gorgeous Englishmen called Led Zeppelin. I listened, enraptured, as she described Jimmy Page, who was once in the Yardbirds, as being the most exquisite man alive on planet earth. He already had an evil reputation among the women of the world as being a heartbreaking, gut-wrenching lady-killer, wielding a whip and handcuffs, a concept that appeared to be in total contradiction to his perfectly poetic, angelic face.

I left Cynthia, with a new respect for her profession, promising to write faithfully and avoid Noel Redding like the plague. (A promise I wouldn't be able to keep, unfortunately.)

It was time to move out of Mommy and Daddy's house in the Valley and become a grown-up. I was getting my own salary, making my very own record, and ready to take the big dive into the Hollywood pool of frantic fools. One memorable night at the Palamino Club, Gram Parsons introduced me to a friend of his, Andee Cohen, a West Hollywood trendsetter and photographer elite. The first time I went to have tea with her in her upstairs apartment off Santa Monica Boulevard, I had to tell Marlon Brando she would return his call when she got out of the loo—*that's* how hip she was. I was in awe of her hipness, of course, but hoped I was ready to enter her lofty ivory-towered league, so when she told me she was looking for a roommate, I was staggered by the prospects and the timing.

While I packed up multitudes of stuff, my mom sat on the couch with her head in her hands; her only baby bird was ditching the nest for digs of her own. I knew she would cry for an hour when I closed the front door for the final final time, and I'm sure a funeral dirge resounded in her heart when I drove off in the pouring rain to sleep under another roof.

Miss Andee was waiting for me with open arms and a hot pot of tea, but had to rush into the night to meet one of her incredibly happening boyfriends. She had made up my little bed in the living room, since it was a one-bedroom apartment, and I was surrounded by her Moroccan wall hangings and exotic pillows. It was magic; I was alone in my very own place, it was raining outside, and Chris Hillman had asked for my new phone number. It happened the night before at the Whiskey; he came up behind me, put his arms around me, and said, "Moving to Hollywood, eh?" He and Anya were separated and she had gone back to England; he and Gram were living in Nichol's Canyon in a bachelor pad that I was aching to enter. So, I sat in my cute kitchen, sipping Constant Comment, waiting for the phone to ring. After three cups, Chris called to welcome me to my new home, and after putting the phone down I slid onto the floor in a delirious heap of mush, with giggling grandiose dreams of the days to come.

> January 10, 1969 . . . Here I am, elated because the lovely Mr. Hillman called ME, *Called ME!!* Dream upon dream upon dream come true. I truly believe in myself and my ability to dream . . . they sometimes come true (if I dream long and hard enough). I'm listening to Byrd songs of yesteryear and "We'll meet again . . ." sigh.

While all of us girls waited for Frank to make time to do the GTOs' album, Mercy came up with the perfect title, since it described her increasingly addled brain: *Permanent Damage*. In fact, I was worried that Frank might hear about all the needles floating around the Landmark Motel, where Christine, Cynderella, and Mercy had taken up residence. I watched them shoot heroin only once, and went running back to my car, shuddering. Mercy never seemed to have any money, so after Christine and Cynderella were finished with the needles and cotton, Mercy would try to get every last drop out of the remnants. She wound up giving herself a blood test, over and over again, kind of a sleazy bloodbath in a comedy of horrors. I loved the girls anyway, even though they thought I was goody-goody gumdrop. I just didn't want one of them to die, or Frank to find out!

Miss Andee took the photo for our album cover (I was holding a country fiddle and wearing a long white dress to impress Chris), but Frank wanted something special for his wacky girls; our album would open up, and on the inside would be solo shots of each of us and a paragraph about what being a GTO meant to us:

> The GTO's to me, dear friends, are a way of life. I'm so in love with everything I see, hear or feel, because I think everything is joyful. There are low points of joy, perhaps dark blue, and high points—pure white. The GTO's are all different shades. Everything is a color, isn't it? Tra La Tra La Tra La, I love people and their smiles. The GTO's smile at people and they stick their tongues out at us. It's OK though, I'm used to it. I love you everyone, I love you! Hugs and kisses, kisses and hugs, Miss Pamela.

> The GTO's, a color with five schizophrenic hues, a complete personality clash. A travelling caravan of players, masqueraders. 630 pounds that came together last year by way of The Log Cabin, now taking different forms, waiting for their big debut (as usual) wondering where it will be this time. Miss Sandra.

> The GTO's are a menace to American maidenhood. Watch out that your teenage daughters don't get their hands on any of the GTOs' literature promoting gayety, kinkyness and flamboyancy. The GTO's are out to corrupt your children. Watch out! There may be one lurking in your neighborhood! Miss Cynderella.

> The GTO's are to me a combination of the world's beauty and ugliness, we are supreme, yet the gutter, that's all except there is no forever. Forever, Miss Mercy.

One of my sweetest moments occurred right after the photo session for these solo shots. Just being in the middle of a huge roll of black paper, in the center of an empty room, in front of a blazing spotlight, dressed in my frothiest fifty-cent garment, beaming a smile for my would-be public as a semifamous Hollywood photog snapped away would have been enough; but when it was all over, on the way out of the double swinging doors, I met my first Beatle. We were squawking about each other's brilliance in front of the camera when Cynderella plowed right into George Harrison! (And we didn't call her "Pumpkin Butt" for nothing!) I was palpitating all over, instant sweaty armpits and gasping for breath, while still trying to appear cool in front of one quarter of half my life. He was soooo charming; he said he had *heard* of the GTO's and was looking *forward* to our album. I could have passed out right there on the A & M blacktop and become one with the Maharishi Mahesh Yogi.

Rolling Stone was doing an entire issue on the groupie phenomenon, and wanted the GTO's to star in the centerfold!! We lounged on the couch like casually reclining celebrities, spouting important opinions to our (har-de-har) adoring public:

> The GTO's are a sociological creation of Frank Zappa's. He didn't "create" The GTO's, he merely made them a "group" . . . and is now presenting them in concert as well as recording them. The GTO's are not lesbians, they're girls who happen to like other girls' company. The GTO's in all their freaky splendor are . . . outasite. Each has a personality all her own, and together they are not to be believed—chattering, laughing, telling stories, leaping about. The visceral reaction is full freak, but once you get into it, you don't even notice. "Girls don't show their emotions like they should," one of the girls said. "When I say: 'Sandra, you have the most beautiful breasts in the whole world,' that's not homosexual, it's just what I feel. You know how it is when you don't have a boyfriend and there's a girl to hold your hand, to kiss you, to say nice things to you, it's so important." Sparky says: "We don't ignore each other at all." Cynderella says: "We compliment each other. There are closer relationships between girls than boys." Mercy says: "We love boys to death, but you shouldn't be pushed into things. Some people think we're dykes and they're disappointed when they find out we're not." Miss Christine says: "This is Hollywood . . . but in Ohio, maybe they're not ready for this. We're trying to spread our philosophy."

Cynderella and I joining forces in London

SHEPARD SHERBELL

Radiant Zappa summer

My precious Moon Zappa

The GTOs' first publicity shot

MICHAEL CRAVEN

Mr. Zappa with his Girls
Together Outrageously

JULIAN WASSER

The GTO's at the
mixing board

JULIAN WASSER

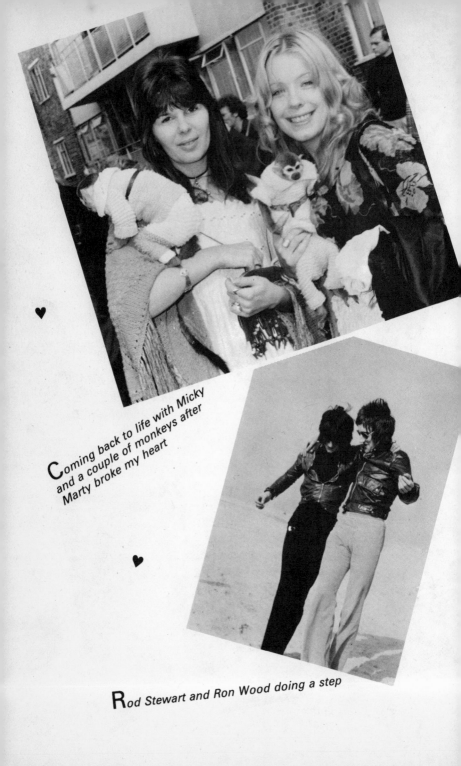

Coming back to life with Micky and a couple of monkeys after Marty broke my heart

Rod Stewart and Ron Wood doing a step

Me and Marty, dedicated follower of Granny's

There was always somebody
to pose with on Portobello Road.
He came in handy.

PHIL FRANKS

It was a lonnng article, and each of us got to tell our story, with lots of pictures. I carried the issue around in my briefcase along with my lyrics and journals and Flying Burrito Brothers photos.

Gram had a lady-love who lived in Santa Barbara with their baby daughter, Polly Parsons. Once in a while he felt the urge to subject them to his Hollywood life-style, and they would arrive at Burrito Manor with bundles of diapers and baby bottles for a brief stay before being shuttled back off to the Santa Barbara solitude. I was evening-dreaming about Chris when the phone rang, and Gram asked me to come up and meet Nancy and baby Polly. It was a joyous occasion, and I flew up to Nichol's Canyon with a one-way ticket to Burritoville in the pocket of my suede fringe jacket. Nancy was a stunning brunette with the biggest green eyes I had ever seen, and so in love with Gram that I could smell it on her skin. She called him her "old boy," and I was a little in awe of her as I was with all wives and nearly wives. Polly was a perfect doll-baby, with Nancy's green eyes and Gram's frighteningly long fingers, and she liked me!! I hadn't been around many babies, but this was one baby I wanted to get to know!

January 17 . . . Polly and I got along so well that Nancy asked me to baby sit while she went out with Gram, and I said "of course!" She went to get dressed and I sat in the living room with Polly while Gram, Chris and Brandon de Wilde (new friend!) sat talking in the dining room and I realized a lovely thing. When a man's head is with his friends—or somewhere that he's fond—he doesn't know you're there, but it's not because of you or that he doesn't care! He's just elsewhere momentarily. Also Chris and Gram's idea of a woman, a wife, and what she's supposed to do . . . Chris, especially has such good down-home ideas of wifery, but I see that I'm not nearly ready for marriage. (Ha! I should be so lucky!!) Gram told Nancy he thinks I am a star! I felt truly at home, like one of the Burrito family. When they all left, Brandon stayed with me for hours, he never left! We talked all about him and me and liked each other very much. People I truly love stand out and glow in a crowd. A thousand people could be in a crowd and if someone I love is among them, they shine like the sun. For instance, Gram and sweet Chris at The Palamino. I couldn't take my eyes from them. Oh my Chris, someday I'll tell you the story of my love for you. Once upon a time there was a golden-haired girl with blue eyes who was entranced by a golden-haired boy with blue eyes . . . what a story.

Gram invited Mercy, Andee, and me to come sing on the chorus of "Hippie Boy," the final song on the Burrito's first album, *The Gilded Palace of Sin*. Captured on vinyl with Chris Hillman!! The glory of it all!! When we arrived at A & M, a big blond girl in glasses stood up and announced, "*I* am the original Burrito fan." I'm sure I begged to differ, but she was *so* convinced that I kept it to myself. Her name was Michele Myer and she was a Chris Hillman devotee, but she liked me anyway, and we discussed the Byrds at great length. After we all screeched out, "There will be peace in the valley for him now we pray-aaay," Gram took Andee and me into a little room with a piano to play his new ballad for "his two favorite girls." Before he sat down, he looked down at his longest of long fingers with a confused look on his face and said, "Sometimes I wonder where these hands came from, I keep expecting to see stitches around my wrists." I don't think he knew where he came from, or what he was doing here. He cried while he sang a sorrowful song for Nancy: "You may be sweet and nice, but that won't keep you warm at night, I'm the one who let you in, I was right beside you then . . ." I figured they were having trouble that I didn't know about. I was right.

I again took care of Polly the next night and Chris asked me out on a date. The pounding in my heart was heard all over the world. After everyone left and the house was quiet, I sat in front of the fire with Polly sleeping next to me and the pouring pouring rain spattering on the windows, and I wept with thankful womanly joy.

January 19 . . . I fell asleep last night by the fire and Chris came home and covered me with his bedspread, he brought a girl named Lizzie home, but fell asleep beside me in the living room.

I watched his lovely face in peaceful sleep and . . . there are no words . . . My feeling for him is so true, boundless love.

I mooned around my new house, twinkly-eyed and trembling. My heart was doing a new dance, skipping beats, in the throes of something scary. I wanted to DO things for him, I wanted to sew and cook fried chicken and vacuum his rug. I did GTO interviews, went to meet the Rowan and Martin people, did a cover for a magazine, all in a love-daze, waiting, waiting, waiting.

Dear Father,
I want to thank you
for the golden-haired boy
with blue eyes that
finally see me
Blue eyes that smile at me
with me
Years passed and I prayed
each night for his joy
Now I am a part of it

A few days out of thousands
To be remembered until . . .

I want to thank you
for each tiny second that passes
with him near me
Words that sweetened within me
throughout the years
can chime now like bells
around his ears
How can I thank You enough
for his words that dance around me?

January 23 . . . He came to me and held my face and kissed me everywhere. I knew from the touch that all had changed. He wanted to go for a ride and he told everyone we were going to park up on Mullholland. Ha! We held each other and talked of everything, everything. Oh, I shall remember this forever and thank God nightly that it happened. I know I will cry, cry, but the tears of sadness will never be as strong as the pure happiness of being together and looking at each other, seeing the same thing in our eyes. I tucked him into bed and held onto him until I couldn't. I felt so much like a woman, powerful maleness overwhelming me. Oh, how I knew years ago!

5

♥

EVERY INCH OF
MY LOVE

I didn't know how soon I would cry, cry, and the tears of sadness would more than equal that pure happiness I gushed so sappily about. I spent the night with him, and succumbed savagely to my new womanly desires, moaning love words in his ear all through the long sweet night. In the morning, when he climbed over me, ice-cube cool and silent as a sting, I realized he didn't want me to be his new wife: In fact, he didn't even want me to be his new girlfriend and vacuum his rug or cook his chicken!! The torrential rains poured, setting new records, and I was stuck in Nichol's Canyon with the man I loved who didn't love me.

He was the strong, silent type anyway, but this silence was beating down my eardrums. I couldn't wait to get home and cry.

January 25 . . . The misery has so overcome me that all I can do is sleep. There is no time to dwell on the lovely Mr. Hillman and wait for tears to drown me.

I spent two days in bed, wondering if I would ever have the energy or desire to get up, get dressed, get famous, or get even. Miss Andee tiptoed quietly around the house in flamboyant Chinese silk robes, whispering through her many important phone calls as if she had a dying patient on her hands. The shades were drawn and it rained on and on outside. I suffered for as long as I could and allowed myself to surface long enough to take a call from Brandon de Wilde. He wanted to take me to a swap meet on Sunday, and I just loved a good swap meet.

January 28 . . . As usual I expected too much from Chris and gave too much to Chris. Such is life with me, too much of everything. It's as if all the anguish poured from me with the pouring rain, and today there is calm acceptance, peace. I'm glad I'm like this; a couple days of misery is better than a dull ache lasting too long. As Scarlett O'Hara said, "Tomorrow is another day!"

I thought of erasing the Burrito Brothers from my mind for about five minutes, and then drove up to Nichol's Canyon to try and catch whatever medicine ball Chris threw at me. I visited with Nancy and Gram, and was in the middle of cleaning the kitchen when Chris came home.

January 29 . . . Things taken for granted before are such a huge part of my life now; female things that I *must* know (and, oh, how they come naturally!) Oh, how I bask in his appreciation of the things I do for him; a kiss on the base of the neck while I do the dishes, a hug as I clean the stove . . . a dance around the living room.

Kind of sickening, eh? I was determined to fit the mold I imagined
he had hammered out, bending and folding myself into the shape
of woman I hoped he required. I went to Santa Barbara to stay with
Nancy for a few days, taking a cowboy-shirt pattern with me to sew
for my man. "Stand by your man, give him two arms to cling to,
and something warm to come to, when nights are cold and lonely
. . ." Tammy Wynette and I shared the same sentiment, and I sewed
the night away, listening to the demo that Gram had given me of
The Gilded Palace of Sin.

**February 3 . . . The shirt looked lovely but his eyes didn't shine.
Can I keep my goodness of heart? Purity? How many times can
I give my heart and have it cut in two and thrown back at me?
It's as if none of it ever happened. I feel like a wilting rose, a
lovely piece of fabric that's faded, the sun with a black cloud
covering me, a precious cowboy shirt hanging in the back of
the closet . . .**

To my divine relief, the Burritos got on a train and went on an
extended U.S. tour. I was at the station to bid them farewell, and
so was Brandon de Wilde.

The Burritos were rolling down the track like a Merle Haggard
song, and little Burrito cowgirl was sniffling and sobbing as though
an era had ended. They were supposed to be gone for six months;
half of me collapsed with good riddance and the other half just *knew*
I could have made Chris love me if I had had more time. I vowed
never to give up on him.

My car was on the blink, so Mr. de Wilde politely asked if he
could take me home from the train station. I hopped into Brandon's
van and spent the next six weeks right next to him, through incredible
amounts of thick and thin. I was entering a triple Aries Twilight
Zone, and plunged in heart first, as I always did.

Brandon had just split up with his wife of eight years and was in
high gear. He didn't know if he was agonized or available for con-
sumption by the first free female. He was irresistible when he smiled
and laughed, which was all the time, and he was blind as a bat,

always messing with his contact lenses, bumping into walls, or wearing his thick Coke-bottle glasses. His career was topsy-turvy; he quit acting after twenty-five successful years in front of the cameras to sing country songs like Chris and Gram. He was bored with acting, he was bored with marriage, he had bags full of drugs, and he was bumping right into my lonely walls. Brandon and I rebounded into each other very loudly, with a clutching, clamoring passion that defies discretion.

February 8 . . . Brandon. It can't be purely sexual. Oh God, it never will be, there's too much going on between us, but our attraction for each other is boundless. This stuff is definitely no good for the head. Gram was practically stuffing it up people's noses on the train last night—big globs of it. Oh, GP, stay safe, my dear friend. Brandon and I had strawberry and spare-rib flavored kisses, we make love *so* well, so completely satisfied, we sometimes laugh and scream and roll all over with joy. Am I not a good girl anymore? At least when I give my body, I give a chunk of my heart as well. Poor poor Nancy, Mr. Parsons didn't phone Nudie about her thousand dollar wedding dress, and she hasn't heard from him. I had the feeling at the train station that he wanted to be wild and free. Brandon and I are driving up to see her.

I snorted so much coke in Brandon's van on the way to Santa Barbara that I forgot who Brandon and I were and where we were going. I had to go lie down in the back and fidget with every part of my person to convince myself I existed and could breathe in and out. I was not a good drug-taker. I became guilt-ridden and perfectly paranoid, but wanted to remain on Brandon's "level," so I did it anyway. Sex with him was awe-inspiring. He had the energy of ten men and required very little sleep, so I was always exhausted, stoned, worn-out, and in heat.

February 21 . . . My first experiences of honest-to-God love-making, Brandon and I lift from this earth, I climax every two or three minutes and the feeling is not to be believed, there are no words in the dictionary to describe it. Brandon feels the exact same way and is "with me" *every second*. But, alas, too many drugs, God forgive me. What would Chris think?

Brandon was staying in David Crosby's guest house on Beverly Glen (he was an original Byrd!), and I just about moved in to share his trials and tribulations. Brandon was achingly addictive, and I fell in and out of love with him hourly. He demanded full attention, insisting that I sing with him, cook meals, do laundry, and play with his son, Jesse, whenever he came to visit. We also spent a lot of time upstairs with David. He was the last holdout of the heavenly hippies, his pudgy body always naked as he passed around humongous bowls of coke and pot. He played us the tapes of his new group, Frozen Noses, and they sounded blissfully beautiful; the most ethereal harmonies I've ever heard. They changed their name, thank goodness, to Crosby, Stills and Nash, and went on to sell trillions of records.

When I came up for a breath of fresh air, the GTO's were on the cover of *Teen Set* magazine, and Miss Andee had two letters for me from Chris Hillman, sent from the middle of the road. I, of course, had the Burrito itinerary and sent many sentimental gew-gaws across the wilderness, never expecting a reply, so I was literally struck dumb. Despite my rabid lust for Brandon, the image of Mr. Hillman hovered over me like a halo.

While I sequestered myself in a bacchanalian sex cave, the GTO's got in trouble. The police found a syringe spinning round and round in the Landmark loo, as well as three wacked-out, wildly dressed females, completely under the influence. Two sets of somber grieving parents coughed up bail money, while poorpoorpoor Mercy was trapped like a rat, coming down in Sybil Brand, a cage for dumbfounded damsels in distress. When Frank caught the sinful scent on the wind, he postponed our album indefinitely and cancelled our allowance. Naughty naughty GTO's! I had to think of a way to make some dough that wouldn't crease my style too much, or take up too many precious seconds.

When I extricated myself from Brandon's arms and came home to take care of beeswax, I realized the full extent of my rebound. I couldn't take much more of dear Brandon anyway; he only slept two and a half hours a night, and needed constant adoring care. His blind eyes were wild with a need that no one could fulfill, so I decided to stay home and let him collect himself without me. My decision wasn't without dramatics, because despite the double-barreled rebound, we had been able to dig up some real love for each other. He was the first man who didn't leave me out of his important male thoughts. He let me pull aside the macho curtain and get a glimpse into the manly mind. It was a jaw-dropper.

Once again, I nestled into the room I had left behind at my parents' house to regain my sanity and composure. I developed strep throat whenever I abused my tender body, and my mom would bring me Campbell's chicken noodle and rub my chest with Vicks. She and I would talk the nonsense out, and I would leave feeling like I could never really go wrong.

> **March 20 . . . I'm very numb, I just got back from Mom's and Gram called. The rest of the tour was cancelled, and they're here. Completely numb, I'm off to Burrito Manor. God help me.**

I was wrapped in Mr. Hillman's arms for slightly more than three days, then he got silent again and I went home. Since I had been through it before, the trauma was slightly less horrific and I was able to carry on with my flipped-out life, after shedding a mere twenty thousand tears. I had several things to think about: Frank was bringing Cynthia Plaster Caster to L.A. to continue her career, and I knew she would expect my undivided attention, and the Jimi Hendrix Experience was due to arrive at about the same moment (real cute timing); I received an ecru lace invitation to attend the wedding of Nick St. Nicholas and his betrothed beauty, Randy Jo (So kind of him, don't you think?); and . . . Mercy was still whiling away her time in the outer sanctum, Lucy had quit the GTO's, stating very loudly that we had "gone commercial," and Sparky was weighing her options. Christine and Cynderella weren't even allowed in the log cabin, Sandra was weighty with child, and I was out of money.

Despite my unfailing inner voice shouting that I was crazy, I started another cowboy shirt for Chris Hillman, hoping to get proficient enough to sell my wearable wares to many would-be hopalongs. I expelled every ounce of love I had inside me into this turquoise number, stitching some of my long blond hairs, a few driblets of blood, and plenty of tears into the hand-embroidered beadwork. Long and deep into the long deep night I slaved away on this masterpiece, and Chris finally graced my doorway with his presence. He put on the work of devotion and it embodied his inner being. The next time I saw the glorious item, Michael Clarke was wearing it at the Whiskey a Go Go, and he told me the amusing little story of how Chris had lost it to him in a poker game. Ha ha ha!!! Sadness enveloped me once again, but through the gloom I had found a way to make a few creative bucks.

The Burritos had become my reason for drawing breath. I thought about Chris a zillion times a day; he was plastered all over the inside of my brain from the time my eyes rolled open in the morning until I pulled my Mickey Mouse sheets around me at about three A.M. I heard Gram's sweet, piercing voice lamenting through Miss Andee's rare and wonderful window shades as though he were standing in the courtyard serenading me. One Burrito night I caught a glimpse of myself in the mirror at the Whiskey, decked out in total cowgirl fringe, looking just like Annie fucking Oakley, and I knew I might as well be living in Mike Clarke's drum kit. Had I finally realized there was more to life than pedal steel twang and Nudie suits? Perhaps.

Even in light of this final realization, I got a hold of a country fiddle, determined to fully master "Orange Blossom Special" by the time Mr. Hillman came to his senses.

Noel Redding decided he was crazy about me at a club called Thee Experience right in front of Cynthia Plaster Caster, who had just arrived in Hollywood. While she looked on, he said he would like to take me to the north of England someday. This may not sound like much, but to be thought of in long-term terms by a British Someone, to hear your name spoken in conjunction with EN-GLAND, was the ultimate pinnacle. Meanwhile, Cynthia looked like she had just lost her last cast, and we never frolicked under a ruffled canopy again. Whenever Noel came to town, we got up to lots of no-good, and even though I wasn't in love with him, and he never apologized for leaving me in the game room, I always saved space on the calendar for the scrawny lad.

> April 28 . . . What are looks anyway? Just because My Father God blessed me with some prettiness, makes me *no* better than anyone else! Cynthia says we'll never be close friends because of what I'm doing with Noel, and I feel like an unfeeling cunt. April 30 . . . Miss Pamela did the right thing tonight. I waited on Noel to "do his thing" at Thee Ex, and he was finally ready to leave. He had another chick and wanted me to come too . . . No deal. He kept saying, "No scenes, I promise" . . . No deal. After much persuasion, he saw I wasn't coming and said, "You're the sort of girl I want to marry." Good heavens, I didn't think he had it in him! P.S. Big news! Led Zeppelin are arriving tomorrow.

The next night my dear Mercy accompanied me to the Whiskey to see Led Zeppelin, having served her very hard time. I got sticky thighs over the very naughty Jimmy Page while I watched him reinvent guitar playing. He was wearing a pink-velvet suit and his long black curls stuck damply to his pink-velvet cheeks. At the end of the set he collapsed to the floor, and was carried up the stairs by two roadies, one of them stopping to retrieve Jimmy's cherry-red patent-leather slipper. After this thrilling display, we made our way to Thee Charming Experience, where I peered through the sticky din at Zeppelin carousing at the darkest table in the back, and was very proud not to know them. One of the guys in the entourage was carrying a young girl around upside down, her high heels flailing in the air, panties spinning around one ankle. He had his face buried in her crotch and she was hanging on to his knees for dear life, her red mouth open wide in a scream that no one could hear. It was impossible to tell if she was enjoying herself or living a nightmare. Someone else was getting it right on the table. Horrible things were going on, but I was finding it difficult to keep my eyes from straying to the salacious display. Jimmy Page sat apart from it all, observing the scene as if he had imagined it; overseer, creator, impeccably gorgeous perfect pop star, and he was staring right at me. I turned away, and luckily he couldn't see me blushing in the dark. Mercy leaned over and whispered, "Dangerous man."

I took mescaline and went to Disneyland (Walt and I had always had a very special relationship). I sat in front of the robot version of Abraham Lincoln and startled the lady next to me by asking what year it was; I was chased through the House of Tomorrow by three horny little pigs; and I trailed behind Mickey Mouse like he had a British accent. In fact, I had such a good time that I decided it was time for me to take LSD and find out what was really going on.

May 8 . . . Amazing revelations in my head. What is life about? Something pretty much like I thought it was, only it's all clearer now. My needs are so simple; love between a man and a woman. Now I know why hippies "see God" when they take LSD. Everything is opened up; senses, perception, spirit un-boundless forever.

I looked in the mirror and saw my heart beating in my eyeballs, the galaxy throbbed through my quivering veins; I could see trees growing up my cheeks and animals being born in distant dimensions. Ghostlike souls endlessly circled inside my bulging brain, and I was one with them all.

When a soul is born, it never dies; it is ETERNAL, traveling like the earth around the sun. Multitudes *inconceivable.* Things can be looked at in so many ways, we're just put in a set of surroundings and *we* create our world. If there is hate within you, you're missing the opposite feeling of love. It's blotted out by the hate. How close they are together; love and hate, good and evil, pure and impure. They are really the same and you draw the lines yourself.

I took my country fiddle and left the sleazy temptations of Hollywood to Led Zeppelin's roadies and Noel Redding's three-way partners. I was hitchhiking south, to Lovingspoon, Kentucky, where my

Aunt Mildred and Uncle Edwin resided with the Lord. I was hoping to clear my muddled head by dangling my feet in Pond Creek, and find some authentic old Southern fiddle player to teach me "What a Friend We Have in Jesus."

> **May 8 . . . 9 AM . . . I'm sitting in the car with "Silly," my ride's rather retard wife, and their three-week-old son, "Billy," who hasn't moved or made a sound. Larry is trying to hotwire the car, and I hope we'll soon be off. My destination: Tulsa.**
> **May 9 . . . I am trying to find some good in this. Creepy Louisiana Larry thinks he adores me and we've just had our third flat tire here in fucking Needles, California, at 110 in the shade. Why? We had to sleep in this fucked up Studebaker with only one door and the back seat full of crap, and that creep wouldn't keep his hands off me. I repeat, why? He just stopped to buy bullets. He feels a need to shoot rabbits. Won't THAT be fun? *Fuck*.**

While Larry blasted away at the innocent cottontails, I made my escape from the Studebaker asylum and silent infant, trundling through the tumbleweeds until I found a four-dollar motel next to a truck stop in the middle of nowhere. I sat down on the lumpy bed and opened my fiddle case, hoping to soothe my worried mind by sawing on it for a few minutes, and to my abject dismay, the dregs I hitched a ride with had weighed down my fiddle case with a rusty old electric razor I couldn't even hock! Woe woe woe was me. A fitful, tragic, sleepless night ensued. After scouring the two-bit pawnshops, I met a man who looked like my favorite Dodger, Gil Hodges, and when he suggested that we hitch across the country together, I was humbly grateful. A few hundred miles later, he announced that we would have to "act like man and wife" if we were going to be traveling companions, and I was alone again. On the side of the road, in the lavender New Mexico twilight, I said aloud to no one, "Will the real Gil Hodges please stand up?"

> **May 12 . . . I don't like regular cities or suburbia one little bit. How can people live their lives out in one little spot? Why is it**

that people in bus stations look so miserable, forlorn and completely beat? I join them here now in my misery, oh please, get me down in those hills right now!"

I took a Greyhound to somewhere in Kentucky and then got a ride from three Kentucky teen-boys who tried to put their big paws all over me as we cruised through the blue grass. I cried and screamed so hard that the one boy with a thin shred of decency made the other two remove their mitts from my tits, and I was able to hurl myself onto the highway. I arrived in Lovingspoon a bone-weary traveler, and slept for sixteen hours straight as the sorrowful oil-paint eyes of Jesus watched over me.

For the first few days in isolation, I worked in Aunt Mildred's garden, kicked pebbles into the creek, and took long walks in the glorious mountains, trying not to fret about my long-gone fiddle. I wrote letters to Chris Hillman, pointing out the many virtues of country living, I wrote poetry about nature, slept long hours, ate lots of fresh turnips, and then Sunday rolled around. My Grandpa, Pop Miller, had been a banty rooster preacher, crowing long and hard about hellfire and damnation, but I barely remembered feeling like a guilty sinner. (I was "saved" when I was eight years old, walking petrified down the long aisle at church to admit to the entire congregation that I, a pig-tailed girl of tender years, needed redemption for my wicked ways.) That beautiful spring afternoon in Kentucky, I began to wonder about my ill-defined relationship with His Nibs, Jesus Christ.

I sat down in the long wooden pew, looking forward to humbling myself to The Man Upstairs. After the initial hymns and prayers, the testifying began and the fifty-year-old walls quaked as the fear of the Lord was propelled into my soul. Wait a minute! I tried to fend off the impending frightmare as the moaning and sobbing surrounded me. The parishioners were all begging forgiveness for the horrendous sin of being born, banging gray-haired heads against the walls. Through the din, I spoke to God in my own way, attempting to explain why I dabbled in drugs and gave head to Noel Redding *et al*. Thunder crashed in my head and I shivered all over, knowing I was all tangled up in the age-old pressure of living inside the flesh.

> **May 22 ... My head hurt all day and I called Mom. I started crying and telling her about the religious thing I'm going through, and she said the relatives' way of life is different from mine and that I was a good person, and I was young and had a lot of life to experience. She said I definitely wouldn't go to Hell. (Is there such a place?) My sweet mama.**

I sat under a weeping willow eating rhubarb pie, wondering if I was a Christian or not. I was determined not to stick a label on myself, but I desperately needed Pearly Gates insurance. I went round and round inside while my Aunt Mildred sang, "Safe am I, Safe am I, in the hollow of His hand." Jesus seemed to make her so happy.

> **May 29 ... For some reason I don't want to be here anymore. This lovely place is where all the confusion began with my soul and what's to become of it. I can't decide if certain things are right or wrong! If fornication is supposed to be evil, then why did God make male and female bodies fit together so perfectly? Don't "saved" people wonder? I guess they're happy enough not asking questions. Maybe it never occurs to them? I'm *not* defying God, I'm defying the way it's done. It doesn't have to be this way. There's a lot to do out there, and many ways to do it. I pray to Him inside, and He hears me just as clear as if I were shouting.**

I went deep into a lush Kentucky rain forest and sat down in a thick pile of leaves and tried to figure out why I didn't like going to church. As I sat still and quiet, watching the mist glimmer through the ten million shades of green, I realized for a flickering instant that the whole planet earth was my place of worship.

And then, the night before I left, Aunt Mildred and Uncle Edwin called me into the living room, and I got down on my knees with them in front of their TV set to pray with Billy Graham, and afterward I wondered if all the acid trips in the world could help me make sense of it all.

I got on a plane with the first of many religious migraines pounding my head apart, and when I got home, I realized it wasn't MY home. I loved Miss Andee, she helped me to see that I was an important piece of the pie, and I always sat rapt when she decided to shower me with heady info, but I was also feeling shrouded by her importance. I needed my own room, this became clear to me one night when Miss A and Cynderella brought the entire Bonzo Dog Doo-Dah Band into my bedroom (which was the living room). Not being in the mood to cavort, I washed my hair three times, painted my toenails, wrote several letters, scrubbed the kitchen sink, and tried to learn to throw the I Ching, when all I wanted to do was crawl under the covers.

June 19 . . . I can't go to sleep because Bonzo Dog are in my "bedroom," Ha! The Bonzo's were astounding tonight, it's impossible to describe their brilliance. They did one song called "Head Ballet" where they all sat on the edge of the stage and moved their heads in bizarre unison. The lead singer, Vivian Stanshall, came out in a massive muu-muu with a gigantic lion's head on, beating a hand painted drum, and when he whipped off the lion's head, he was wearing a sheep's head, and he kept taking masks off until the finale when he had blood-shot ping-pong balls stuck into his eye sockets. It was enthralling and he was my type, but Andee got in there. It's hard to imagine they're out in the living room. Legs Larry Smith is one of the funniest humans I've met in years, but I guess this section isn't for me. What section *is* for me? I wish whatever I know right down deep would surface and give me some answers. The GTO's seem to be at a standstill, I wish our album would come out. I miss Miss Lucy, and Sparky wants to quit. What I really need is to feel accomplished. I bet people like The Beatles and Leonard Cohen feel accomplished. One thing for sure, I always want to feel like a free person. The only presence I want to feel owned by is God . . . and maybe later in life, the man I marry.

Michele Myer, the girl I met at the Burrito session, had conveniently moved right next door, and I approached her on the wonderful idea of having me for a roommate. Her apartment was bigger than

Andee's, and I hoped to convince her that the dining room could be turned into an adorable bedroom. Michele was, as you recall, the original Burrito fan, and since I saw her at all Burrito gigs, we had gotten pretty friendly, despite our many and varied dissimilarities. She shlepped down from San Francisco because of the lack of local show biz, and because Chris Hillman lived in Laurel Canyon. Her dad was a cop, her mom was a lush, and she had pretty much been raised by the nuns at Catholic school, which conflicted constantly with her adoration of pop stars. Her bosom was the biggest I'd ever seen, and she kept it well hidden under many wraps, she wore glasses, and had never had s-e-x or a real boyfriend. Her IQ probably reached the moon, however, and she was highly quotable and a sweet softie under the wary, unamused sheen. I moved in and got my very own baby-blue phone. I missed the Burritos, and the first call I made was to Gram Parsons. I believed Gram had been blessed with the magic stuff, but he was so tormented and confused that the magic came out in little blurts. I felt honored to be with him when one of these blurts occurred. The GTO's were rehearsing because we were finally going to finish our album, and I invited Gram to come pick up the purple beaded shirt I had spent weeks creating for him.

> June 26 . . . and he showed up, bombed out of his mind. He looked around for a piano, and I followed. "I could sing for you all night, Miss Pamela . . ." and that's what he did, three hours of beauty, pure shining love and brilliance. I'm so inspired and awestruck once again, full of him to the brim. I'm content just knowing he's alive. Never has anything I've done been so appreciated, GP loved his shirt so much. He said, "She doesn't do this for money, there is so much love in this shirt, I can feel it. This shirt will never be entered in any poker game!" On and on he went, gosh I was so happy. The GTO rehearsal went A-1, and we put tracks down on Friday.

Frank conducted us with his baton while we recited our loco lyrics. He glared at the bad girls, and no one glared more efficiently than

Frank Zappa. In fact, he was still so angry at the busted chicks that Sparky and I did most of the reciting. I was so relieved and happy the album was being completed that I took the news about Chris Hillman getting married for the third time without too many hysterics; I knew my Prince Charming was trotting around out there somewhere on a white charger, wondering where the fuck I was.

While we were recording our album, Brian Jones drowned in a swimming pool, all alone in the middle of the night. It was the first major pop-star death and it put me into a ministate of shock. The invulnerable became tragically vulnerable, and it shook some of the glitter dust out of my baby blues. Mercy became catatonic with grief because her fave-rave would never hear the song she had written for him.

> July 3 . . . Poor poor Mr. Jones, drowned in a pool all alone. Poor baby had nowhere to go, nothing to do since The Stones relieved him of his duties, so sad . . . "Prince Jones smiled as he walked among the crowd" [From Eric Burdon's "Monterey"] God bless Brian Jones' rock and roll heart.

I loved living with Michele; she worked during the day and I could cut out my cowboy shirts on the floor in the living room while listening to the Burritos or my new country fave, Waylon Jennings. I could pull down the shades in my dining-room boudoir and sleep until noon, dreaming of fame and precious British pop stars until I started my day with a cup of English Breakfast Tea and cinnamon toast. I had pictures of Noel Redding, Rod Stewart, Chris and Gram, Jesus, Mickey Mouse, and Mr. Z hanging over my bed, which was covered with my grandma's handmade quilt and a bunch of heart-shaped pillows. I had guests: Alice Cooper, Kim Fowley, Rodney Bingenheimer, "What's Happening" Bob, my wacky GTO's, Gail Zappa, parades of people passing through my very own pad. I paid the rent with my made-to-order cowboy shirts, and while I waited for the GTOs' album to come out, I listened for the clatter of hooves on my front porch.

Mr. Carlos, one of the BTO's, was in Europe with the Living

Theatre, and he wrote a letter to Mercy, describing the gaygaygay life in Gay Paree, and as a postscript he added, "I ran into Jimmy Page and he wants Miss Pamela." From across the ocean, this sweet scary news found its way into my delicious dining-room boudoir, where I reclined on my handmade quilt and pondered this brand-new hair-raising possibility.

July 31 . . . Jimmy Page is coming to town today, I don't know whether I want to be with him or not, who knows what diseases I'd get? Such a sweet and lovely precious looking cherub, why is it that he's perverted? Maybe he's not?? Perhaps I'll find out??

When Led Zeppelin was due to hit town, the groupie section went into the highest gear imaginable; you could hear garter belts sliding up young thighs all over Hollywood. LZ was a formidable bunch, disguised in velvets and satins, epitomizing The Glorious English Pop Star to perfection; underneath the flowing curls and ruffles lurked slippery, threatening thrill bumps. The two sides of me were fighting it out, and the sinning side I hoped to squelch in Kentucky was about to score a major knockout.

Thee Experience was reeling as Bo Diddley took over the dance floor, duck-walking back and forth with his big boxy guitar. I was all in white, trying to prove my purity in this dodgy den of iniquity, sipping red wine through a straw, waiting nonchalantly for Led Zeppelin to arrive. I was feeling haughty one minute and petrified the next, trying to get a little tipsy before the demonic darling darkened the seedy doorstep. Robert Plant was the first to walk in, tossing his gorgeous lion's mane into the faces of enslaved sycophants. He walked like royalty, his shoulders thrown back, declaring his mighty status in this lowly little club. He was followed by the king of rowdy glaring roadies, Richard Cole, who seemed to be scanning the room for likely-looking jailbait. They were surrounded in seconds by seductive ready-willing-and-able girls, who piled up at their table like clusters of grapes going bad. I was noticing that the whole group was there except for Mr. Page, when Richard Cole stumbled over and handed me a scrap of paper with Jimmy's number at the Continental Hyatt House scribbled on it. He leaned into me and mumbled thickly in my ear, "He's waiting for you."

The Continental Riot House was just a few blocks down Sunset Boulevard, but I didn't leap out of my seat to dash out the door. I hadn't fully decided to make myself readily available for him anyway. I was intrigued, and wanted to be intriguing. So I sat there on my ass, watching Bo Diddley repeat history, tingling all over, thinking about Jimmy Page waiting waiting waiting in his lair.

August 1 . . . Earl Warren Showgrounds, Santa Barbara, 8 PM . . . I must sneak some writing. Jimmy Page was just here to greet me and asked 92 questions as to why WHY *WHY* I didn't meet him at The Hyatt House last night. Someone gave him my number and he called today asking me to come here with him, but I came down by myself to show a little more hard-to-getness. I think my hard-to-get just got up and went. He seems so shy and delicious, grey eyes gazing into mine, sweet sweetness, pale white skin, gentle gentleman with something to hide. What does he want from me?

11:20 PM . . . I'm in the limousine while Jimmy takes his fourth encore, some girl attacked him on stage and it took two big guys to get her off him. Richard Cole escorted me to the car and made sure I was well taken care of. What's going on. Oh, here comes Jimmy . . .

Led Zeppelin live in 1969 was an event unparalleled in musical history. They played longer and harder than any group ever had, totally changing the concept of rock concerts. They flailed around like dervishes, making so much sound that the air was heavy with metal. Two hours after the lights went out, as the band sauntered offstage, the audience was a delirious, raving, parched mass, crawling through the rock and roll desert thirsting for an encore. Twenty long minutes later, mighty Zeppelin returned to satiate their famished followers.

The long ride from Santa Barbara was one of those dream experiences that leave you glowing in the dark. From the moment Jimmy slid his small velvet-clad ass across the seat of the limo, right next to mine, until the door was thrown open in front of Thee Experience, we cooed and giggled like doves in heat. It was a hundred-mile drive, which gave him plenty of time to come out with "*all the lines*." He told me he had gotten my number the last time he was in town but was too nervous to use it until the last day, and he called and called but the line was constantly busy. Mmm-hmm. He said he wanted to spend time with me MORE THAN ANYTHING IN THE WORLD. Tell me more. I kissed and slobbered all over the inside crease of his slim white arm until he rolled his head back against the plush seat, gasping, "Oh, Pamela, yes, yes, yes." Yeah yeah yeah. He warned me that his previous L.A. girlfriend would probably be in the club and that I would have to give him the chance to "explain" to her about me. Uh-oh.

I climbed out of the warm, dark backseat womb, full of wet kisses and flaming glazed eyes, and found myself in the precarious position of sharing this splendid divinity with Catherine James, the most gorgeous rock courtesan alive. She and I hissed at each other from a dark distance, and I beat the old hasty retreat back to my cozy pad, where I tossed around in the sheets with the vision of Jimmy's back-yard peacocks strutting across my latticed brain. I was turned inside out, pulsating with creamy pink desire for this most coveted hunk of drool material, but I was too thin-skinned to take the chance of being scorned this soon.

> August 2 . . . Morning, not much sleep . . . Michele said Jimmy couldn't even believe I left last night, he was asking everybody if they'd seen me. He looked all over the club after "explaining" to Catherine, and left alone. Hmmmm.

I knew he had gone to Texas, and I couldn't hang around the house waiting for his call—I'd go mad. So I went to a friend's pool and lolled in the sun, perspiring over my brief but pungent memories of Jimmy Page. When I arrived home I saw the phone was off the hook, and I thought, "Oh no, even if he tried to call, he'd say, 'Your

phone was busybusybusy again.' As soon as I set it down in the
cradle, it rang. "Long distance, Mr. Page calling." The first thing
he said was, "Oh, the elusive Miss Pamela, you took your phone
off the hook because you knew I was calling."

He knew what to say all right; he could have given a Master's
course in how to turn a fairly sane girl into a twittering ninny. No
one had ever gushed over me, or given me all the lines before, and
I could feel myself falling apart and turning into one of those gooey
unrecognizable substances. He told me he was going to come to my
door, sweep me off my feet, and take me away in his white chariot;
he told me he was my knight in shining armor; he told me he didn't
know what was coming over him, he had never felt like this before.
He taunted me with those freaking peacocks that walked by his
bedroom window, as if someday in the near future I might be able
to lift my head from the pillow and see them for myself. He acted
like he couldn't believe I ever gave him a second glance. When I
told him I missed him, he came out with, "Oh Miss P. Really? Are
you telling me the truth?" My melting heart wasn't ready for this
guy. I swallowed it all whole, and it was fucking delicious.

**August 4 . . . Just wakened by my dearest Jimmy, calling from
Houston to tell me he'll call at ten minutes after nine tomorrow
night, and "Oh, I thought I'd lost you when you didn't answer
your phone yesterday." His face is so new, SO new, everything
seems unreal; a new thing has taken me over. The agony with
Chris is over, now I feel *so* good, such a floaty feeling of anticipation, silly, silly, silly. I sit here while my body fills up with
little bubbles—each one full of soft, crazy, loud, gentle, screaming, lovely, odd, joyful things, bursting within me and spilling
all over my heart. This time tomorrow I shall be throbbing.
What am I doing getting this carried away?**

Well, he came to my door with his roadie Clive, and swept me
into his white limo, and took me to see the Everly Brothers at the
Palamino. We got all caught up in those glorious harmonies. Jimmy's
eyes misted up and he squeezed my hand on certain meaningful

lyrics: "Mmmmmm, I never knew what I missed until I kissed you . . ." He looked hard at me with a tiny smile on his rosebud lips, making me sweat with suspense about the long night to come. He put something into my hand, and it turned out to be a silver ring with twenty little pieces of turquoise embedded in it, and I wondered if I was going steady with the best guitar player in the world. He always messed with his black curls, poofing and fluffing them around his flawless face; he wore emerald velvet and white chiffon, thin little socks, and the most perfect brooch on his lapel. I couldn't wait to get back to the hotel and take it all off.

> August 6 . . . We got carried away into some enchanted land and were swept into each other like the tide meeting the sand. . . . Our bodies were meant to be together and he said, "I hope you know you'll never get rid of me, please keep me around until you don't want me anymore . . . I'm not like this, what's happening to me? All I can do is look at your face." I held him so close and told him, "I feel like I've been holding you forever," and he said "You will be, we'll be together for a long long time if you want it that way. I've known you for a thousand years, don't you feel that way?" Yes yes yes, Mr. Page. We tried to sleep, but woke up every ten minutes and kissed. Every time he touched me he would moan and sigh and call to God. Such a face, so gentle and soft, I'm amazed at his sadistic tendencies; they're such a part of him that I doubt if he'll ever stop. It was really frightening, he changed into another person, but all he did was chew me and slap me a little. We talked about our ages and he said that five years between couples is perfect. Everything he said drove me nuts. His beautiful grey eyes always there beside me, beneath me, above me. Everytime I feel doubtful (which is constantly) I look at this ring and all I can see is his perfect face.

I saw Jimmy's whips curled up in his suitcase like they were taking a nap and pretended I didn't, looking quickly away as if I had seen someone's personal private peep show. He came up behind me and put his hands gently around my throat and said, "Don't worry Miss P., I'll never use those on you, I'll never hurt you like that."

Then he sucked on my neck, and when I could feel the bruise being called up out of my bloodstream, he tossed me down on the bed and told me he would throw the whips away to show how much I meant to him. After ripping into my antique-lace dress and making raging, blinding love to me, he wrapped the whips round and round his forearm and slid the leather coils into the plastic flowered wastebasket, where they remained until he left for Somewhere U.S.A. a week later.

We talked about how much better it would have been had we met before all the pop-star–groupie business started and got in the way of a meaningful and honest relationship. He vowed not to let it get in our way, but inserted a clause that allowed him to "do things" on the road because he got so "bloody bored." I shuddered at what those "things" might have been, and inwardly craved impossible monogamy with my precious Mr. Page.

When he picked me up late one night, I opened the door and our gaze locked for many entrancing moments before I collapsed in his arms at the sheer relief of seeing him. This unpremeditated display prompted him to say, "Your insides are so sensitive, I knew you were different." Clutching me to his thin, trembling chest, shaking with the outrage of our positions in life, he moaned, "Oh Miss P., how are we going to get rid of them all?" He had been in my life a mere few days and was already driving me wildwildwild. We only saw the rest of the group ("Percy," "Bonzo," and "Jonesy") at gigs because he wanted to hole up and be alone with me. He invited me into his private world, and I was hope hope hoping that the glass slipper would fit my size-seven foot.

On his day off, we stayed in my bedroom, listening to the test pressing of *Led Zeppelin II* over and over again while he took reams of notes. I had to comment on every solo, and even though I believed the drum solo in "Moby Dick" went on endlessly, I held my tongue and went on pressing his velvet trousers and sewing buttons onto his satin jacket. I told him about Nudie, "the rodeo tailor," and the whole team, including their massive manager, Peter Grant, got fitted out in cowboy clothes. We went to the Glass Farmhouse, where

Jimmy got a long antique coat embroidered with a dragon and a silly velvet hat with a feather in it. I was holding his hand, and in my ultimate glory by his side. The roadies, even Robert and Bonzo, began to tease us about how long our fling was lasting, how Jimmy never spent so much time with a girl on the road before. All the other guys were married, so they watched Jimmy's love life with envious glee. Not that they didn't get up to their own bedroom antics. In fact, a good friend of mine, Michele Overman, was spending time with Robert, and she made a little inscription in my journal;

"My dearest Pamela, Now that my lovely Robert and I are together, I have a nice bit of information for you. Robert said, 'She's the best thing Jimmy's found and he knows it.' Speaking about *you*, of course!"
August 12 . . . Anaheim Stadium, 8,500 screaming raging people, a twenty minute standing ovation, Jimmy treating me like a princess. There was s'posed to be a Zeppelin party, but Jimmy and I smoked and drank at Thee Ex and went back to the hotel, made exquisite love and crashed out. We woke up around one and talked about him leaving and how lonesome and miserable we'll be. He even said he would send for me somewhere so we could see each other before he goes home to Pangbourne. AAAaaaaaHHH! We had a hilarious fight, screaming and kicking and carrying on, so much fun! He said that he always has such a fantastic time with me every minute, etc. etc. etc. I wish I could remember all he said; it's back there in my memory somewhere. We're off to Vegas now to see Mr. Presley. Mr Page takes care of me, doesn't he?? I adore him so much.

We stayed in this elegant suite with a king-sized bed up on a platform, and sat right in the front row to see the King reclaim his throne. He was wearing black leather and looked like ten greek Gods as he tore through "Love Me Tender," "Don't Be Cruel," and "Jailhouse Rock." He was sweating, he was in the flesh, he was alive, inhaling and exhaling. And there I was in Las Vegas, breathing the same air as Elvis Presley, sitting between Jimmy Page and Robert Plant, completely and entirely beside myself. Some sideburned grease monkey appeared after the show, asking Jimmy if he would like to meet Elvis. He said, "No, thank you," and I never quite got over it.

August 14 ... Gone ... My lovely Jimmy. How amazing it all was ... is? So full, every second taken up, two weeks full of one never-ending moment with JP, and the grand finale last night; a million fireworks going off at once in my soul. Lime sherbet gushing like geysers from holes in the earth. I was floating on top of peppermint clouds, his lips turning into another amazing fruit after every kiss. Soft screams floating from my lips, my entire being pouring onto his face, buried in my body ... My whole self was opened up and everything sweet was entering my pores. Every piece of Jimmy, every piece of me; interlocking with raspberries, oranges, pistachio ice-cream, cherries, grapes, and tons and tons of lime-green sherbet. I had an orgasm every minute, and each one was a different flavor.

I had taken some very intense mescaline, and Jimmy watched over me, making sure I was having a good time. He liked to be in control, and didn't take many drugs or drink much alcohol. I think he believed his beauty was too important to tamper with. He was always in the mirror, primping on his splendid image, and putting perfect waves in his long black hair with a little crimping machine. He used Pantene products, and whenever I smelled them, for years afterward, I remembered being buried in his hair.

I was a fool for him, and prayed to anyone who might possibly be holy that I wasn't just a one-tour wonder. I could be true-blue to his image forever if I had a hinting hope of another healthy slug of him. More than anything, I ached to meet him somewhere on the road, which would be a miraculous accomplishment indeed.

August 18 ... I was sweetly awakened at 9:40 by Jimmy telling me of how he misses me more than I can imagine and how he took some girls back to his hotel and became so repulsed that he kicked them out. He said he's so miserable without me, he's going to send for me around the 25th because he has five days off. I'm in a state of shock.

August 20 ... Where are you, James Patrick, where are you? Every time I get any confidence, it's shattered. Damn it all to Hell. Yet, I know him, he'll call tomorrow and give me every sweet excuse ... I hope.

August 21 ... No word from James Patrick. No word from

James Patrick. Can you imagine? Is there a creature somewhere on this earth called Jimmy Page? Good-night imaginary James, wherever you may be.

August 23 . . . (Beatle day '64) What can one say when one is this miserable? I'm just walking around like a lump of clay.

August 24 . . . Here I am on another exciting afternoon with the friendly sewing circle. I just made a nice dress, but who cares? Who's going to see it? I have these lovely visions of myself leaving the plane in it, running to Jimmy with wings on my feet. What an ass I am.

August 25 . . . What a draggy hot miserable day. When I dare to think about what this day might have been, I cringe. Jimmy has a chick in every city, what was I thinking? All I know is what I felt. I guess what I feel won't be able to count anymore. I went to see Crosby, Stills and Nash, and they were so inspiring; goosebumps sprang up all over me. Oh, I was *so* happy for David. Praise God for them all. Even though I'm miserable about Jimmy. I'm always thankful that I'm living in these times and that I appreciate what I appreciate. Oh, why am I left hanging? Even if he said, "Fuck off," at least I'd know where I stand. I'm not even standing anymore, I've fallen down.

August 26 . . . Complete breakdown of everything, moaning his name, screaming his name down in my throat . . . empty words spilling into the hot empty air . . . "Jimmy Jimmy, where are you?"

I was pacing around the apartment in a numb fog, so when the phone finally rang, Michele answered it. "Pamela, it's Jimmy, it's Jimmy!!" I was like Sleeping Beauty waking up after a hundred years of death sleep as his sweet voice told me how "the scenes" he was having were like "eating hamburger," and how he really "needed" to see me. While my tears of relief dribbled into the receiver, he told me, "The boys really like you, they usually hate the girls I see." He promised to send me a plane ticket the next morning and I said a silent prayer that he would. As I started to pack my suitcase to go on the road with Led Zeppelin, I felt strong because I had called to Jimmy like a cavewoman deep down inside myself, and it had worked.

I waited all morning for my airline ticket to arrive, and when it didn't, I started shivering and couldn't stop. Michele was trying to

hold me up, because I was a quivering heap, curled up on the floor
in a fetal position. I asked her to hand me my journal, and with
shaking hand I wrote: "Why did he even bother to call me? At least
I wouldn't have heard his sweet voice, and the hurt would be healing
instead of fresh blood still flowing . . . where is the white chariot,
Mr. Page?" Michele made me a cup of tea, and I stood in the
doorframe to steady myself. After two sips, I dropped the cup of
steaming Earl Gray, grasped the doorframe with one hand, clutched
at my heart with the other, and slid dramatically down to the floor
as the doorbell rang. Suddenly I could run, and standing at my front
door was a messenger boy holding my TWA ticket to New York.
"Miss Pamela Miller?" he asked, and I kissed him like Blanche
DuBois kissed the "young, young, young man" in *Streetcar*, then
whirled around until I got dizzy, and fell down again. The sun was
shining; I was a twenty-year-old blonde with blue eyes and a ticket
to New York sent to me by Jimmy Page, the most beautiful Englishman alive.

The next three days on the road with Led Zeppelin were classic
rock and roll heaven; I was exactly what I had always aspired to be:
the girlfriend of the lead guitar player in the world's biggest and best
rock and roll band. I was the only girl allowed backstage, and while
the band went over the set list and got all dolled up, I sat on the
ample lap of the world's greatest and most monumental rock and
roll manager, Peter Grant. I had heard horrendous tales of Mr.
Grant's kneecap-breaking escapades; his reputation as being a teeming Goliath preceded his paunch, but he and I developed a special
relationship, and I was bounced on his knee on many occasions. He
was always *right there* for "his boys," and nothing, not even his
family, took precedence. Peter and the whole group called me "P,"
and I accepted the endearment with slavish gratitude.

I was on the left side of the stage where Jimmy entranced eighty
thousand Led Zeppelin maniacs with his magic guitar fingers and
black-satin suit emblazoned with gold dragons climbing up his long
legs. The audience was in a frenzy, and from my vantage point,
sitting up on Jimmy's amp, I almost felt like one of the group; I

could see what they saw, and feel what they felt pouring from the frenzied fanatics. The wild-eyed girls looked up at me and wondered which member of the group I was sleeping with, and I was so proud. I wore four huge, clunky turquoise-and-silver bracelets all the way up my right arm that each member of Zeppelin had given me to take care of during the show. Turquoise was very big in 1969, and these particular bracelets were the heaviest, gaudiest pieces ever made by American Indians in the entire state of Arizona. I gazed out at Jimmy under the bright lights with his violin bow, tears filling my eyes at the thought of being able to take off his soaking-wet chiffon shirt after the show, tell him how magnificent he had been onstage, and climb into the long black limo with him and head for the hotel.

August 29 . . . Well, here I am in New York, JP is on stage, pissed off at me for forgetting his shirt. Oh well, he'll get over it. I have two things urgently to report: Bonzo came and sat down with us and said, "What's this? A happy couple?" and Jimmy said "Yes, yes, yes," and Bonzo said, "I approve of this one, Jim, do with her whatever you will, I really like this one." Bonzo, JPJ and Percy made a bet with Peter that Jimmy takes me to Pangbourne, and Jimmy said about the matter: "You never know, P, you never know how my luck runs." It's SO hot in this dressing room, but Bonzo is doing his drum solo . . . it's almost over, Percy is introducing the group. 10,500 people just screamed for Jimmy. God, he drives me nuts, I can't fuck him enough. Today he said he would be upset if I was with other boys while he was away. It's so great running around in limousines, eating the best food, being treated like a queen by everyone. No one can believe that Jimmy brought *anyone anywhere*!

August 31 . . . Jimmy and I stood alone by the plane (ah, romance . . .). He held me and said, "Bye, baby . . ." I haven't heard that much emotion in him before, and I've never seen quite that look in his eyes before. My God, I wish I could write every little thing that happened; walking down the windy streets of New York, seeing our reflection in every window, him introducing me to people as, "Pamela, she's from L.A. . . . This is Mrs. Page." People coming up to me at The Pop Festival, offering me presents because I'm with someone they worship, our bath last night and his words, "I can't bear to hear about other scenes you've had, I don't know why, P, it's never happened to me before." Richard Cole got me right on stage by saying, "This is Mrs. Page, you wouldn't deny her seeing her old man, would you?" The guy said, "No one allowed up here, there's not one girl up here," and Richard said, "Right, and there's only one Jimmy Page." I sat right on Jimmy's amp, he was so close I could touch him. The crowd of 80,000 went NUTS! The end of the night was sad though, Bonzo was so stoned, Peter had to carry him off stage and they couldn't do an encore. Jimmy was so worried he couldn't sleep, and he tossed and turned all night. I'm waiting for the plane to take me to L.A., wearing Jimmy's clothes, I feel completely enfolded in heaven. If my ears weren't deceiving me last night, Jimmy was falling asleep and he raised up and said, "If I were to marry you, P . . ." then he stopped and finished with, "Oh, never mind, I'm too tired and I'm saying things I shouldn't."

Sparky quit the GTO's and went to New York with Miss Lucy, and Frank had to delete her from the album cover. When I clambered off cloud nine, I missed her sorely, and questioned my position in life. When would the album come out? Would Frank even put it out with two of the girls on hiatus-never-endus? I found it hard to relate to the remaining girls because they were bombed out and I thought their priorities were pointless (except for Sandra, who had a brand-new priority named Raven). I was making shirts for the Hollywood rock elite, I was taking acting classes, I was keeping up my journals, I was dancing at the Whiskey every night, I was madly in love with Jimmy Page, but I nagged at myself constantly for my lack of accomplishments. "What am I doing with myself? What a complete dunce, on my way to being 30 with nothing to show for it. I'm so far behind, I took LSD last night and freaked out all over the place. I was up against the wall, realizing what a huge nothing I am. Where is my creativity?" Whenever I was around a mighty slug of innovation, like Led Zeppelin, I found a big empty hole in myself that clamored to be filled with some type of creative brilliance.

It was my twenty-first birthday, and what I wanted was an exciting lengthy résumé or an engagement ring from Jimmy Page. I settled for a big birthday bash and invited one hundred of my closest friends, who brought one hundred of their closest friends. "What's Happening" Bob provided many crates of champagne, and stood at the door like the official host, wearing an ancient tuxedo with tails, bowing to all the pretty girls as they paraded in wearing their finest finery. I had accumulated an insane conglomeration of wack-jobs during my hours of hitchhiking, and they were lined up on the couch like several different kettles of fish. Dunco the Clown, a shy oddity with a very low IQ, was the first to arrive, and sat anxious and hopeful, wearing his tatty outfit, clutching his pail of balloons and party favors, eager to create animal hats for the crowd. Next to Dunco sat an old black guy named Ellis in a puce leisure suit, who had a mellow crush on me. He gave me loads of polyester dresses from his clothing store in Watts, and had brought two large plastic sunflowers with happy faces to brighten up the party. An Indian guy named Ray completed the picture; he woke up one morning completely bent over, and was spending the rest of his life trying to figure out why. He liked me because I didn't laugh at his affliction and would occasionally accompany him on his spiritual quest for a straight spine. I wandered around the living room wearing a pink teddy and satin slippers, waiting for the mescaline I had taken to kick in, listening for the phone to ring, watching the circus begin. I didn't know half the people who showed up, and two infamous groupies from New York, who came with a friend of a friend, stole all my wonderful birthday gifts. I watched Eric Burdon squash pink icing into my carpet with the heel of his boot, and from my vantage point on the floor, the gooey fuchsia sugar seemed to slide all the way to China. I listened to one of Spooky Tooth serenade me on my rented piano (another attempt at creativity), and I was thinking so hard about Jimmy that I almost missed his call. The shrill ringing blended with the melody in my mind, and when I realized what the sound was, I crawled through the many pairs of legs in a desperate race to the phone. His sweet British accent barely cut through the din, and I kept asking him to repeat himself, which did not enhance conversational spontaneity. The fact that the picture of him by my bedside was winking, blinking, and grinning didn't make for much normalcy either. Just when he was about to say something profoundly romantic (the mescaline helped me to read his mind), the ravishing, uninvited Catherine James walked up to me with the cute guy from Pink Floyd and said, "Happy birthday." In my condition, I could tell she didn't mean it. All of the remaining GTO's ganged up on her with glaring looks, and she slinked out, but it was too late to recapture the precious tender moment. Jimmy said good-bye, and I couldn't wait for the party to be over.

September 14 . . . It's hideous being 21. It makes me feel as if I should run out and do something before it's too late. Our album comes out soon, really this time. I wonder if I'll be sorry for not developing some sort of real "career." At least I'm creative which is more than I can say for a lot of people. Everyone flips out for my shirts, at least it's artistic; I'm making something someone will enjoy and I'm putting MYSELF into it, it's better than sitting behind some desk or working at some store . . . isn't it??? I *can* play "Home on the Range" on the piano. What kind of person am I, really? Not a whole one yet. It sounds corny, but I haven't found myself. I'm not truly sure of anything . . . except God and Love; two things I must have to exist (and both are the same thing). I'm not up to my expectations, I mean, somehow I'm limiting myself; not living up to my fullest potential. But does anyone? What counts anyway? Does it matter what someone *does*, or rather who he IS?
September 29 . . . Nothing should ever bore me. There is always something to look at, something to think of, or another position to put your body in, or something to feel. If we realized every little thing, we would never be bored. How great to be that advanced. Please, God, have I advanced AT ALL this year?

6

♥

IT'S A GAS GAS GAS

I climbed my Snow White wall-paper waiting for a long-distance call from my demented prince across the sea, and my baby-blue phone sat mute and mocking, only ringing when local yokels felt like saying hi or if some poor fool wanted to order one of my cowboy creations. I really wanted to avoid sleeping with someone new, to prove to Jimmy that I was dead serious about sleeping with *him*, but this pent-up passion didn't keep me from looking, gazing, staring, dribbling, and contemplating. Michele and I went to the Palamino and sat right in front of Waylon Jennings— the sexy country-stud he-man with the dirty look in his eye. He played a hand-tooled leather guitar with "Waylon" carved into the strap, and he had a cigarette dangling from the corner of his mouth as he promised to take sweet mental revenge on the unlucky lady who had dared to break his heart. I sat with my legs slightly spread apart, staring hard at him, sweating over his black-leather wristbands and greasy pompadour, and he couldn't help but notice me licking my lips. He growled and sounded threatening, a big, tall grown man with a serious chest and big cowboy boots, picking on his guitar with an incredible lip-curling suave. I believed he was out of my element, but I desired him immensely, and passed a note to Michele, just like in junior high: "What a hunk! He's staring at me, can you tell? I could be tempted."

After his set, we sidled up to the bar to tell him just how *really* great he *really* was, and he called me "angel" with a very unangelic look in his eye. I'm sure he was surprised to see two freaky little hippie girls panting in his presence, and he kept hiking up his belt and squinting out from under his black cowboy hat ringed with silver conchos, saying "I'll tell you what," before every sentence. "I'll tell you what, it sure was great havin' you girls up front tonight. . . . I'll tell you what, I could hardly get through my set with those panties staring me in the face. . . ." Sweat was trickling down my side, so I poked Michele and we sat down to wait for his second set.

I thought about Mr. Page in between gadding about Hollywood, attending any event I could get myself invited to. The most bizarre party I ever went through was for Frank Sinatra, Jr. He was so desperate to be talented, it broke my heart. An entire crowd of major celebrities was forced to endure an hour-long screening of a TV special that featured Mr. Junior and his special guest, a pair of boots that were made for walking. I like being in a room full of movie stars; Robert Culp and Sammy Davis, Jr., were chatting away like two normal people, and I was awestruck by Rod Serling. I couldn't help but notice how many something-on-the-rocks he was putting away, and I worried about his liver. Toward the end of the screening, I sat in the back of the room as Danny Thomas blathered on to Jack Haley and George Burns: "Just think, Jack, imagine George, from

our loins, from our loins . . . your kid, Frank's kid . . ." I wondered
which genius involved in the show sprang from the loins of Danny
Thomas. Rod Serling walked me to my car in a very intoxicated
state and requested that I make him a cowboy shirt. When the phone
rang the next morning, I thought I must still be asleep, or maybe I
had entered the Twilight Zone at last. "This is Rod Serling . . ."

I got a letter from that swankpot Rod Stewart, along with a photo
of him and his best friend, Ron Wood, asking if they could please
crash on my floor:

> Dearest Miss Pamela, A picture of me and the lovely Ron Wood,
> doing a step. Thank you very much for letters and such. We will
> be in L.A. in October if all goes well. My dear Pamela, could I
> ask you a small favor if I may? Could Ron and I sleep at your
> place? The floor would do. My solo album comes out around
> September 22. Could you please send me one, along with your
> own long-playing effort? Hope and trust you're being good. . . .
> See you soon, Rod.

I had previously entertained the idea of sharing more than my
floor with Mr. Stewart, but he was now a temptation I had to do
without. I was determined to walk the straight and narrow, hoping
against hope that Jimmy would make an honest woman of me. Noel
Redding also wrote to me, announcing the date of his arrival and
asking me to please make myself available to him. Old times' sake
wouldn't work this time. It was with this attitude, and with chastity
belt attached to my 1930s pink-satin tap panties, that I found myself
face to face, body to body, with Mick Jagger.

> **October 22 . . . 6 AM . . . I did something, or shall I say, I *didn't*
> do something, and I'm wondering why not. I think I'll wonder
> about it for a long time. Mercy and I went to see the Burritos
> at the Corral in Topanga Canyon, twirling and spinning to-
> gether. Jagger, Richards, Watts and Wyman came walking in
> and the roof lifted off the dilapidated old dump. We carried on
> like nothing astounding was going on, and kept dancing to The
> Burritos. Luckily I had on a long black velvet dress, cut real low,
> and lots of chi-chi rhinestones. I could feel *his* eyes upon me,**

and I rocked out even more. Gram noticed what was going on from the stage, and said into the microphone, "Watch out for Miss Pamela, she's a beauty, but she's tender-hearted." My sweet Gram was so thrilled that his new best friend, Keith, was there to see him play. Mick came up to Mercy in between sets and said, "Introduce me to your beautiful lady-friend," and then he kissed my hand and bowed. Those lips!

Mick invited Mercy and me back to the huge house the Stones were renting in Laurel Canyon, and number one on my farfetched fuck list was literally within my grasp. Mick, Keith, and I sat around the fireplace, listening to Mercy predict profundities through her beaten-up tarot cards. She carried her cards everywhere, hoping to bump into the likes of Keith Richards, spread them out on the rug in a triangle, explain the Tower and the Hanged Man, and create answers for unasked questions. After the reading, which went on for half an hour, Keith picked up a guitar and Mick sang, "I followed her to the stay-shun . . . a SUITcase in my haa-and." I entered rock and roll heaven and was hanging out on cloud nine; my heart was beating below my waist, just like it did at the Long Beach Arena. Mick and I danced around the living room to the Stones' unreleased album, *Beggar's Banquet*, and when he asked for my opinion I was tongue-tied, but smiled like I had written a rave review. Within seconds he was right in front of me, holding my arms down at my sides, kissing me so hard that I knew I would have swollen lips for a week.

6 AM, continued . . . After he kissed me, he began to caress my face with his lovely hands. He came on and on and on to me; delicious huge kisses from that amazing mouth, caresses everywhere, I was melting, but holding back. Terribly shy, I was. "You're *shy*!" He couldn't believe it. I went to the pool to put my toes in the water and look at the full moon, Mr. Jagger followed, kissing me and kissing me and tangling my hair.

"I'm going to bed, Miss Pamela," (sexiest voice I've ever heard.)

"Have a nice sleep."

"Do you want to come to bed?"

"I don't know."

"You want a week to think it over?"
"Yes."
(silence)
"Well, do you want to come to bed?"
"No."
AMAZING!! So amazing that I had to write it word for word.
And where was Jimmy when I told Mick Jagger "NO"? Probably
fucking some CUNT!

I was trying to be true to my pink-velvet prince who was probably
tying girls to bedposts all over America. Led Zeppelin had once again
hit the U.S., but I lingered around my telephone to no avail. On
October 28, Jimmy finally wakened me with some sort of vague
greeting, sweetly announcing that he would see me in two weeks.
It was a depressing conversation and I wept for forty-five minutes.
Why didn't he fly me to the Midwest, throw me on top of the flowered
bedspread, and make me yelp with delight? Absence obviously didn't
make his heart grow fonder, and I could only hope that the sight of
me would make him salivate. I would wait out the two weeks, and
if Jimmy didn't show me he truly cared, I would find Mick Jagger
and flagrantly fling myself upon him. Before the two weeks were up,
however, I saw Mick two more times, and it was hot and heavy.

October 30 . . . Wonders never cease . . . I just left Mick, still
saying "no." This time he begged me, he even said "Promise
me you'll stay . . . just once" over and over again. Sigh. Kisses
and caresses, more gentle this time. I even overheard him ask
Mercy how he could convince me to stay with him. When other
people are asked to leave by big roadies, we're asked to stay
on, and I feel so privileged. MJ was supposed to sleep with
this chick, but he was with me every second; they finally had
a conversation and she split. I guess he was convinced he could
get me to stay. He said, "You're pretty, so pretty, the prettiest
girl I've met here, I really mean it." Mercy told him that Jimmy
was my boyfriend, and I'm sure he snickered. He probably knows
what Jimmy gets up to, and thinks I'm being a prude. Oh well.

I was being downright masochistic by not sleeping with Mick, but
I really was worried that Jimmy might find out and think I was just

like all the girls he left whip imprints on. I wanted to prove to myself
and to Jimmy that I could keep my urges from usurping the pure
love in my heart. But still I needed to be near Mr. Jagger. I made
him a black crepe shirt and took it to PJ's, where I knew the Stones
would be in the front row for Ike and Tina Turner. I had to entrust
one of Mick's roadies with it because he was home with the flu, but
as I was leaving, the roadie winked and said, "Mick told me if I ran
into Miss Pamela, to tell her to drop by tomorrow."

November 3 . . . MJ tried his best to seduce me last night, and
somehow I held on to my sanity throughout his *thrilling* caresses. AAACH!! My body was hurting, aching for him; "Miss
Pamela, don't leave now, we should be together, I really dig
you, you know. We're acting so silly, like a couple of kids, we
both know we'll enjoy each other." Still, I didn't relent and at
first he was pissed off, but he returned, saying, "You're really
too good, aren't you? What do you think Jimmy is doing right
this minute? You're a GTO, remember? Not some school girl
from Oklahoma.

I had a real short dress on and he slobbered all over my thighs,
chewing me up real good. I was breathing in heaving gasps and he
inched higher up my thigh, leaving a sticky trail like a snail had
been crawling into my panties. Devouring my legs like they were
edible, he left one massive swollen bruise on my right inner thigh
and I excused myself and fled wildly into the night. I hoped hard
that I wouldn't be classified as a prick-tease, and I prayed the hickey
would heal before Jimmy got a load of it.

I needn't have worried. Jimmy called me from San Francisco, the
final spot on the tour, promising me he would fly down to L.A. on
his only day off to see me.

November 7 . . . My beloved never arrived. I don't know how
much of this stuff I can put up with. He keeps pouring it on to
me; you'd think I'd be saturated by now. He woke me at 5:30
with his tenderest voice and every excuse you could imagine.
I wept and sobbed. So now he says he'll be here this afternoon.

I'll believe it when I see him. Bitter, bitter, bitter . . .

2:45 PM . . . I have no feelings of his arrival. Still, my anxiety knows no bounds. I am still, the world around me is still and quiet; yet within me is this turmoil, it feels as if my blood is bubbling. I shall have to fly out alone tonight to see him and the thought appalls me . . . but I must. Jimmy, how much of this will you give me? How much can I take?

I flew out alone, a pathetic beaten puppy, my perfect glossed-up smile painted on with a lipstick brush, my cracking heart palpitating on my ruffled sleeve; I had to see him, no matter what.

Jimmy made a big display of being overjoyed to see me, but the "something" that everyone sings about was not in the room with us. I took achingly deep breaths trying to recapture the sweet sleaze that developed between the starched white sheets at the Continental Riot House, but he smiled his most enigmatic smile and fluffed his curls. We wandered around Sausalito, hand in hand, loitering in art galleries where he bought a bunch of Escher etchings for five hundred bucks apiece. His timing was perfect. Escher died a couple of months later, and when I read about it in the papers, I was transported back to ritzy hippieland, standing on the cobblestones, watching Jimmy's profile through the rustic window as he perused lizards crawling into each other, two hands drawing each other, and black-and-white ducks turning into each other. We carried the rolled-up Eschers around the breezy waterfront, and I gazed up into his face, searching for a sign of devotion. He bought me a book of Sulamith Wülfing's ethereal paintings and I clutched it to my chest, trying to contain the flood that was forming in my tear ducts. I loved him so much, and he was slipping quietly away from me. The sorrow I felt was so sincere, so lonely, I knew I was finally a grown-up.

Jimmy flew off to England, and he didn't offer me the seat next to him on the plane. Instead he told me at the airport, "P., you're such a lovely little girl. I don't deserve you, I'm such a bastard, you know." I felt like I had just been handed a one-way ticket to Palookaville. Alone at the airport, I knew what it was like to be crippled. I could hardly walk, and sort of slid along the wall until I reached the exit. People were staring at me and I was glad to share some of my wretchedness with the shocked strangers.

It just so happened the Rolling Stones were playing Oakland Stadium that night, and I decided to drown my sorrow among the multitudes. My friend Michele Overman was also in San Francisco, and having just sent Robert Plant back to his wife, Maureen, she was raring for some diversion herself, so we hitched to Oakland Stadium to see if we could scam our way in. None of the hippies at the gates believed I knew Mick Jagger, some of them even guffawed in my face, which made me more determined to get in. Most groups stayed at the Edgewater Inn, so we stuck out our thumbs and found ourselves pacing the hotel hallways, listening for music. We heard a guitar being tuned and bravely pounded on the door. The beauteous Terry Reid, the Stones' opening act, opened the door and graciously admitted us entrance. We listened to him practice for a while and I casually asked if the Stones were also in the hotel, and he answered in his sweet high falsetto, "They're right down the hall." I excused myself, and just as I opened the door, Mr. Jagger happened to be passing by.

November 10 ... MJ spotted me and came after me; "Miss Pamela is here!" Hugs and kisses and all that. He put me into a limousine and I was taken to the concert ... unbelievable! We sat together in the dressing room and I massaged his neck. I got a little paranoid, feeling like I didn't belong in that high and mighty scene, but then I remembered the quote from Mick that I have on my wall: "Don't worry about what others think of you, or you'll never get it together yourself." He held onto my hand, and the dirty looks I imagined I was getting from everybody in the room faded away. They rehearsed for awhile, and they're all SO amazing; brilliant personalities. MJ is magical, truly spiritually evolved. He awes me. I was put ON STAGE for the concert, and I got to see the audience FREAK OUT from The Stones' perspective. Everyone came together; surging like a sea to the stage, thousands of eyes never leaving MJ's magical being. Such power with a capital P. How would it feel to have thousands of kids "under your thumb," ha! He was wearing a long red scarf, and got down on his knees to whip the stage with it during "Midnight Rambler," and it was the most sensual thing I've ever seen. He asked me to fly back to L.A. with him for the night, but I promised Michele I would stay here at her sister's for a few days. Oh well, he'll be back in L.A. soon, I'll see him then. I want MJ, why not? About James . . . I AM going to accept it the way it is and groove. That's all. I'll do as I PLEASE while he does as he pleases. If I felt love from him, I would wait the three months until he returns, but WHY SHOULD I?? I couldn't be promiscuous anyway, and there is no one I truly desire except the tangy MJ.

Why I didn't fly back to L.A. with Mick that night still remains a mystery to me. I guess I still had Jimmy's scent all over me, and wanted to hold on to it for as long as possible. He smelled so fucking sweet.

November 18 . . . I dig musicians, I feel they have the most to offer me mentally and emotionally because they think basically along the same lines that I do; extremely creative people. Music is Life. As Captain Beefheart once said, "God is a perfect musical note." It's a shame there's a whole competitive scene surrounding most musicians. I want to see MJ because he's a groovy exceptional person. Ah, well . . . life goes on.

Groovy?

The GTO's album finally came out to mixed-up reviews, and I dedicated it to Jimmy Page, the Flying Burrito Brothers, and Jesus (not necessarily in that order). Nobody knew what the record was all about. Besides our revelatory songs, there were a lot of suggestive, whispery conversations, giggling, and panting going on; also a phone call between me and Cynthia Plaster Caster over the telephone, discussing the merits of Noel Redding: "I was a virgin last time he was in town . . ." Frank threw in a lot of perfectly timed sound effects, and snippets of intimacies we didn't even know had been put on tape. The review in *Rolling Stone* was a big, long nonsensical story that had nothing to do with the record. Once again our painted-up faces were plastered across teen magazines. A paperback called *Groupies and Other Girls* by Jerry Hopkins came out at the same time, which reestablished us as pillars of our community:

Groupies in Los Angeles are crass, supercilious, pretentious, beautiful beyond description or reason, freakish, cultish, aggressive, mad and young. Groupies in Los Angeles are extreme. The GTO's epitomize an international groupie type, The Freak. It is fitting that these five young women record for a record company called "Bizarre," for that is what they really are, bizarre. They travel in a pack looking much like that section of The Goodwill store where clothing is sold by weight; worn cowboy boots, rotting thirty-year-old blouses and acres-large skirts and dresses, limp boas, pink tights, 75 cent army belts, and on top of everything sartorial is an amazing display of the cosmetic arts—mascara and rouge looking as if it were applied from a toy sand bucket with a small shovel. Zappa's publicist says: "Because of their many close relationships with rock stars, the girls are constantly accused of being groupies, which they deny vociferously." "We don't just sleep with them, we go beyond the physical level with all of them and they respect us for that. Musicians are really very intelligent people, and that's the way we treat them; not like studs. That dehumanizes both us and them. The GTO's seem to offer comment on society, serving as social critics, serving as a peculiar Rorschach test, forcing the public to react. What the GTO's have going for them is, really, a dream come true! Now they're a group! Now they're making records! Now they're appearing in public! Now they're being interviewed and photographed! It's as if they've become the stars they have so long worshiped."

Mick Jagger was really a very intelligent person, but I wanted to treat him like a stud, and maybe even get into a little dehumanizing.

My new friend, Ray Davies, was playing with his group, the Kinks, at the Whiskey, and I dressed up like a cream-puff coquette, heady for conquest. I knew the Stones were leaving town the next day and would most likely be luxuriating in the red plastic booths, swigging down the overpriced cognac, leering and bleary-eyed, cheering on the British. I was right. Leering the least, however, was the highly dignified Mr. Jagger, who was wearing a two-tone velvet suit from Granny Takes A Trip, the trendola trippy hip shop on the Kings Road in London. I passed right in front of them, pretending I had no interest in whoever might be occupying booth number one (it was always someone *very* interesting), and what I was hoping would happen did. "Why, if it isn't Miss Pamela, looking just lovely . . ." I was invited to squeeze into the booth next to Mick, and no bomb threat, no terrorist action, no fervid groupie maneuverings, no desperate urge to pee, could have convinced me to remove myself from his presence. He ordered me two Harvey Wallbangers at a time, and my hands developed a mind of their own. Under the table I got a hold of the inspiration for the abstract oil painting that got me an A in my Cleveland High School art class. I slunk down in the seat, transcendental with desire, glancing up at Mick, who was all dimples, and I knew I would finally see his trousers down around his ankles. In my teen dreams they had always been corduroy, but velvet would do just fine.

He gave new meaning to giving head, which did not surprise me in the slightest; those lips!!! Please!! But looking down and seeing Mick Jagger between my legs kept me from surrendering with the wild-animal abandon I had anticipated. We made love for hours, but I kept flashing back to squatting in front of my hi-fi, touching myself for the first time while Mick groaned about being a Kingbee coming inside, and here he was, right on top of me, doing *just that*. It was all too much. I was dizzy with the reality of that very instant. I was dying for him to say "Let me put it in, it feels all right," but it probably would have left me comatose.

November 25 . . . I am extremely happy. I left with dear Mr. Jagger last night, and we got along *so* well; honesty, freedom and joy. Genuine. I helped him pack his seven suitcases, and he gave me some lovely clothes. One is a black velvet beauty that was *made* for me. The sexual experience was quite a joy. The most luscious "plating" and kisses. "You're warm, Miss Pamela . . . I really like you, you're a sweet, kind lady. I wish you had decided to stay with me weeks ago. Think of all the time we've wasted." All I really care about is the fact that he LIKES me, genuinely. He told me about the craziness of the road . . . Detroit tonight. There was a mad rush for the plane, Gram took Keith to Nudie's on his motorcycle, and they came back late. Keith scares me, he's like a foreign object, and my sweet Gram is becoming his clone. Such a beautiful, wonderful time I've had, but I wish I had someone to cuddle with every night. If only I could settle for some normal groovy guy. Good Heavens, he'll have to be some super-human person because right now, the only people I could see myself being with are (get this . . .) Mick (how absurd), Jimmy (useless), or Chris (totally unthinkable). What a pathetic case. Why can't I meet a nice engineer or CPA? It's too late now.

> "You can't always get what you want . . .
> You can't always get what you want
> You can't always get what you want
> But if you try sometime, you just might find . . .
> You get what you need . . ."

Oh yeah.

The Stones decided to do a free concert at Altamont Speedway near San Francisco to thank their many fans for being alive. It was supposed to be a HUGE giveaway for as many lucky humans as could fit on the premises. I debated with myself about attending for days, and finally decided to hitch a ride up north with a friend of Rodney Bingenheimer's who had a colossal crush on me.

December 6 . . . As a matter of extreme principle, I left Altamont an hour before the Stones came on. Scrunge and filth unlimited! I have come to the conclusion that I am spoiled. I just wasn't satisfied to sit in the dirt with half a million smelly, grubby people and wait for The Stones. I really thought that people would be united and brought together in a lovely way . . . but NO body cared about each other. I lasted until The Burritos were over (they were wonderful) and the SLIMY FUCKED-UP Hell's Angels started throwing beer on me and no one around me cared! I started crying and cursing and we *split*. I don't have to go through that crap to see MJ. In the first place, after seeing him so many times, I can close my eyes and see him ANY TIME I PLEASE. The reason I didn't go to the hotel is because I'm still so nervous around the rest of The Stones. I am formally spoiled. I hate concerts unless I go with the group. They're on right now, but I'm going to call the hotel a little later and see what happens. PS . . . Would you believe The GTO's played

ONE YEAR AGO tonight. What has happened to us? I'm supposed to be world famous by now!"

I called the hotel and Mick asked me to come straight over. I was
thrilled, but since he sounded flipped-out, I asked him what was
wrong, and he said, "Don't you know what happened?" A guy had
been knifed, and died right in front of the Stones as they played free
for the masses. He also told me someone shot at him, and he was
a nervous wreck, "Please come right away." I told my diary later,
"Poor angel, trying to sing for 500,000 people who didn't deserve
his abundant gift . . ." I arrived and sat around with the group as
they rehashed the sequence of events that led up to this odd death
right in front of their eyes. Mick kept saying he felt like it was his
fault, and maybe he would quit rock and roll forever. Everyone was
extremely high. I felt like some inadequate female fly on the wall,
stuck in the middle of No Laughing Matter. Gram was there, leaning
against the wall wearing black leather and eye makeup, nodding out.
Keith was wearing cowboy clothes. It looked like they were turning
into each other. Mick held my hand and seemed slightly reassured
that I was there, but other than that, I was feeling stuck in awesome
flypaper. I wanted to say something insightful, something so meaningful that it would lift his heart. I was conjuring up this enlightening
tidbit when Michelle Phillips from the Mamas and the Papas walked
in, and it seemed that Mr. Jagger wanted a three-way to take the
load off his weary mind. He sent Michelle to his room, and gently
eased me down the hall a few minutes later, tantalizing me with his
tongue down my throat, telling me what a good time I was going to
have. I don't even know if Miss Phillips was aware of his illicit
intentions, but I had to escape because I didn't want to share him,
and I didn't want to share her either.

No matter how many shirts I made, my needs weren't met and
my ends wouldn't meet, so I took a day job at a simple little sleazy
bar called the Moon Pad Inn. I was serving beer to hardworking sad-
eyed hard hats who taught me to play pool and get a good head of

foam on many glass of Bud draft, but I was bored sappy and not making enough money. Hitching home from work one evening, I climbed into a plush emerald Mercedes and said hello to the manager of Danceland. Kurt was a middle-aged, curly-haired, sun-tanned German who convinced me that the answer to all my problems was on the corner of Pico and Figueroa in downtown L.A. He pulled an application out of his hip pocket and I was hired on the spot to "dance and converse with interesting men for eight cents a minute." Eight cents a minute! After reverting quickly to B-3 math, I calculated that I could make $4.80 an hour if I danced constantly. It sounded ideal, except for the fact that six nights out of seven would be spent with lonely old farts (I imagined) who felt they weren't worth the price of a candy bar, so they had to pay fifteen cents a minute for the privilege of a dance partner. If I danced five nights a week, I would only make seven cents a minute, so my social life would have to be curtailed immensely for the almighty dollar. I wanted to save up and go to England, meet the elusive British Someone, and have loads of pink-cheeked children.

As I ascended the dismal, dingy, droopy staircase, I became sorely depressed. Tattered crepe paper from some long-ago saggy celebration hung ragged and fading against a peeling backdrop of once-serene scenery. At the top of the stairs was a podium that looked as though a minister should have been standing behind it, saving souls; instead, a rotund, rubber-faced, bleached-out B-broad of about fifty-five was peeling tickets off a huge roll and handing them to the gentlemen customers. Each ticket represented five minutes with the lady of their choice, all of whom appeared to be relaxing on an orange plastic couch, the looks on their faces ranging from extremely eager to dance to wishing they were dead. I put my "personal belongings" into a locker and found an empty spot on the Naugahyde next to a tatty-teased nail-biter who would only scooch over about half an inch to make way for the newcomer. My butt barely grazed the seat before I met the first of my many, many patients. It didn't take me long to realize that most of these bungled souls were there for conversation and companionship, and before the week was out I was Dr. Pamela Miller, a highly underpaid psychiatrist, listening to guys pour out their aching, cheating hearts for eight dollars an hour. Most of the "beautiful dance hostesses" were having a hard life themselves— single moms, or wives of out-of-work down-and-outers. If you didn't try to think about something else while these guys spilled their sorry guts, you got *involved* in their problems, and *felt* for them. I could tell by the glazed looks on the dance floor that most of the hostesses weren't listening. I tried, I really did. Frank Sinatra played over and over while the men dreamed on and on . . . "Love was just a dance away, a warm embracing glance away . . ." A lot of men from far-off foreign lands came to Danceland to meet the American girl of their dreams, and even after they realized it would never happen, they kept climbing those seedy stairs. I knew they were pretending they were on real dates, and it killed me.

"Regulars" were an imperative part of the dance hall, and I had quite a few. Jackson was a young Filipino who came to see me twice a week for an hour. He wanted to spend more time with me, but he was saving his money to bring his mom out from the Philippines. He rarely wanted to dance, and he held my hand and told me his life story in hour-long segments until I had heard it all. One evening, as I sat pondering Jimmy Page, Jackson arrived, all spiffed up. After buying his hour's worth of tickets, he presented me with a little box, his face expectant and gleaming. Inside was an engagement ring, complete with itsy-bitsy diamond. He had called his mom long distance to tell her he was proposing marriage that night, and I was sitting in a cross-legged trance because Jimmy had called from Pang-bourne on my way out the door. Now I had the absurd chore of telling a total stranger that I could never be his bride. Jackson attempted dignity as he clutched his velveteen box, turned on his heel, and hurried down those unremarkable stairs. It was pitiful.

Jimmy called and asked me to find him some Aleister Crowley paraphernalia that might have wound up in some old Hollywood bookstore, and I took this as a sign of love. The reality was, of course, that he knew I would go dig up this horrible stuff and send it straight to England. I didn't know it, but he was in the process of buying Mr. Crowley's estate in Scotland. He also got a hold of his cloak somehow, and I could picture his white skin draped in grandiose darkness and I worried that he might be getting obsessed with the black vibe. I scoured Hollywood Boulevard and found a killer-diller item: a typed manuscript with notes in the margins written by Al himself. Jimmy wired me seventeen hundred dollars and I sent this treasure across the ocean, wishing I could go with it. On December 22, I received a package unmistakably from Great Britain, written in HIS hand. I stared at it for a long time before gently removing the tape and ribbons that HE touched, and beheld a more meaningful little box than the one poor Jackson had presented to me. "For my dear P. With all my love at Christmas, Jimmy. XXXXXXX" Inside was a necklace like I had never seen. Gasping at the sight of the antique turquoise phoenix, wings open wide, holding a big stunning pearl, I bellowed and blubbered with pain and delight. I wanted Jimmy SO BAD. Hope surged anew within me, adrenaline was pumping hard and fast, and despite my horrid job, it was going to be a wonderful Christmas.

December 22 . . . Ah, so much thinking about Jimmy, and so warmly. The sun shines sweetly within me once again when someone speaks his name. . . . Noel Redding called, he's had a nervous breakdown, poor little man, always miserable on his holy birthday. Sad, but it's good that I'm not going to be with him. I don't want to be with anyone until I can touch my beautiful James. . . . Think of me sweetly, Jimmy, your black hair wild on your white pillow of sleep.
December 25 . . . 'Twas a lovely day with my beloved parents. I had Dad pick me up at "Danceland" early last night. Money is money, but enough is enough! I look down at Jimmy's phoenix constantly, and hope he gets through to me on this day of days so I can hear his soft sweetness. Michele and I went to John Phillip's for "frozen noses," beautiful people and weirdness. Whole pigs (poor things) were being eaten. Sleep is coming . . . Love and joyous Christmas thoughts and wishes . . . Thank my dear Jesus for being. XXXXXXX Pamela.

I slogged away on the dance floor, meeting one complete weirdo after another. The men never spoke to each other because they were all embarrassed to be there, so each evening I eyeballed a different silent squad of goons, wondering which one would make my night. The spitting image of Wally Cox wandered in several nights in a row and stared hungrily at my feet, and I knew something strange was about to happen. Somehow they always chose me, those guys with eyes like the laughing demento in the old werewolf movies. The eyes of Mr. Cox were magnified fifty times by his three-inch specs, and there was no doubt about it, he was looking right at my feet. It was a slow night, so I accepted when he weaseled over to request the pleasure of my company. He dug his pointy chin into my shoulder, and Mr. Peepers and I glided goofily across the floor for a brief clumsy spin, and then he wanted to have a little chat. "Out of all the girls in this place, your feet have the most appeal," he said, with such sincerity that I was forced to look right into those grossly huge eyes and see that he truly meant it. What do you say to that? I thanked him a lot and waited for the punch line. He wanted to "caress and massage" my feet, and offered fifty dollars to do the honors. He told me he drove out from Michigan in his trusty Corvair because he figured women were freer in Los Angeles and might understand his feeling for feet. He had dedicated his life to the specialness of feet: "They support the entire body!" We sat in the back of the room where it was dark, and it wasn't bad at all. It actually felt pretty good, and he was ga-ga with ecstasy. I didn't take his fifty bucks, I just couldn't do it. I took twenty, and felt guilty for a week.

January 4 . . . I got the foot fetishist tonight, I mean, he's REALLY nuts. What happened to *him* along the way? Oh well, I was chosen to have my feet tickled by this great gentleman. Can you imagine? Left work early 'cause I was feeling so crummy.

I wrote a love song for Jimmy with a Burrito twang . . .

Feelin' so low
There's no place to go
To keep you off
Of my mind

Nothin' is gained
By feelin' this pain
'cause in the end
I'll just be left behind

There's no time for laughin'
No time for cryin'
I just keep prayin' that
People are lyin'

Feelin' so blue
'cause they say I'm losin' you
And the ocean is
So deep and wide

I'll keep on waitin'
While you keep on datin'
And I'll be here
When the glory has died

There's a sign on my door
That you overlooked before
Come in from the storm . . .
Come Inside

January 9 . . . I often wonder how I get so carried away, to the extent where I forget what is important, what matters. It took Danny, a Chinese boy in cancer research who danced with me in "Danceland" tonight, to show me where it's at. We got to talking about people; Mick Jagger is made of the same stuff that he is, I'm made out of the exact same stuff as Liz Taylor and Lady Bird Johnson, EVERYone is grand, they're just taking different pathways to ultimately the same goal (even if some aren't aware of it). In the creator's eyes, Jimmy Page is no better than a skid row bum. NOW we come to my preference; tho' they are NO BETTER than lawyers, doctors, engineers, mechanics . . . I dig musicians. There are girls who dig sailors, you could call them "sailories," chicks who dig doctors, "doctories." So, go ahead, call me a "groupie." It's Jimmy's 27th birthday today . . .

Close to me now
On this day of birth
Your day of dawning

Jimmy met a girl named Charlotte on his birthday, and fell over backward with love. Word of this scalding news filtered across the sea and hit me in the face like a pot of boiling Earl Grey.

Miss Christine wrote to me from London, where she was hanging out with Todd Rundgren, enclosing a shot of Jimmy from *Melody Maker* in which he was wearing the most beautiful shirt I had ever made. It was a pink-and-white velvet creation with fringe that hung down to his knees. His hands were clasped and he was looking heavenward, his ringlets black as night against the soft pale velvet. Her letter told me of "Lady Charlotte," and my heart clenched like a fist.

January 20 . . . Oh, my sweet blonde head is forever in fluffy pink clouds of make-believe. God help me as I go through another empty month of trying too hard to forget his beautiful black-as-night hair and his incomparable loveliness created in God's finest hand. Who is there for me? Every relationship ends in utter emptiness: Nick St. Nicholas, Mr. Hillman and James. I *should* marry a C.P.A. or a ditch-digger in Iowa. [*Many* tear-stains blurring this entry.]

Before the empty month was out, Waylon Jennings came back to town to thrill the cowpokes at the Palamino, and I was front and center to thrill Waylon Jennings. It was a big step for me to choose this particular gentleman as my next conquest, because he was entirely out of any element that I had ever been in. I had been listening to his albums since Chris and Gram played them for me, and I thought he was incredibly sexy, but he was a MAN, with hair on his chest. I had only slept with a handful of people, but none of them had much hair on his chest, except for Mr. Hillman, and I don't think he ever dreamed of owning black-leather wristbands. Brazen and daring, I sat in front of him while he sang, teasing him flagrantly by peeling off several pieces of clothing, one by one. He was totally disarmed and astonished, because by the time his set was over, all I had on was a skimpy satin chemise, "come hither" written all over my face. When he didn't arrive by my side at the end of the night, I wasn't dissuaded. I met a friend of his in the audience who invited me to Waylon's session right after the show, and I planted myself on the couch, staring through the glass as he swaggered around, working up a hot version of "Honky Tonk Women." I couldn't believe he wasn't taking advantage of my obvious wicked lust for him, and by three A.M., I was tired of oozing desire with very little response. I said good-night to the good old boys I had been hanging out with, and left the session. As I got to the exit, I saw that Waylon was right behind me with that squinty, indecipherable look in his eye. "What's your phone number, baby?" I gave it to him, and he said he'd call me in an hour.

> January 28, 3:30 A.M . . . If Waylon "comes" (ha) tonight (I still have my serious doubts), it will be my first one night stand, *and* my first "older man." Also, it will really test my ability to get along with a person not in my surrounding element. Well, sweet adieu, if the big country man makes an appearance, won't it be grand?
>   9 A.M . . . I made love to Waylon. It certainly was one of the oddest nights in my life. Waylon Jennings in my bed. We were honestly crude and crudely honest with each other, and learned a lot from each others' worlds. Two worlds combining (colliding?) for sure. He would apologize for being so steamed up, and kiss me on the forehead, calling me a "sweet angel," and would get up to leave, then come back with a vengeance saying, "I'll tell you what, you really know how to please a man, baby." Such a huge *hunk* of man.

As he finally got dressed to leave, he roamed around my little room, littered with pictures of Mick, Jimmy, and Noel, lit a cigarette, picked up his black cowboy hat, and said, "Do you really like all this long ha'r and everthang?" I assured him it was sexy *and* fashionable; he shook his head like he couldn't figure it, smoothed his pompadour, kissed me on the forehead, and put on his ten-gallon tipping it gallantly. With a squint and a smile, he was gone. I sat up in bed for a long time after Waylon left, pondering a new fact of life, the one-night stand. I didn't feel guilt-stained, even though I didn't know if I would ever see Waylon again, but I did feel like a grown woman. My roommate, Michele, heard all the noise coming from the dining room, and had to climb out her bedroom window to go to work. When she came home that evening, she suggested I find another place to live.

A girl named Mickey, whom I had grown to know and love while Zeppelin were in town, was also looking for a pad, so we linked up and found a beautiful old garden apartment on Fountain Avenue. She was hanging on to John Paul Jones while I was with my darling Jimmy, so we already had a poignant past. I showed her the ropes at Danceland, and she was rapidly accumulating regulars. We grinned over puny shoulders and peeked around sad flabby middles, helping each other through many fraudulent, fruitless nights. I collapsed one horrible evening, making Mickey think twice about her new job. I was lost in a sweet, thick memory about Mr. Perfect, Jimmy Page, when I realized that the small Chinese man I was doing the two-step with was inhaling me deeply, sniffling and snurfling to his heart's content. *He* smelled like rancid cigars, so I could see his point, but when I demanded that the sniffing cease, he couldn't even hear me, he was so far gone in my Shalimar. The more I protested, the harder he inhaled, and when I tried to pull away, I found he was clamped onto me like a petrified crab. I let out a screech and became a bundle of lace and nylon on the floor. It happened to be "Nighty Nite," and all the hostesses were wearing nighties. Thursday night was "Hawaiian Night" and we all had to wear bathing suits and collapsing worn-out leis. The rest of the world went around and around, but Danceland just sat there, smelling up the universe. As I was being escorted from the floor, an old guy who was being jacked off in the corner craned his neck to see what the wailing was all about. I never jacked anyone off, but I danced and chatted constantly. I was making seedy money and saving every tarnished cent.

February 6 . . . I am sweet, delicious, and a juicy 21! Somebody claim me!!

I was adrift in a big world with no boyfriend, so I dug up old flames and trysted again like I did last summer.

February 12 . . . Very happy, spent a lovely afternoon with The Burritos. Chris was so sweet, we got high as helium balloons, and talked of many things. He and Gram said they would come in to Danceland, and then Chris said, "You and I will have our own private Danceland someday." I feel so good with MY Burritos. Gram took me in the studio and said, "Look at this luscious little thing I found all alone in the parking lot." I was with Mr. Hillman all afternoon, and it was very smoooooth.

February 19 . . . I saw Brandon's joyful face today. He moves in 78, while everyone else moves in 33 ⅓. 92 memories got side-tracked on my mainline. When he opened the door, energy and joy poured out. He is so incredibly ALIVE; draining at times. He came over for ten hours, we necked and stared and cooed and goo-gooed, seeing him again was like someone turned a lightbulb on in my brain. I'm a "thrill, a joy and a delight" to him right now.

February 22 . . . Here I sit, full of Tuinal, stuffed with coke (a quarter oz. to my left, and a joint of ice-bag in my hand). Never having purchased coke, I can't believe this tiny bottle is worth $250.00. We just got back from the movies, and now Brandon is out playing music somewhere. We got so coked up in the theatre, nobody gets me higher than he does, in every way actually. We really get along superbly, such a good friend to have. Being with him comes so natural, I just love him. You can't imagine what happened after "Butch Cassidy"; some guy grabbed me on the street so Brandon yelled out, "Fuck off, you wetneck pachuko," and the guy pulled a gun on us! I ran down the street, trying to stop cars while deWilde tried to talk them out of shooting us. He's a real sweet talker. All very interesting. Tra La.

February 24 . . . Here I am, on an airplane, involved in another odd one; Noel (dear thing) called this morning and sent me a round trip ticket to New York. It should be interesting. I love planes. Ah, me, James and Charlotte . . . the rumors hot and heavy that he is residing with her in France. Anyway, dear friend Noel is lonesome over there, and I'm gonna go have fun with him!! Oh, won't everyone be talking about this one? It's incredible how fast news travels in this pop-star circle.

February 27, NYC . . . here in strict nudity, in the potty, writing, so Noel can't see. He went through another number last night about Brian Jones and how he should join him in death (Brian was his idol). He called his mother and almost cried. God, what a split personality, he's in there right now, laughing his head off over nothing.

March 2 . . . I had a grasshopper for breakfast (3 pm) after an extremely lovely fuck, and I'm still zonked. Noel said I was one of his "loved ones," "And I don't have many."

March 4 . . . Only home for one day, and guess what? I was just with Nick St. Nicholas. Mercy and I went to The Whiskey, and I flipped, *really,* to see his face. He came over and we talked of Randy Jo at length, they're having lots of problems. Too bad. We got high and listened to Judy Collins, and he gave me such a beautiful kiss. Good heavens, I'm trembling, it's absurd. God knows I can't get the least bit involved in this one.

I saw them take their vows, and the married man was a no-no in my little red book.

The GTOs' album didn't make it onto the *Billboard* charts, but the *très, très* avant-garde FM stations were playing it, and it was about to be released in Europe, so the girls got together and worked up a new act to show Mr. Zappa. He was heartily enthused, but no plans were made and I was aching to redebut. Miss Christine was going steady with Todd Rundgren and he suggested we tour Europe with his group, Runt, but it wouldn't be until the summer and I didn't know if I could wait. We weren't really getting along, and it was becoming what Sparky and Lucy had predicted, a business venture. Christine and Cynderella thought I was a phony-baloney fickle sweetie-pie, Sandra was Miss Mom, and Mercy had started inhaling angel dust in startling amounts. One night as I held her hand, she demanded that many dead rock stars appear before her. On her knees she beseeched Sam Cooke and Otis Redding to make an appearance;

she then attempted to conjure up her idol, Brian Jones, pleading with the vapors. At this precise instant, some blond stranger walked into the room and found Miss Mercy wrapped around his legs, her rainbow-afro wig askew, her eye makeup smudged beyond compute, laughing and sobbing, gazing into his eyes as though he were the second coming. I'm sure he never forgot it.

March 6 . . .

> *The scene is ending*
> *Images fading into the walls*
> *Cloth roses tossed*
> *Into trashcans full*
> *Of tiny pieces of empty dreams*
> *Never fulfilled to the fullest*
> *Stepping from an invisible vision*
> *Shedding garments*
> *Rose colored taffeta*
> *Musty and rustling*
> *Looking into the dark*
> *And sticky smelling past*
> *I leave each of them to themselves*
> *And each other*
>
> *The whole thing*
> *Has matted my hair*

I feel so many things for so many people, I really do, and it IS true and honest. Does it seem phony? Obviously it does. SHIT, I'm *not* phony, and I'm not going to ever let it bother me. It's me, I'm a willow and I admit I do bend with the winds, wherever I'm taken . . . I love it. I feel like I'll never be depressed or bored anymore. Although I have no particular love now, maybe I'm not supposed to—I love so many. It makes sense to me. How can I be fickle when there is no one to be true to?

The fact was, I desperately wanted someone to be true to. I needed a rock and roll rock to lean on; a foundation, some gorgeous hunk to wake up with in the steamy afternoons. I cried dreary tears, waiting for someone to tell me he loved me, and while languishing on my bed of thorns, I inhaled, imbibed, and swallowed several foreign substances. I tuned in, tuned on, and dropped out one too many times. As I cruised the strip with King Dale (I was the Queen of the Hips and Rocks, remember?) one glistening afternoon, the hash I swallowed turned into a living creature in my heaving chest cavity, attacking me from the inside out. Sunset and Fairfax became a war zone with unidentified hurtling objects whizzing through the air and spilling squishy sludge onto my feather boa, which, of course, grew a head and began to eat itself. I clutched the bucket seat to keep from toppling into the trenches, so consumed with fear that I started gagging and sputtering, begging Dale to pull over, pull over, where am I, pull over!!??! I can still see Dale's dry mouth opening and closing like Shari Lewis had her hand inside his hippie head. "You're losing it, you're blowing it . . ." Just what I needed to hear. He finally steered his miserable vehicle to my front door, and I crept into bed, missing several appointments, while my entire life played in my tortured head like a rerun of *Leave It to Beaver*.

March 10 . . . I left yesterday for some far-off land on Dale's hash. I ate *so* much of it that I went bizarre. I truly thought I was dying. I saw myself as a little baby, then as a tiny child, all the kids I knew and things I did. Then I realized I was seeing my life flash before me in seconds, just like right before you die. I kept trying to take control of myself; such a fine line between sanity and insanity . . . I was walking that line on a circus tightrope. I slept for fourteen hours straight in all my clothes and lace-up boots.

"She blew her mind out in a car."

Cynderella had a pen pal in England, Gene Krell, who co-ran Granny Takes a Trip on the Kings Road. She was having a pen-and-paper romance, and suggested that I write to Gene's partner, Marty, a boy from Brooklyn who was making good in swinging London. I would have preferred to receive mail from an Englishman, but Marty was a trendsetter, and dressed Robert Plant and Mick

Jagger, so I condescended to dash out a few pages a week. He sent chic chic T-shirts that nobody in all of America had ever seen before, so Mickey Mouse and James Dean smiled and glowered from my bosom, all covered in rhinestones. He also sent photos of himself, which weren't too bad; he had a thick mop of hair that was blatantly frosted and blown dry to perfection, he wore immaculately hip garments that hung from his slim frame, and he had a sunny, seductive smile underneath the biggest hooter that I, personally, had ever made contact with. His letters were real funny and he signed his name backward, so when he announced he was coming to L.A. to scout for a new location for Granny's, I began anticipating his arrival.

March 20 . . . Very strange about Marty, I was so shy with him and bashful. It's the oddest to meet someone you've been writing to. He was tired from the flight and fell asleep in my lap, I played with his pretty hair and he kissed me real sweetly. Right before he left, we *really* looked at each other and liked what we saw; the realization was lovely.

I was ripe for the plucking.

March 26 . . . Michele slept on the couch and Marty and I went to bed . . . very nice, though I still don't know how I feel about him. He said he wanted to take me to England when he goes back. My feelings are very different; no freak-out-ness like with Jimmy and Chris, but it's not like a rosebud blooming either. I guess I'm just trying to explain it because I plucked him. I should just stop trying to figure everything out.

Who plucked whom?

March 28 . . . Well, Marty is in love with me, or so he continually says. Lots of "You're my baby," "You're my beautiful girl," etc etc etc. . . . It's so nice that he says those lovely love things when we make love, it makes it so much better. Just off to Danceland (yucchy!), Marty is taking me to Disneyland tomorrow. Oh, what different lands I romp in.

Waylon Jennings the
night I nabbed him

ASPER DAILEY

Me and Theodore Bikel's big
slacks on 200 Motels

CALVIN SCHENKEL

Please, Mr. Zappa, give me some direction

CALVIN SCHENKEL

HUNT SALES

Tony Sales, teen dream

Within the same four walls as
Ringo Starr. Howard Kaylan is
napping on my shoulder.

Donnie Wayne Johnson/
Pamela Ann Miller

FRANK EDWARDS

Donnie is wearing one of my handmade fall-aparts

Cuddling ♥ All is calm, all is hot

MARGARET MILLER

Duet with a madman

RAEANNE RUBENSTEIN, COPYRIGHT © 1986

Keith Moon and I with
Pete Townsend. I get excitement
at your feet.

RAEANNE RUBENSTEIN, COPYRIGHT © 1986

RICHARD CREAMER

Keith and I in the
middle of an improv

RICHARD CREAMER

Keith in drag—Miss Moon and Miss Pamela

PHIL FRANKS

Sandy and I before I stamped on his heart

I quickly learned that Marty loved to fuck, he needed the conquest constantly, and I wasn't enough. Unfortunately, by the time I realized this (he fucked my neighbor, and she told me *all* about it) I was hooked on him.

> April 5 . . . I had no idea I could ever get so *mad*! I WAS RAGING!!
> I went through the ragies, the weepies, and then the sulkies.
> Man, I just can't understand whores, and that's what he is. I'll
> have to put up with it tho'; it's him. There are fuckers and there
> are nice ones. He's a fucker. I must bear in mind that he "loves
> me so much" . . .

He called me "Dollin" and grabbed my titties in the market, he was brash, outspoken, and loud, throwing his New Yawk accent all over Hollywood. He was proud of his hot temper, his sexual prowess, and the way he could string curse words together until he was out of breath. He ran the hippest clothing store in the hippest city in the world which catered to the hippest people on earth, but he wasn't quite satisfied. He wanted to BE one of his own clientele. He grabbed hold of little me, the concubine elite, and kissed my ass until I was convinced I could love him.

When Led Zeppelin came to town for two nights, I paced back and forth, pretending to be composing new GTO material. Marty watched for a while, looking amused, and said, "Why don't you just *call* Jimmy, Dollin'?" I couldn't figure why Jimmy didn't call me! By this time I believed he had fallen in love with the girl named Charlotte, but felt I deserved to hear the facts from his very own rosebud lips. The last time I heard from Jimmy was when he sent me the phoenix, and even though I fell for Marty, I needed to clear Mr. Page out of my system.

> April 10 . . . Jimmy is in town and hasn't called. I DO NOT
> understand. I smile at dear Marty while inside I'm freaking out.
> Oh, Lord knows, why why why why!!!? My Jesus, what an-
> guish; the oddest bruising pain in my heart that beat only for
> him for so long . . . pink velvet pants, angel-faced precious

Jimmy, why oh why don't you be so kind as to call and say "hello" to the broken-hearted girl you left behind?

April 11 ... God is truly with me, Marty and I went to The Whiskey, and there was Jimmy's sweet face. I sat with him and he told me he would always be my friend and that I was the only person that he cared for in this country, but we really couldn't talk there, so he took my number (that's why he didn't call!) and wants to see me on Friday. He told me he was happy and in love, and hoped I was too. He invited me to the show, but I don't think I could bear it.

April 13 ... Robert Plant called and insisted I come to the show, he left cab money for me at the gate, so I'm on my way now. He said they wouldn't go on until I got there. Marty got angry at first, but then he said, "Do what you have to do, Dollin'." He's so incredible at times, but I'm sure he'll go out tonight and pluck someone.

April 14 ... Well, James was tremendous to me at the concert, tho' I have seen them better. Robert had a headache, and John was on smack, of all things. I went back to the hotel with Jimmy and we talked until 5 AM about happinesses, sadnesses, truths, untruths, Charlotte and Marty. He showed me pictures of her which I could barely look at, and he told me he was "being good," which for him is a miracle. When I left, we hugged tightly, "Are we still friends?" "For sure." "We're still friends?" "For sure." "Be a good girl, P."

I walked slowly down the dismal Hyatt House hall, but before I reached the elevator, I did one of my collapsing acts, sliding down the wall into the customary heap position until I could pull myself barely together, get into a cab, get into my bed, and rock myself to sleep.

Marty had indeed plucked some available tart, and it took me awhile to convince him that I didn't sleep with Jimmy. (But oh, how I wanted to.) Marty pretended cool, but the double standard lurked beneath his bushy eyebrows. He was the first "regular" boyfriend I had had since Bobby Martine, and even though our sex life was thrilling and constant, my feelings for him fluctuated every day. He couldn't find a store hip enough, so six weeks after he blasted through my door, I was weeping at the airport as he flew off to

London. We were both going to save our money, and I was going to wing my way back into his arms as soon as possible.

Miss Christine was still in the midst of a lasting relationship with Todd Rundgren, and he still wanted us to go on tour with Runt, starting in New York in one month. I worked seven nights a week at Danceland, still saving every grubby cent, and bought a cheapo ticket to London to surprise Marty.

April 27 . . . Well, friends and neighbors, two weeks from to-morrow, I leave for London. I'm going to stay two weeks before I have to meet the rest of the girls in New York for the tour. There. That's what's happening. $150 a week and expenses for three months, and then . . . God knows what.

Before I left, I had the urge to see beautiful Beverly. We spoke on the phone once in a while, but she was always sorry to be alive, so I rarely saw her. I was thrilled to be alive, and we got on each other's nerves. She was living in a tiny hovel on Honey Lane in Laurel Canyon, and it took her a long time to crawl to the door to let me in. I sat with her while she sorted out piles of dark-colored velvet rags. She had been sitting there all day, moving the rags around and shooting heroin. Her boyfriend had been busted, and she wasn't in a very good mood. She wasn't in any mood at all; just a vague semblance of life, cowering, sniffling, and crippled among her collection of dusty frogs. Her windows were blacked out and I begged her to let in a little light, a little air; she said the candles were enough, and offered me some heroin. I shied away from that doomy stuff, but I wanted to get near her, so I sniffed a little. She didn't seem to notice that I had done anything out of the ordinary, so after the nodding and nausea went away, I did too.

I called Chris and Gram to say good-bye, and found that Gram had been in a motorcycle accident. I rushed off to the hospital, not ready for the pathetic sight that greeted me.

May 3 . . . Went to see GP with Mercy and Carlos, took flowers

and all. He's so beaten up, such a mess. It was hard not to scream, his face was blown up like a purple and blue balloon. God bless him and keep him through this, maybe it'll help somehow, he's been SO high all the time. I've been calling him Gram Richards. He hasn't heard from Keith, so I sent him a telegram. I hope he gets it.

I said all my good-byes, sent back my rented piano, packed up all my many items, and put them in my parents' garage.

I took a trip to Ensenada with my daddy for a night, just to hang with him before I left. He was always driving down to Mexico because his best friend and partner in the gold mine lived there. We had a pleasant, uneventful time, but my dad brought a bottle with him to swig on the trip back to L.A. He was already pretty tipsy, having knocked a few back with Ruben, but no matter how I begged to drive, he held on to the wheel. He was telling me all about the bad old days in Pond Creek, going about fifteen miles an hour, when we heard a siren. At least I heard the siren; he was whooping and hollering, dredging up some long-lost long-ago event that cracked him up as he weaved all over the freeway. The policeman took Daddy to jail in San Diego and told me to come back in the morning. I sat in an all-night movie until some wack-job started beating off next to me. I ate pie in a coffee shop next to a poor guy with only one thumb on one of his hands and no arm at all on the other side. I thought I had problems. I prayed right on the spot, thanking God for all my limbs. I sat in the big Caddy sled until the sun came up, and then went and retrieved O. C. Miller from the clink. When I left Mom to go to the airport the next day, she was happy I was going to see the world, but very sad she would have to be without her baby daughter for so long. She wasn't sure about Marty, but she never inflicted her misgivings on me.

May 12 . . . Lovely talking to Mom, I love my folks so much. My stability in this *crazy* world I live in. I'm listening to Linda Ronstadt's new album. She dedicated a song to me at The Whiskey last night while I was dancing. So sweet. God knows what this beautiful life holds. If only I could realize how full it is *all the time,* and never ever get bored. Boredom is a COP-OUT! A terrible excuse for not living every second and drinking God's air (no matter how polluted) into your lungs! Ah, breathe deeply of this life! I'm so fortunate to be blessed with the freedom I have; travel is at my doorstep, new places, new people, new adventures constantly. I want to reach out and learn from every person I meet; take their stories and intertwine them with my own so I can live MORE than my allotted years on this earth. I've been thanking God for my comfort lately. How incredible to feel continually pleasant. I feel like I might lift off the ground at any moment!! Hey, I *will* be lifting off the ground any moment!! England, watch out!! Here I come!!!

7

♥

DEDICATED FOLLOWER OF FASHION

*T*here was some kind of mix-up and I wound up in first class, downing champagne and sucking on lobster tails. I took this to be a glorious sign of things to come. I met a stunning songwriter, Jimmy Webb, who happened to be sitting right next to me, and we got chummy on the long flight. He wanted to show me a castle in the English countryside that he was hoping to buy, and he paraded me through the airport, completely bypassing Customs, and into a waiting limousine, full of his gorgeous English boyfriends. He promised to take me into London after checking out the pad, and since Marty had no idea I was coming, I could take all the time in England to get to the Kings Road. The place Mr. Webb wanted so badly was once the headquarters for a famed reveler's paradise called the Hellfire Club, which boasted such infamous revelers as Benjamin Franklin and one of the princes of Wales. I was very impressed with the perfectly carved penises that lined the many alcoves, and since I couldn't feel any remaining Satanic vibrations, I gave this beyond-description mansion my stoned seal of approval. We smoked joints on the bank of the River Thames, and while I communed with the fairy-tale splendor of the countryside, I discovered several shades of green that I never dreamed existed.

When I finally got to Granny's, Marty was next door getting his hair done, so Gene hid me in the dressing room until he came back. "You have to see the beautiful chick in the dressing room!" Of course, Marty peeked in, and I had taken off all my clothes except for my spiked heels from Frederick's of Hollywood.

Marty worked every day except Sunday, so I had plenty of time to see the entire city of London. I was the ultimate sightseer, and I saw every sight until I was worn out. I viewed every painting and sculpture at the Victoria and Albert Museum and the Tate Gallery, and I studied the handwritten *Alice in Wonderland* in an antique glass case. I was stunned by the heavy bad vibes in the Tower of London as I trudged through the dismal joint with several pairs of Bermuda shorts in front of me and behind me; I was an ogling spectator at Buckingham Palace, waiting for the white glove to wave back and forth, back and forth; and I saw Tommy Steele suspended in midair at Madame Tussaud's wax museum, his wax fingers pressing the appropriate piano keys for all time. Five pounds found their way around my middle as I stuffed in Cadbury's Flake, Smarties, and Murray Mints, "the too good to hurry mints." The GTO's album was in every record-store window, so I was an instant semicelebrity and did a bunch of interviews for the rock press. I went to Portobello Road and bought many thrilling antique bargains, I went to the zoo to see "Guy," the famous gorilla, and I sent a hundred Big Ben postcards to make sure everyone was aware that I had become a gallivanting globe-trotter. At night, Marty and I hit the happening night spots, mingling with his many in-crowd customers. I waited for the phone to ring-ring to find out when the GTO's were supposed to meet Todd in New York, but I just went right on waiting. Lucky for me (unlucky for her), Michele Overman had followed Robert Plant to England. She was in the process of having her heart wrenched out because he wasn't rushing to leave his wife, Maureen, and his two kids. She was weepy and miserable, but at least she was company. I even befriended Catherine James, who was in London having a horrible time with the father of her baby boy, Denny Laine, the pipsqueak from the Moody Blues. He was treating her like a second-class citizen, so she had secretly taken up with Gene, Marty's partner, and they were in the throes of a divine clandestine entanglement. When she finally took the big walk out of Denny's life, the four of us (five, including baby Damien) lived together right off the Kings Road for a brief happy time.

Marty was angry that he had to be true to me. He loved me a lot, and the swell part of him intended to be faithful, but the rotten-to-the-core part wanted to spread venereal diseases throughout the entire country of England. These two sides were in a constant battle, and he was often cold and distant to me when we weren't in the sack. Making up was always magnificent, but I wasn't doing a damn thing to make him mad. He typified the pissed-off young man, and I wandered around the flat in circles, bemoaning being in love with an angry young New York Jew who was caught up in his angry young penis. He said he didn't feel like a man when he couldn't pick up chicks. I tried to relate his infidelities to his insecurities, and we had umpteen as-deep-as-I-could-get-him-to-go conversations. What it boiled down to was this: He thought he deserved to share his cock with whomever might enjoy it, at the same time loving me totally. These girls, of course, meant nothing to Marty, he just needed the conqest; the fact that he was wanted and desired was urgent. I asked him if his mommy had loved him, and he got a big kick out of that. He howled.

In an attempt to make myself more desirable, I was getting

my hair done next door to Granny's when Gene ran over to tell me that Mick had come in to pick up a suit and would I like to say hello?

> May 23 . . . I finally met up with Mr. Jagger, let me try to express how grand it was!! I flew to "Granny's" when Gene told me he was there, and when he saw me he dropped all his packages and opened up his arms for me. He wanted to know everything, who, how and why I was here!! After he paid for his suit, we went for a walk. He sent his driver on and we walked along the embankment to his house . . . he always had his arms around me, and said I made him feel good, and wasn't it great how we bumped into each other. He told me of his constant ups and downs with Marianne Faithfull, then he showed me his first flat with Keith and Brian, we checked out each others' buns and had a great laugh. . . . "I must have your number!" He went to Ireland, but will be back Wednesday. Uh-Oh.

Mick started dropping in on me while Marty was at work. One afternoon, I could hear him singing as he came down the stairs: "I love to dance, I love to sing, I love to ding-a-ling . . . Yoo Hoo. Miss Pamela, I've brought someone to see you!!" I was stark-raving dripping, having just hopped out of the tub, when he strolled into my bedroom with Charlie Watts in tow. When he saw my wet ass, he clapped his hands over Charlie's eyes and admonished me: "You wanton woman, you mustn't let Charlie see you like this!" He treated Charlie like an innocent lad of twelve, fresh from boarding school, and I must admit, he always did seem to have a couple of buttons missing.

Marty was uncontrollably crazy about me one day and utterly unenthused the next, which introduced me to the unfun world of the ulcer. I went to one of those amazing free doctors in London, and he pronounced that I had the beginnings of a bleeding ulcer and I'd better get my emotions in check. *Very* unfunny. I watched Marty inhale plates full of curry and lasagna while I chewed chalky tablets and piddled around with my porridge and warm milk. I couldn't drink any booze, and I felt like a tired old bag, despite the delectable Granny's dresses that I clothed my ailing body with. I needed a shot of new spunk.

I invited Mick over to lunch, and we wound up grappling and panting in a pulsating frenzy on Marty's double bed. I believe he entertained this idea on first seeing me at Granny's, but was waiting for me to put my hand on his upper thigh or some other strategic warm spot, which I finally did. He still made me nervous, because despite the fact that I was going with Marty, a seemingly regular guy, I was truly the ultimate groupie, and Mick was in the ultimate group. I casually reached over, in between bites of turkey roll and processed cheese (which he chastised me about: "*Processed* cheese, Miss Pamela!!"), and nonchalantly fingered his zipper and surrounding area. My nerves flew out the window as he threw me onto the mattress and turned me into a cheating trollop. It was fantastic. Just as our moans started harmonizing, we heard a key in the door, and footsteps on the stairs. One-two-three, Mick came and went, I got up and ran into the bathroom, my clothes bundled up in my arms, and threw them on as fast as I could. When I tiptoed out, all was quiet, the cleaning lady was making the bed, and Mick was nowhere in sight. My shoes had been neatly placed next to the bathroom door, and I was overwhelmed by his thoughtfulness.

We kept carrying on, and although I did feel a smidgen guilty, Marty's indiscretions and rotten moods kept me from confessing my sins.

June 24 . . . Ever since I spoke to Mick last night, I've been getting really "strange vibes." Marty's not treating me properly, and Mick just called again from the studio, wanting me to come down. He's acting very strange; asking questions about Marty, stuttering and stammering. When I told him it hasn't been going that great, he said "Good," and we decided to see each other tomorrow. If I didn't feel so in love with that bum, Marty, God knows what could happen! Life is, once again, very interesting, tho' it should ALWAYS be, and it always WILL be if I make it so!"

June 25 . . . When I arrived at Cheyne Walk, Mick was really

happy to see me, said how pretty I looked, etc. We went up
two flights of stairs to the sitting room and had orange juice
while he woke up, then went to the "Chelsea Fair." We walked
there, holding hands, and I looked at him and thought to myself,
"I *like* you, Mr. Jagger!" and just before I was going to say it,
he said, "I like you, Miss Pamela!" I got a spine tingle for sure.
The Fair was so old-fashioned, so many tourists that he got 97
autograph seekers, but we had a lot of fun with it, he said to a
fan, "You really think *I* look like Mick Jagger? You're the third
person today who told me that." We went up and down Kings
Road, making comments about everything . . . laughing, skipping and holding hands. He remembered how we danced in
L.A. even the dress I wore and the song that was playing! He
doesn't even walk, he prances!! We went back to his house and
I put on Dylan's album and we got high on some incredible
maryjane and fell into such a beautiful mood, we fucked on a
pile of pillows, . . . bodies so gentle; him saying how I make
him feel so relaxed. I was relaxed too, I felt so floaty and warm.
Just what I needed.

As we walked down the Kings' Road in the sunshine, holding
hands, everyone stared at us. Two gawking American girls said, "Isn't
his girlfriend pretty?" and time stood still for Pamela Miller from
Reseda, California.

Marty took to staying out all night, and I was overwhelmed with
pacing-the-floor, worn-out grief. He was sometimes remorseful, asking why I put up with his shit, or he was insulting, telling me if I
didn't like it, I could leave. I wrote to Michele Myer: "Marty has
gone out on his own again. He needs to be alone sometimes, I
suppose. He's not going to change for me, or anybody. I'm going
to try to see things his way, and understand. If I can't, I'll just have
to leave him . . . shit."

Todd Rundgren called to announce trans-Atlantically that the tour
was off, too bad. I felt helplesshelplesshelpless and pennyless-
pennylesspennyless. I had my hopes pinned on touring with Runt,
resuming my GTO career, and recapturing my fleeting infamy. The
plug had been pulled and it was all dribbling down the drain. I
needed to get away from Marty for a while, but didn't want to go

back to Danceland, so I called our manager, Herbie Cohen, and pleaded for some dough to see the world. Marty acted like he couldn't bear the thought of me leaving, but I could tell he needed some time off for bad behavior. One of Vito's dancers, a girl named Renee, was also in London, selling hand-painted shoes in a flea market, and I convinced her that life would have no meaning unless she saw Paris.

> July 13 . . . I'd like to have a lovely affair. The French men really know how to look at a girl! I've heard about it, and now I'm seeing it first hand; they look you up and down in a split second, their eyes piercing. People of the world; they all do the same things, only in different ways. Ooo La La!!

Renee and I posed in sidewalk cafés, went to decadent discotheques, and frolicked on pillows with rambunctious French men. I tried not to think about Marty or Mick as I trembled beneath Venus de Milo and the Mona Lisa, stuffing my head full of culture, and my gut full of Gruyère. I met a stunning eighteen-year-old beauty, François, as I lounged on the floor in a flashing, spinning den of iniquity. I had smoked a ton of hash, and this boy in my face was a true work of art. I followed him to his hovel and we had a sweet, endless, enchanting fuck. His little bit of English spoken in that luxurious accent made my heart quake, and by dawn he was down-on-his-knees mad for me. He was the singer/songwriter in his very own rock group, and he spouted deep poetry at me while tears formed in his eyes. He was brooding and political, worried and profound. Three days later, he announced to the world, "I love this woman," and begged me not to leave.

> July 17 . . . We made love three times while it rained and rained outside, and the light from the streetlamp filtered through the window . . . ecstasy.

Renee wanted to go to the Riviera, she was bored with Paris. She was my traveling companion, so I complied, and François beat his chest in teenage anguish. I could hear the sound of his heart cracking wide open. As I trudged through the pebbles and aqua water in my bathing suit, with leather-skinned men leering at me, I thought of that exquisite young boy with the weight of the entire universe on his sweet young shoulders. The last thing he said was, "You don't love me, but you will never forget me."

We bought seven pair of shoes in Milan, spending lots of lire, and carried them around in ill-gotten pillowcases. We searched for "The Last Supper" in the hot empty streets while locals snoozed, and finally stood beneath the masterpiece, mesmerized. I had only been in Italy one day and I had already realized that when an Italian guy pinches your ass, he actually latches onto your labia for dear life. Many smooth, swarthy, finger-happy creeps were knocked over by my humongous purse in the sweltering summer of 1970. We tramped through the ruins in Rome, floated around in a gondola in the Venice canals, and camped out under Michelangelo's David for several hours. I was struck dumb with wonder, and couldn't leave him until his caretaker got suspicious and asked me to move along. I touched his cool thigh and tingled as if he were warm and alive, regarding me with silent supremacy. I cut him out of a postcard and stuck him in my wallet next to James Dean. We checked out the churches, but I was disheartened by the ragtag beggars, mournful and bleating outside the ornate golden doors.

> July 25 . . . St. Peter's was dismaying. The Catholic church is so overly powerful in Italy; brainwashed people. I'm sure Jesus is more depressed with the Pope (who seems to be an extreme money-monger) than he is with an old drunk in the street. Perhaps I sound blasphemous, but it's what I believe. They charge 500 lira to see The Sistine Chapel. Michelangelo would turn and twist in his grave.

I ate wiener schnitzel in Salzburg and reclined on velvet grass in Vienna, listening to Strauss waltzes being played right in front of me by an ancient orchestra of wizened white-haired geniuses. Birds twittered, and children's laughter tinkled like bells all around me.

It was idyllic perfection until I opened my eyes to gaze out at a family of ducks, serenely paddling across the pond, and directly above me stood a pervert, his eyes bulging, his grin berserk and rabid. He clutched his flaccid member and, with optimistic delight, began to wave it in my face. Why me, Lord? Renee and I dashed from the glorious park, but on the way out we saw the deviate again, hidden in the bushes, shaking his dong as he waltzed to Strauss with a nonexistent partner. When he saw us again, his glee was unsurpassed; he let out a wild banshee shriek and poked the air with his now-poised pole as if it were a poisonous spear. We left immediately for Amsterdam.

When we hit Holland I found a newsstand with *Rolling Stone* displayed, and, foaming at the mouth, I perused the pages rapidly. Much to my bitter sorrow, Gram Parsons had quit the Burrito Brothers to branch out on his own, and I grieved as though a death had occurred. I wrote to him, sobbing onto a postcard, while I chewed *pommes frites* from a paper cone. "My dear GP, I could cry that I missed you all playing together one more time. Your music has made me so happy, at times I thought I would pop open with joy. . . ."

We stayed with a bunch of hippies and a psychic gay man who told me I folded men like paper and shot them down like soldiers. He obviously had *not* been following me around, but I thought of poor little François and saw a grain of truth hidden in his goofy words. The hippies sold *keef*, a crumbly, potent ocher-colored substance, stronger than hash. I was flat out of dough, so Renee and I went to a sleazy club called the Milkweg and sold a ton of it to the locals. For a few days we made the rounds at the hostels, selling it to the traveling students, and one afternoon I decided to try a dab of the merchandise. I landed facedown on another planet where no one spoke English. Using incoherent sign language to get my non-existent point across to no one, I took an endless stream of buses to Nowheresville. It wasn't as bad as the time I lost my mind on hash, but it was nearing that level and I swore never ever to repeat that nerve-wracking, mind-blowing-in-the-wind experience.

Renee and I finally sold enough *keef* to cross the ocean in a big old steamer. After I bought my ticket I had about fifty cents to my name, and I was looking forward to a hot bath full of British bubble products and a long satisfying session in the sack with Marty. My six weeks abroad made me appreciate the bit of bourgeois buried beneath my beau monde garments, and as I accepted this comforting thought, Anne Frank's bookcase hideout, the Eiffel Tower, Michelangelo's gravesite, and the hundreds of cats living in the Roman ruins faded into the great European distance.

Marty opened up his arms and I fell into them, unaware that he had already given me the boot. I'm not talking about a pair of boots from Granny's either. I resumed the maddening relationship with renewed fervor, not knowing for a full week that his pilot light had been extinguished and the gas turned off. As the nights went by and Marty preferred to stare at the TV set and reread old *New Music Express* articles, I began to realize I was alone in the room. After the initial shock, I tried to engage Marty in some love talk, and a horrible look came over his face. Nobody home. No room at the inn. He had come to a decision while I was away: He had made up his mind to share his eight and a half inches with anyone who had tits. He told me it wasn't in him to be true; he said I was welcome to stay, but I couldn't ask questions. I fawned and wheedled, I flattered and squirmed, I wanted Marty (God knows why), but I couldn't compete with half of England.

I packed my many clothes and girlie-goop and staggered down the four flights of stairs, weeping as loud as I could, hoping Marty would grab me around the ankles and beg me to stay. He didn't, so I kept on trudging, into a taxi and across town to a one-room flat where Mickey, my Danceland roommate, was residing. Her married popstar boyfriend had set her up in Ladbroke Grove, a colorful tie-dyed area where many a jingle-jangle morning had taken place. I was so wrapped up in sniveling, groveling grief that I hardly noticed where I was for the first few days. Cowering on the floor, I smoked joint after joint, staring off into the haze, writing my own agony column: "Alone, a woman alone without her love . . . I must stop dwelling upon it, but how? I've shed so many tears, my eyes are blind with sorrow." I was so stoned I couldn't see.

> August 8 . . . My soul is devastated, it's like the emptiness of a city when a bomb has blown it to smithereens. The closest thing to Hell I've ever felt. The same old story; my need of him, wanting to know how why and where he is at all times . . . and his need for freedom. What kind of woman could accept *that* kind of freedom? At times I thought my search was finally over, and I know it will be very hard for me to give in to a relationship like this again. Unless an affair is for eternity, it will always end in heartbreak. So Jesus, sweet Jesus, what is the use?"

"Don't you remember you told me you loved me baby? Baby baby baby baby oh baby . . ."

I've always been blessed with the world's greatest girlfriends, and Mickey nursed me through yet another heartache. I staggered back and forth, putting sixpences into the heater, rolling hash joints, smoking opium, and whimpering into my vodka. No one can say I didn't revel in my bad fortune. Amazingly, I woke up one afternoon and didn't grab for a reefer, and I knew I was on the mend. I crawled into the bathroom and saw we were out of toilet paper. Good old Mickey had stacked up old newspapers for this likely occurrence, and when I reached down to grab a fistful of newsprint, I saw myself staring haughtily back from the pages of *Melody Maker.* So I wiped my ass with myself, laughing and crying, and came back to the bountiful land of the living. (I had just come back to the land of the living when Jimi Hendrix slipped through the cracks. It made my head spin to think that this mighty rock and roll force choked on his own upchuck and would *never* be coming back. Ah, the frailty of legends.)

> September 20 . . . I just read something that Joan Baez said, "You can't dwell on the past and memories of old, or you miss the minute of NOW." I must realize that it all happens for something better to come along, if your heart is good. I shall benefit,

becoming wiser and stronger. I shall hold my face to the wind, drink the sunshine and love all. . . . God be with me and help me to better just one person's life.

Bravo, Pamela.

I put on a brave voice and called Mr. Jagger to tell him of my unblushing availablity and how we could crawl out from under our clandestine covers. A lady named Bianca answered the phone. With a husky growl she told me never, ever, under any circumstances, to call Mick, ever ever again. Get the picture? Yes, we see.

I turned twenty-two at Noel Redding's country house in Kent, comforting him, and profusely pondered my future. The GTO's were nil, I had no career, no money, and an extreme lack of boyfriend. I loved England, but missed my mommy. In spite of the blatant negatives, I had been looking forward to twenty-two, because Paul McCartney had been twenty-two when I loved him so. I just knew it would be one swell year up ahead, and I turned around and there was Sandy. I had always felt a deep kinship with bass players —Paul McCartney, Nick St. Nicholas, Chris Hillman, and Noel, to name a few. Sandy was the bass player in a Ladbroke Grove supergroup, the Pink Fairies. His eyes were the color of hot fudge, and his thick hair cascaded down his slender back in clean, wavy clumps. He looked like a sensitive prince in search of Sleeping Beauty, and unfortunately for him, he found me. I wanted to fall *in* love so I could fall *out* of love with Marty, and Sandy would do just fine, thank you. The first day we met, he gave me a pinwheel that he had in his lapel, telling me it was a corsage. That's the kind of guy he was.

September 23 . . . Feeling amazing on the full moon, Sandy and I have an amazing affinity; beautiful eyes looking at me, soft touching and gentle trust. He told me "I love you, but quietly." People seem to come on to me so soon.

Poor Sandy, I was in the royal rebounding mode, and sank easily into his elegant arms, happy to remove my mourning rags and slip into a princess costume. His eyes got damp just looking at me, which is just what I needed after the callous treatment I had received from the sex king of Kings Road. In fact, Sandy and I didn't indulge in sex. He understood the trauma I went through, and didn't put the screws on me to screw him. He was content to hold my hand, recite beautiful poetry, and breathe the same air I did. He should have worn velvet cloaks, but he wore denim because the Pink Fairies hadn't hit the Top 100 yet. The drummer, Twink, sprinkled multi-colored glitter on everyone, calling it fairy dust. I had glitter in my hair and on my shoulders for weeks.

I was a rebounding fool.

October 1 . . . I've been spending every moment with the man of my dreams, I think I have finally found him. Last night he gave me his ID bracelet that his mama gave him on his eighteenth birthday. He said it was the ultimate sacrifice, as he hadn't taken it off since he put it on. I want to be with Sandy forever, I've certainly been with him in another life; spiritually, heavenly, cosmically, simply, somewhere over the rainbow, or maybe right here. God always does this for me. When I lost Nick, Noel came 'round. When I lost Chris, Brandon was right there. When I lost Jimmy, Marty was sitting in my lap, and now, Sandy. I feel as if God has blessed this life I'm living for some divine reason. I want to be closer with Him, the ultimate Lover.

Renee and I sang "Angel Baby" with the Fairies all over England, and I got a taste of the good old glory I craved. I looked over at Sandy, who gave me his adoring gaze as I sang, "It's just like heaven being here with you-ooo, you're like an angel, too good to be true . . ." He was too good to be true, and so was I. I *wanted* to be true, and I *wanted* to want to be with Sandy forever. I figured we had spent a few good lifetimes with each other already, so how about one more? He was gone on me; he inhaled and exhaled when I did, watching my every move as though a miracle were taking place. This may have been one of the reasons I decided to talk myself into swooning. I poured my heart out to my journal about my dashing new prince.

> *Before me*
> *You sit gazing*
> *Your eyes*
> *Drinking the waters*
> *Of my love*
>
> *I pour onto you*
> *The waters of my soul*
> *May you no longer thirst.*

Not only was the poor guy going to drop dead from lack of liquid refreshment, he was going to be folded like paper and shot down like a soldier.

I had come to England for two weeks, and stayed six months. Since I was flat broke, and Sandy was a struggling group member, I decided I had to go back to L.A. and get a job to make enough money to bring my miraculous butt back to England in style, with enough left over to pursue some sort of show-biz career. The Pink Fairies had an album coming out called *The Snake* that was sure to top the charts, and Sandy would soon have enough dough to support us grandly. I missed my mom and the GTO's, and I wanted to escape the impending wind and snow, so, with solemn promises to remain chaste and cherishing, I finally used the second half of my round-trip ticket and headed for L.A.

On my way back to my beloved home town, I stopped to see my adorable relatives in Dayton, Ohio. The Mothers of Invention happened to be playing in Cleveland, so after eating an enormous plate of corn bread and cabbage, provided by Aunt Bertie Mae Moore, I hopped a Greyhound and entered the maladjusted world of the Mothers. Frank had added the two lead singers from the Turtles to his line-up, Mark Volman and Howard Kaylan. I had met them at the Bath Festival in England, and we had instant rapport on a high level. We all loved TV theme songs, and hummed the *Father Knows Best* ditty and any silly lyrics we could remember. "Because they're cousins, identical cousins, and you'll find, they walk alike, they talk alike at times they even . . ." At times they even what?? I still can't remember. It was one of those deals where I felt like the fucking queen of Sheba whenever I was in their presence. The bearded gray-haired one, Howard, made me feel like I had just descended from the top of a Christmas tree. We made heavy goo-goo eyes, but I was supposed to be in love with Sandy, and besides, he was married. The three of us smoked a lot of pot, had a wacky mutual admiration society, and wore our love like heaven. As I staggered from Mark and Howie's room I bumped into Mr. Zappa, who gave me a lovey-dove hug, and I looked up at him with smoky stars in my eyes.

When I got home and moved back in with Mommy and Daddy, I went through a strange period. I wanted to act, I wanted to sing, I wanted to do SOMETHING creative to get myself shoved into the vast public eye. I started taking voice lessons from the wrong person, who concentrated on my nonexistent octaves instead of noticing I had an aluminum ear. I wanted to sing high harmony with the Burrito Brothers or star in movies with Paul Newman, but what I wound up doing was going back to Danceland and taking a job in a little dump in the Valley.

Sandy sent me fairy-tale love letters and mushy poetry books, promising to save his hard-earned gig money and buy me a one-way ticket back to his arms. He kept a vigil over my pictures on his damp Ladbroke Grove walls, and called once a week with the financial update. One night he called from a red phone booth on Portobello Road to propose to me, and I purred like a pussy into the receiver. The next day I met Miss Christine at Todd Rundgren's recording session and made twinkly-eyes with his exquisite teenage bass player, Tony Sales. (*Another* bass player!) The fact that Soupy Sales was his dad was an added bonus. He had been one of my many black-and-white idols, right up there with Ernie Kovacs and Howdy Doody. I didn't mean to go hog-wild over the boy, in fact *he* pursued me in a teenage frenzy. I knew I would be racked with guilt, but couldn't resist the delicious temptation of this green-eyed wonder. Nothing feels better than a fresh, budding, blooming passion. I was an all-day sucker for it, and after several evenings of verbal foreplay and a few slobbery make-out sessions, I accepted the inevitable and kicked my shoes off.

> November 27 . . . I keep thinking of backing out, but after last night, it's doubtful. We got drunk at The Troubador, and fell into his bed, and as he said, "went floating downstream . . ." It was so good, but so many thoughts in my conscience saying, "No, no!" Untrue to Sandy. Shit. I wanted to go to him untouched, have I no will-power? Does the whole world have to fall in love with me before I'm saturated?

Before I could bend down and touch my toes, I was involved with Tony to the extent that I couldn't let go. He was so young and sweet, and he told me he was falling in love with me. Big sigh. I was soooooooo confuuuuuuused!!!! I thought "someday" had finally arrived and my prince had come, trotting down Portobello Road, and here I was, hitting the hay with a nineteen-year-old beauty from Beverly Hills. Couldn't I ever just hit the hay without getting *involved*? Noooooooooo! Once again I was seeing infinity, this time in Tony's sea-green eyes. Sandy poured his heart out to me through the mail, and it got to the point where I cringed when the blue aerogram drifted through the mail slot in my mom's front door. I wrote him that I loved him because I didn't know what else to do. I wasn't too familiar with rebounding, so I really believed I had fallen in love with Sandy. I tortured myself with guilt because Sandy told me he was being true-blue, and I, of course, was coming daily.

Tony lived with his brother, Hunt, and his mom, who was miserable because Soupy had split the scene and moved to New York. She suggested that Tony and I "get a room" one night. I was feeling like a slut anyway, and this didn't help. We went over to Mercy's coo-coo household to see if we could spend the night, and found Mercy in a condition past cure. She had been smoking angel dust again, and all her roommates had abandoned ship. She glommed on to me like I had floated through the ceiling, dragging me to her bed, where I remained while she clutched at me and cried out loud, "Pamela and me, alone together forever!" I guess Tony had become invisible. She went from thinking that the loony-bin guys in white jackets were knocking at her door to believing she was dead with a capital *D*. She peered at me from under the covers and whispered, "Did you die too? Oh, I'm so glad!" The only good thing about angel dust is that it wears off fast. Pretty soon her eyes cleared and she hugged me tight. "You and I lost our minds together." I told her I loved her but to include me out, and Tony and I went to Sandy Koufax's Tropicana Motel, where the prices were displayed inside a flickering neon baseball.

I kept up the literary love front for Sandy, hoping I would feel tidal waves of adoration for him when we met again. My ticket to London arrived and I panicked, but as much as I wanted to stay with Tony, I felt I owed it to Sandy to see if we could recapture what he didn't even know had gone missing.

January 15 ... In the air ... "Dazed and confused," I write at twenty thousand feet. Tony and I have been talking about what's happening between us, and I realized how unsure, *mixed-up* and SCHIZOPHRENIC I am. He told me he wanted me with him when he "came into his own." Oh Sob sob sob. And here I am on my way to someone else. When we said good-bye it was like wrenching off a part of me, an arm or something. The last thing he said was, "I'll always love you."

I knew when I saw dear Sandy at the airport, peering at all the passengers, desperately seeking my face, that the tidal waves of adoration I felt were for Tony. I so much wanted to have tears of love spring into my eyes when we ran to each other and embraced, but the split-second shock was slow-motion torment when I realized I wasn't in love with Sandy. It was impossible for me to fake it, so Sandy knew from the first instant that something had gone extremely awry. I went through the motions, sitting around in his basement flat, smoking a ton of hash, listening to him practice the bass, thump, thump, thump, and sleeping until two in the afternoon. Stunned that I wasn't smothering him with warm and rosy love, he was a silent, pleading devotee, his wounded big brown eyes begging for entry. Behind my blank expression pounded a torment fraught with wickedness because I knew I was battering and bruising one of the world's kindest souls. He looked to my smiling face in the black and whites on the wall for reassurance. It was hellish, but it didn't stop me from collecting a hundred sixpences and running into the rain to call my tempting teen in sunny Beverly Hills.

> **January 19 . . . Is it fair to any of us for me to stay here? Such a triangle, it makes me feel out of it; not really living. I'm not here or there, I'm NOWHERE, always in a daze; Sandy's brown eyes turn into Tony's green ones. I'm going to have to leave, and will I regret leaving here also? If I do, too bad. I don't deserve it if I lose it again. Never have I known such indecision. January 22 . . . I told Sandy after ten gallons of tears that I was too confused to stay with him and would have to leave, and he said, "I'm just beginning to feel alive again." AAAAAHHHHH! He talked me into staying a few more days. I guess he's hoping he'll wake up from this nightmare. How can I shatter this human being?**

My fickle heart pined for another, while I prayed for a miracle. I couldn't *tell* him about Tony, I was too much of a *poulet-merde*. I wanted to slap my own face for inflicting such cruelty on another soul. After all, I had known my own pathetic share of heartache. I felt for him, but I wanted to be anywhere but under his cozy hand-made quilt, cowering in the candlelight. As fortuitous fate would have it, Gail Zappa called, having just arrived in London with Frank and their divine munchkins, Moon and Dweezil. She told me that Frank wanted me to read for the part of The Soprano in his ground-breaking video movie, *200 Motels*, to be filmed at Pinewood Studios. The Provider of Miracles heard my unworthy plea, and I was numb with gratitude. I got the part, solemnly gave Sandy back his namesake bracelet, and trotted off to Windsor to meet my second Beatle.

Frank had written *200 Motels*, a maniacal musical about being on the road with the Mothers—how it drove them crazy, and the lunacy they got up to in Middle America. He was also directing, so he asked Ringo Starr to star as the leader of the Mothers, Mr. Zappa himself. The day I arrived, Howard took me to Ringo's hotel room, where we sat around with a bunch of Mothers, Miss Lucy (who was playing herself in the movie), and my second Beatle, singing "Boys" and "Act Naturally." I lifted my voice in song with Richard Starkey from Liverpool, England. My ex-Beatlefriends, Kathy 'n' Stevie, were probably married to a couple of Canoga Park geeks, and I was rubbing thighs with Ringo Starr. HA HA *HA*.

The berserk drummer with the Who, Keith Moon, was playing the coveted part of the nun, and Theodore Bikel was playing my uncle. My scenes were cut dramatically because Mr. Bikel wouldn't say the word *fuck* or have the word *fuck* said to him. Oh, well. All of the Mothers played themselves in varying degrees of absurdity. I was thrilled because Wilfred Bramble, who played Paul McCartney's grandfather in *A Hard Day's Night*, was supposed to play one of the Mothers who had recently been fired, but his ancient integrity intervened and he toddled off into the dusk shaking his white-haired head, "Tsk, Tsk, Tsk." Ringo's handsome driver, Martin, got the part and was overjoyed at being right next to Ringo at just the right time.

> January 29 . . . I had a nice talk with Ringo today, he's such a pleasant person; unaffected, believe it or not. He told me that Paul is suing the other three Beatles, and kicked Ringo out of his house last week. How horrid, another bubble burst.

The man with the lean, milky-white thighs appeared to be nerding out.

I played the part of an avid minimama groupie-doopie news-hen, and even though I was petrified, Frank liked what I was doing. I looked up at him through adoring rosy lenses and took it all very seriously. When I wasn't sweating under the lights, I was hanging out with Mark and Howard, and started to dawdle in the halls with Keith Moon, who shook the universe with his insanity. He filled a room so full that even breathing was difficult. I felt pressed against the wall because his madness was so bone-marrow deep. He ran around in a nun's habit, sprinkling people with holy cognac, creating constant beatific chaos and hilarity. He was irresistible and dangerous, and heartbreakingly sad.

> February 8 . . . I did my big scene, after much fear, and RINGO told me it was FANTASTIC! Such a teenage dream come true that I cried. MZ said it was perfect and kissed my hand. Keith said he thought I would get a lot of parts because my facial expressions were incredible. Speaking of Mr. Moon, he quite came on to me, asking me to come stay at his place after the movie is over. I went to his room and listened to his new "Who" tracks . . . excellent. Poor little Keith, he's a sad and lonely case. "Tears of a Clown" for sure. If I wasn't so entrenched, I might be inclined to give him a helping hand.

After giving up Sandy for Tony, I wasn't about to tackle Mr. Moon, but I couldn't bring myself to cross him out completely. He really did help me to thrash out the agony over Sandy, at the same time teaching me the fine art of swigging cognac. I figured I would certainly bump into him again somewhere down the lovely line. The movie seemed to be over in seconds because Frank was using videotape, and I was once again hurled into the abyss. I floundered around in front of Gail, so she invited me to stay with the Zappa family, taking care of the munchkins when she went out with Frank for a romantic curry. Sandy came over to bid farewell to his lost love, and marched with me in front of Royal Albert Hall, protesting the ban on the Mothers. It seems Mr. Zappa was much too porno and titillating to perform on the royal boards. Frank and the Mothers marched around with us, and we made the cover of *The Daily Express*. In the photo I'm hovering behind Frank's shoulder, grinning like a goon.

When the Zappas started packing to leave London, I cashed in my pounds and hurried off to Heathrow. Twelve hours later, Tony and I were rolling around in his childhood twin bed, steaming up his childhood room complete with Dodger pennants on the wall. His little prepubescent trophies gleamed on the shelf, reminding me that I was robbing the old cradle.

After several days of private rapture, Tony and I started to go out on the town. Uh-oh. Now that I was HIS, he became insanely jealous and thought my flirting was something to get all wigged out about. He watched me like a beautiful baby hawk, inventing salacious scenarios and stalking off into the night. I would follow him down the street, pledging my love over and over again.

OK. I was back in the land of opportunity, and even though my boyfriend was a jealous guy, my emotional needs were taken care of. So what was I going to do with the rest of myself? Where were the GTO's? Could we make another go of it??? I did some checking around. Miss Christine had fallen for Albert Grossman, Bob Dylan's abundant manager, and was living the hoity-toity life in New York. Miss Cynderella married John Cale from Velvet Underground. Sparky married an actor from the *Hair* cast and was about to have a baby. Mercy had always wanted to be a soulwoman and was entangled with Al Green, the Bar-Kays, and trying to figure out how Otis Redding really died. She carried around pictures of him frozen stiff in the remains of his smashed plane, pointing out the icicles as if they had some significance. She had even fucked Chuck Berry in a trailer in Disneyland, and then traipsed off to Memphis to live a life of soul. I caught her the day before she left. That's how I got to see the frozen shot of Otis and hear all about Chuck's porno prowess. Sandra had taken her baby daughter, Raven, back to San Pedro, where she married a carpenter and became a pregnant housewife with a crazy past. I missed them all and mourned the ill-fated Girls Together Outrageously.

Since the GTO's were officially and finally kaput, I needed a job so that I could get another pad of my own. I always believed I would be world famous one day, and my piddling jobs were usually horrendous bores. I went to visit Nudie, the renowned rodeo tailor from Brooklyn, and he offered me a job selling his world-class cowboy gear to a very classy clip-clop clientele. I was overjoyed, and came to work decked out like Dale Evans. I sold lumpy turquoise belt buckles to the likes of Slim Pickens until the bubble burst and Nudie's wife, Bobbie, canned me after five days. The big boss inundated me with immoral offers, following me around the store like an aging pug-dog. He said I could design my own miniskirt Nudie suit with moons and stars, cascading waterfalls, or wagon wheels and cow skulls, created with masses of sequins and sparkling embroidery thread, painstakingly put together by talented underpaid Mexicans. All I had to do for this remarkable gift was to spend a mere thirty minutes with him in the dressing room, straddling a leather chair shaped like a saddle. Yeah. Bobbie sadly informed me that I just wasn't the right girl for the job. Yeah again.

I hung out with my tempting teen, and repursued my acting career. I sent out lots of photos and got a stunning part in a class A movie entitled *Massage Parlor* with the remarkable actor Doodles Weaver. I suffered for my craft by cleaning a theater every week that was used by a bunch of hee-hawing mule actors, just so I could get free acting lessons. I crawled around on my hands and knees on the sticky donkey-trodden floor, scraping up cigarette stubs and sweeping out the ashes flicked from the Pall Malls of my fellow emoters. The members of the "troupe" looked upon me as the little match girl twice removed, and condescended to speak the speech to me, trippingly on their tongues, while rolling their eyes up to the once-dusty rafters. I read for Peter Fonda, who was curled up in the breakfast nook of his woodsy knot-hole kitchen in the West Valley, and didn't get the part. I read all the cheapo casting rags and went downtown to the Alexandria Hotel to audition for *The Drunkard*, where I met the author and director William Jarvis. I read the silly melodrama to the best of my ability, and he said he would give me the lead but I should take a few private lessons with him first. I was tickled pink when he said I could have my first lesson that very moment. "First things first," he said. "Your voice is too high-pitched. I'll have to take it down a notch or two." He had me lie down on his maroon Naugahyde couch, relax, and close my eyes. I heard a strange buzzing sound and peeked through my eyelashes to see him fiddling with a small vibrating machine and heading in my direction. He placed the little bzz-bzz on different parts of my body, getting lower and lower, asking me to imitate the deep buzzing noise. "The lower I go, the lower you go." When the vibrator was humming into my

crotch area, I jumped up and announced I was late for an appoint-
ment, promising to return the following day for my next lesson. On
the way home, riding many buses, I wondered how long Mr. Jarvis
would sit waiting for me, clutching his buzz box, sweating salty rivers
into the Naugahyde. It was tough trying to break into show business.

After Tony and I wore each other out in the sack, we argued. We
didn't have any money, any means of transport, or anyplace to stay
together. Hitching home from Beverly Hills one night, some sleaze-
ball asked me if I'd like some acid as I huddled next to the door
handle. I told him no, thank you very much, and he said, "I'll take
you on a trip, baby!" and pulled out an enormous fistful of my hair
in an attempt to murder me. The gruesome death of a blond hitch-
hiker was definitely on his pea-brain. I screamed so LOUD that
people started pouring out of their apartments to save the howling
female. The bum threw me into the gutter, leaving me with a bald
patch the size of a silver dollar.

I didn't hitch to Tony's anymore, we didn't see each other as
much, and we spent a lot of time on the phone driving each other
crazy. He thought I was out having a ball without him if I didn't
grab the phone on the first ring, and I was usually on my way to his
house, wasting ninety-three minutes on public transportation so we
could lock ourselves in his mom's pool house. I felt his heart floating
downstream a week before he told me he was too young for a permanent relationship. He was nineteen, I was twenty-two and a half.
I cried a lot and went through the mourning emotions, but I knew
that our love was looking dim way before Tony took his final bow.

May 15 . . . My "weenie" went away tonight because he's only
nineteen and "needs to experience more life." Such beautiful
kisses, such awing love. A teenage experiment? I'm proud of
myself for the calmness I showed. Maturity? Crap! Tony is such
an exquisite boy, but boy is the operative word, and Pamela
needs a man. My Prince Charming dreams are fading . . . I think
he's off with Snow White somewhere, or maybe he died; his
famous white horse threw him and he broke his neck. Perhaps
I got what I deserve after crushing Sandy so rudely. I'm sorry

for that. Truly I am. I'm going to rely more on myself and God;
use all my spare time to improve myself, instead of pouring it
into another person. I am truly all I've got; me and my Maker.
I'm going to forget men for awhile. How about some casual
acquaintances?

Far-fetched, futile, famous last words.

I had seen a lot more of Gail Zappa since *200 Motels*, and she
always put the universe into perspective for me. She was cynical,
brilliant, and eye-opening, going from day to day with her hypnotic
husband and delicious doll-babies without ever wondering what it
was all for. She said I worried too much and pondered the profound
too much, and what was the point? She needed a governess and I
needed a job, so I moved in and learned all about changing diapers
and pouring Rice Krispies at 8 A.M. The Zappas bought a house way
up in Laurel Canyon with a big pool and a cute little guesthouse
that I dolled up and made my own. Gail stayed up late with Mr.
Zappa, drinking espresso, while he worked down in the basement
until dawn, and as the sun filtered through my Mickey Mouse cur-
tains, my buzzer would sound and little Moon would pipe through
the intercom, "Pamela, please come make our breaktess." Sometimes Gail would let me sleep late if I had spent a particularly
wild night, and at around ten o'clock she would buzz me: "Wakey
wakes!!"

I had never spent much time around kids, and being an only
child, they made me nervous, but Moon and Dweezil were the
perfect introduction to small people. Moon was four and Dwee was
two when I started nannying, and the love I felt for them was different
from any other kind. I didn't want a single thing from those munchkins, and it was a refreshing relief. I hung out with them because I
had to, but found out real soon that I also *wanted* to. Gail was real
lenient with them, causing all kinds of unexpected creativity to crop
up. Moon was an amazing artist, and drew tons of pictures in the
pages of my journals of dancing ballerinas and princesses. She wore
fairy wings around the house, tapping her magic wand, turning

commoners into kings and queens. Dweezil was a belligerent, demanding little baby who knew just what he wanted, and would pummel your calves to get it. He was a gorgeous little tough boy, with blond, matty ringlets hanging down his back, dragging his bottle full of warm sweet English Breakfast tea behind him like a club, and I told Gail I had dibs on him when he reached pubescence. He was the sexiest thing in diapers. They both swam like little turtles, and I spent many hours watching them paddle around while I got a scintillating tan.

When the Mothers came home from the road, Howard Kaylan was a frequent visitor at the Zappas', and he was obviously smitten with me. His high school marriage seemed to be crumbling, and he turned to me in his time of need. He wasn't really my type, *and* he wore a wedding band, but we held hands and got into some very romantic heavy petting in my little pad by the pool. I eventually succumbed to his cuddly, captivating charm and goofball sweetness.

July 18 . . . Howie and I made glorious love last night, very much up to expectations; so loving, really. He and the missus are getting a divorce. She called right in the middle of everything, sobbing, and said, "Let me speak to my HUSBAND." It was low. Howie says the more she hates me, the more he loves me. Miss P. in the middle, as usual, not knowing what she's getting herself into.

August 1 . . . Howie and I have been together three nights in a row now. Gail gave me a night off and I stayed at his house last night. We slept on sleeping bags 'cause his wife took the bed with her. We cooked Hawaiian TV dinners and watched "The Wild Ones" and made lots of love. Boy, Howie really gets me OFF! I'm laying here, waiting for Dweezil to wake up from his nap, listening to the soundtrack to "200 Motels." It's very memory making; "Hantoon rantoon frammin!!"

Howard and I went to Disneyland and floated off into never-never land, where Peter Pan said "Come on everybody, here we go-ooo" ten thousand times a day. He made me a piece of eight in "Pirates of the Caribbean" that said "Howard will always love Pamela." It was a different kind of relationship; for the first time, I didn't want to sink my hooks into his back and cart him off to my own private Idaho. In fact, when he told me he had met somebody on the road who was coming to L.A. to stay with him, I didn't agonize or mourn. I knew our feelings for each other were real-to-real.

Alice Cooper had a coming-out party and sent announcements to all of show biz, including the normal-formal crowd, intimating that an important debutante would be making her social debut. Alice was on the verge of prelegendness, but the likes of Rod McKuen had no idea he was alive. After the string quartet took their bows, and the immense black stripper named "TV Mama" peeled down to her bikini bottoms, Richard Chamberlain realized he was out of place in his tuxedo. He was blushing as I sauntered up to him and whispered that Alice was, in fact, a rock and roll phenomenon. Dr. Kildare had been an important part of my life, and I felt sorry for him. It was to his credit that he stuck it out, loosened his uptight tie, and got into the spirit of the lunacy. Rod McKuen, on the other hand, was deeply offended when Mercy, bombed on angel-dust, popped out of a huge cake, poked her grubby fingers into the gooey icing, and hurled it onto his tux and statement-making sneakers. She was, once again, stoned beyond recognition, and went on joyously slinging confection into the dressed-up, disgruntled onlookers until Alice's roadies yanked her out of the cake. Dr. Kildare and I laughed our asses off.

I met someone that night who would alter my life as deeply as Captain Beefheart had almost a decade earlier. His name was Chuck Wein, and he had taken Mercy to Hawaii to be in his movie *Rainbow Bridge* with the late Jimi Hendrix. Mercy swore by him and I was in instant awe. His nickname was "The Wizard," and his brain was whirling with knowledge about the *soul*, the *universe*, space brothers, and vegetables. I grew by spiritual leaps and bounds in his presence. I stopped eating anything that might bleed, and learned how to salute the sun, juice wheatgrass, and accept people who had yet to find the path. I threw the I Ching and studied the tarot deck, looking for the answers I knew they possessed. If I didn't understand something, I would humble myself to Chuck, acknowledging my noviceness.

When Jim Morrison died, I flummoxed around wondering, what was it all for anyway?? He had grown a beard, gotten fat, moved to Gay Paree, and taken his last dive into a bathtub. Had he served any purpose, or what? Was I serving any purpose? Was there any purpose to serve? Chuck explained the workings of karma and how Jim had just worked out some hard karma and was probably already onto the next level. Uh-huh, Chuck, come again??? Oh, how I wanted to *grok* it all.

The Wizard had a team of cosmic seekers, and we were all at a party where I was floundering around a little but wearing a sweetie-pie happy face anyway, like I usually did, and Chuck called to me from across the room, "Stop standing there, pretending you know what's going on." My face turned to happy stone and the rest of me turned into burning liquid, oozing into the ground like when the Wicked Witch of the West was belted with a pail of water: "I'm melting, melting!" Chuck was a bit of a power puppeteer, but I believed every perfect pearl of truth that fell from his lips. He was cracking my contrived persona for my own good.

Whenever my fave-rave groups came to town, Gail was also lenient with me, allotting me some hard-earned rock-out time. I threw on my hot rags and sashayed down to the Riot House to see the Kings of Heaviness, Led Zeppelin. I wanted to go to the concert, and it had been years since I stood in line for a ticket to a rock and roll show. I spoke to Jimmy for a few minutes, for history's sake, then went straight to Robert's room, secretly harboring some hidden pent-up hope, and nestled into his golden blondness until it was time to leave for the Forum. He had also been harboring some interesting ideas about me, and we flirted outrageously in the back of his limo.

August 20 ... RP opened the door, looking stunning and radiant. I had just had a nervous little chat with Jimmy about Aleister Crowley and inconsequential items, so I was ready for

some comfort. Robert caressed my cheek and kissed me, saying, "I've wanted to do this for a long time." In the dressing room, Jimmy watched Robert and me with extreme interest, and after the magnificent concert, Robert whispered, "Jimmy isn't too happy at home, I know he wants you to be with him." I didn't believe it, but guess who climbed into the limo with me? It was so damn *nice* to be near him again. He took me to The Whiskey, and at about one o'clock, he reached over and grabbed me, gave me his wink, and that was it. Glorious yesterdays pouring around me. His best line was, "Last night my entire body was a sheet of pleasure." Bonzo remarked on how good it was to see us together again. Jimmy told me tales of Charlotte and little baby Scarlet. They haven't gotten married, and have lots of disagreements. Oh well, he *could* have had me. I saw Robert on the way out, and he said, "I was a fool to have passed you up." Hmmm.

Robert called me a week later, and told me the boys were making fun of him because he had left his heart in L.A. with Miss P. I was flattered and flabbergasted when he asked me to meet him in San Francisco and begged me to tell him if I had been thinking about him. "Let me in on your thoughts about it, please." I was tortured and thrilled at the same time, but rock's golden Adonis must have had third thoughts, because he never called back with flight information, and then I was relieved and mortified at the same time.

Howard and I kept our sweet affair going, even after the little stub he imported from Philadelphia started to give me dirty looks at Mothers' rehearsals and concerts. I couldn't see him as often as I wanted to, however, so I baited my honey-flavored hook and threw out the line in hopes of pulling in a live one. While I waited for a bite, I studied Stanislavski's method and turned twenty-three. Life went on idyllically at Zappa castle.

September 23 . . . It's a gorgeous day; Moon and Dweezil are down in the garage with Motorhead while he fixes his old truck. Java is cleaning the kitchen, Gail is reading a book, and Frank is in New York promoting the movie. On October 1, I'll be 8 feet tall on the "200 Motels" billboard on the Sunset Strip.

Finally! Brandon brought little Jesse over yesterday to pick up Moon and me, and we all went to "Travel Town." We smiled all day while Moon and Jesse held hands and rode the Merry-Go-Round. So cute. It was a great day. I love my de Wilde, and my little Moonie too.

Just waking up and breathing the sweet air was good enough for me in the summer of '71. It still is.

200 Motels came out to thunderous confusion, but I was singled out in *The Hollywood Reporter*: "Pamela Miller scores as a newshen." Biggie biggie wow wow. The billboard on Sunset Boulevard had me smack-dab in the middle, being clutched by Jimmy Carl Black, my massive hand-painted tits exploding out of my Maidenform. Illusions of grandeur.

Mercy and I spent a lot of time at Chuck Wein's communal abode in the Hollywood Hills, grappling with massive, perplexing concepts, smoking pot and rubbing tiger balm into the third-eye area. I tried in vain to remember who I had been in my three previous lives, but I was pretty sure I had been my dad's mother at one time. Chuck's mom taught me how to make carrot cake, and I studied the big poster in the kitchen about which foods combined properly. "Melon, eat it alone or leave it alone." A lot of the trivial things cluttering up my life began to fall away. I tried to get my parents off meat, but Daddy loved my mom's goulash too much too consider the idea. I got Gail and the munchkins to stop chomping chops for a few months, and I felt like a blossoming saint. It began to dawn on me that I needed someone to share my newfound clarity with, someone who could climb the invisible ladder with me to the unknown realms beyond. I was hoping this advanced soul would also be a gorgeous hunk of stuff.

8

♥

I MET HIM ON A MONDAY AND MY HEART STOOD STILL

Mercy had been telling me about a magnificent young actor who lived right next door to Chuck, and after Moon's huge birthday party, where I organized all the games, served the cake and ice cream, passed out the party favors, and lost my mind, Gail gave me two hours off to shlep down to Hollywood Boulevard to see *Zacharia*, the first (and only) rock and roll western. It starred Chuck's next-door neighbor, and I wanted to ogle the goods undetected before I committed to a blind introduction. After salivating into my popcorn and peanut-butter cups, I dribbled out of the theater and back home, where I told Gail about this splendid blond dish with the juiciest red lips ever, and she suggested I get on the phone to Mercy and get my ass over to his house without *any* further ado. Unfortunately, she wasn't home, so I met him the following evening, which was a Monday, and my heart stood stick, rock, stock-still. It was a sweltering September dusk when we rang the doorbell and stood waiting on his porch. I was all aflutter and wiped my sticky hands across my newly purchased antique, hand-embroidered Mexican peasant blouse, while also attempting to reconstruct my lip gloss. Mercy had the most knowing gypsy look smeared across her face as we stood listening to the music and laughter that preceded the footsteps; then the door was thrown back and standing in front of me was Donnie Wayne Johnson. The big screen hadn't done him justice and I wondered where this absurdly beautiful specimen of manhood had been all my life. He hugged Mercy and ushered us into his Hollywood bachelor pad where many a burgeoning actress had been successfully seduced. It reeked of male conquest and female acquiescence. The furniture was big and beige, the rugs were white, the ceilings were high, the lights were dim, and I was reduced to a lump of blushing flesh. The guy was a hunk a hunk of burning love. A sex god. A good time. A very good time. At least that's what I was hoping as I sipped a glass of red wine and listened to him play his Gibson and sing in a pure sweet voice that defied description. I was enthralled. I accepted his offer of a gnarled ginseng root and chewed it while I danced all over the living room. I could dance anytime, anywhere, but I had a hard time making interesting conversation. I made a valiant effort to be witty and droll despite the tremblies, because I wanted to be invited back. Real soon.

When I told Donnie that I had to get back to work, he wanted to know what I did, so I told him about Moon and Dweezil and my role in the Zappa household, and he thought it was cute. "Don't you want to get a little closer to me before you go?" I snuggled up to him, sinking into the big beige couch, and he kissed my neck and ran his fingers through my hair. It was a giggly playful little moment that I would recall twenty-five times a day for the next two weeks. When we left, he opened the door for us and lounged against the doorframe, steaming up the already steamy summer air. When we had made it down the stone steps, I turned to wave, and noticed that the doorframe he was leaning on had started to melt. I guess it was a figment of my wild imagination. Or maybe not.

I dawdled through my domestic grilled-cheese and potty-training duties, daydreaming endlessly about Don Johnson from Flatcreek, Missouri. He was a struggling actor, but I didn't see much of a struggle going on. He was a totally self-possessed roost ruler, with talent oozing from all ten million pores, and I was dying to see him again. I hung around at Chuck's house, hoping his neighbor would drop in for a friendly cup of Mu tea.

Meanwhile, my spiritual life grew steadily, and Chuck was fast becoming my guru. I mooned around the Self-Realization Lake Shrine, feeding the swans bits of whole-wheat bread, and joined a Japanese church where I learned to channel healing light through a piece of holy paper folded up into a locket that I wore around my neck. The church was open day and night, and you could sit on a stool in front of an ancient Japanese crone, or a young aspiring novice, and have purple healing light channeled to any ailing part of your person through the palms of their hands. I practiced on anyone who would let me, and I'm sure I saw a jet of purple deck my mom's headache one afternoon.

On the earthly level, I continued my acting classes with a method guy on El Centro Avenue, and still planned on winning an Oscar. I got an agent with the most preposterous name, "Velvet Amber," and she walked out of *200 Motels* due to her extreme lack of intelligence, wit, humor, and sense. Ten days after Donnie melted his doorframe, Mercy called and invited me to a party at his house. I squealed like a joyful piglet.

October 13 . . . Don Johnson had a great party. I rocked out. He gave me EVERY line in the book; very beautifully done, very romantic and full of promises, but I presume he was full of shit because he didn't call today, and he said he would. Who knows? I rapped with Desi Arnaz Jr. and also met my idol, Jack Nicholson. I met lots of lovely men, but Don wouldn't have any of it. Whenever I was talking to a guy for too long, he would

scoop me up and pull me into a hallway and kiss my lips off.
Chuck was there and I got off spiritually when we did a cheek
to cheek slow dance. He's still so far out of my league, way up
and out there. He told me he has been to Venus. I believe.

More days went by, and I didn't hear from His Majesty. I fretted
and mewled and fidgeted, trying on outfit after outfit, dragging the
mirror over by the phone so I wouldn't miss his call. I devised all
kinds of things to do with the munchkins that wouldn't take me too
far from Ma Bell, and one afternoon, while we were doing a puzzle
on the kitchen table, right next to the fateful phone, it actually rang,
and Don Johnson said, "Hi, baby!"

And so it came to pass that Don and I entered into a romantic
relationship. I thanked God for my daily bread, my healthy body,
and my new could-be, would-be boyfriend, whose looks could have
prevented World War II. I couldn't take my eyes off him for more
than a few seconds at a time, sometimes stopping in mid-sentence,
flagrantly dumbfounded by his face. He loved to laugh and I could
really send him reeling. That first week of blissful prelove, precom-
mitment was one big too-good-to-be-true party.

After our first date, eating avocado and alfalfa sprout sandwiches
at Help restaurant, he escorted me gallantly to his bedroom like I
was the heroine in one of those paperback romance novels, picked
me up at the door, and carried me to his bed. I was vibrating with
desire run amok and could hardly wait to peel his Jockey shorts down.

November 7 . . . I'm trying hard not to let my imagination run
away with me, but it appears that we're both madly infatuated.
It would be quite nice, for *here* are all his attributes: 1. Really
into acting; in love with it, secure in it. 2. Getting very into
music; writing it, learning guitar. 3. On THE path. 4. *HUGE* cock.
I'm getting off like I haven't in AGES. We do "get it on" perfectly,
last night was heavy wildness. I kept seeing myself in his eyes
so beautifully, and forever it seemed. We were either fucking
or laughing, sounding like a hysterical comedy team! Abbott
and Costello, Martin and Lewis, Miller and Johnson!! I could
get it *real* REAL bad.

And I did.

November 13 . . . Donnie keeps saying things like, "How can this be happening?" I guess I can safely say I'm falling in love.

We saw each other every night, which meant he would usually sleep in my little bungalow and leave in the morning when I went on Cream of Wheat duty. We went to chic-chic-chic parties and screenings, where I hung on his arm like an appendage, beaming so big that my teeth lit up Lucille Ball's living room.

We went to a screening of a Desi junior TV movie in Lucy's den, bringing Chuck with us to make it interesting, and he wowed Desi's date, Liza Minnelli, with his talk of past lives and high-colonics. I Love Lucy peeked her flaming red head into the room to call her darling son, and I swooned, finding myself in babaloo-land for a split second. I swallowed my oohs and ahhs and settled down with a plate of artichoke hearts to watch Desi's thespian heroics. These superstar evenings were secondary, however, to the ever-increasing pitter-patter of my lovesick heart. When we weren't together, every thought of him sent a searing geyser of adrenaline through my entire body, singeing the roots of my hair, making it impossible for me to stand up, stand still or stand it. I had been in love before, but not like this. All those corny love songs reverberated in my skull. "I hear your name, and I'm afla-a-a-ame . . . aflame with such a burning desire, that only your kiss, *kiss* KISS can put out the fire . . ." And sure enough, slowly but surely, Donnie started spouting words of love into my waiting ears.

November 22 . . . We were discussing reincarnation, and how we thought this was our last life, and he said, "My dear, do you know how long it's taken me to *find* you?" We're still being very careful not to say too much. I can't believe how good it is; how damn rational and healthy.

I was confusing rationality with reincarnation. I could close my eyes and picture this beautiful, naked blond man, spiraling through many lifetimes in search of Pam Miller from Reseda, California. When Moon drew a picture of Don and me in my journal, holding hands, I knew an unprecedented plateau had been reached. I was waiting impatiently for the big *L* word to join hands with the big *F* word.

Donnie didn't call me for three days, and it was bad timing, because the Who came to town, and Keith Moon crashed into my life with firecracker force, demanding unobstructed attention. I went to the Who concert/bash and he followed me home, grinning wickedly as he tumbled out of his velvet Granny's suit and into my bed. I hadn't planned on a sexual encounter, but I was on a "Tommy" high, as well as totally bombed on crème de menthe and an assortment of multicolored capsules. I backslid, let's face it. And once I was in the backsliding mode, I reveled in it, becoming several different people with Mr. Moon, including a rich older lady in pursuit of a gorgeous young steward, a hooker accosting a young virginal kid from Connecticut, and a schoolgirl being raped by a priest. Whew! Sometime during the postmidnight madness, Keith pulled a sordid story out of his past that had crippled him for eternity. It seems he was stoned one night and backed his Rolls-Royce right over his personal roadie, killing him stone dead. The coppers tried to indict him for manslaughter, but he got off even though he thought he deserved to burn. He broke down while playing the priest and started to cry, calling himself a murdering fuck. Needless to say, this toppled our improv, and I smoothed his weary, wacky brow while he reeled in masochistic terror. Just as suddenly as he had slithered into this self-loathing, he leaped up—the priest made a mighty return—and proceeded to finish his job on the trembling schoolgirl.

These racy little improvisations went on long past dawn, and as Keith freed himself from my kitty-cat undies and pried his feet out of my leopard-skin spikes, Moon announced her demand for breaktess and I literally crawled across the patio and through the laundry room to make cinnamon toast.

Donnie had called while I was at the Who concert, insisting Gail tell him who, how, where, why, and when. She was evasive for my sake. Mercy happened to be visiting Donnie, and he stuck her on the line and *she* asked where I was. Gail said, "She's at the Who concert, but don't tell Don." Unbeknownst to Gail *or* Mercy, Donnie was on the other line and had heard every damning word.

While I was attempting to sprinkle the right amount of cinnamon on Dweezil's toast, Gail got up, and just as I started to tell her about the insane night I had spent with the Ultimate Maniac, he pranced into the kitchen in high spirits. After tossing the kids around and drinking several cups of tea, he asked Gail could he please take the governess out shopping. As we were making an exit, Gail sailed out onto the porch and announced, "By the way, Donnie called." All during our Tower Records excursion, I wondered what Gail had told Donnie, what Donnie had said to Gail, and if anybody had peeked in my window and seen Mr. Moon wearing my high heels.

I arrived home with twenty albums, worried and tormented. Gail told me she didn't let on to Donnie that I went to the Who party, but as the hours dragged on and he didn't call, I started berating myself for my incorrigible groupie behavior. Something came over me in the presence of rock idols, something vile and despicable, something wondrous and holy. I couldn't control myself. I couldn't help it. Aaaaaaaahhhh!!! Should I see a therapist about it? *Group* therapy?? Oh, no!!! I needed blinkers. I needed to take Donnie to a desert island and peel mangoes for him. I needed major surgery to sever my groupoid artery. I was pacing around in sackcloth and ashes by the time the blasted phone finally rang, and I humbly accepted the articulate torrent from my hot-tempered precommitted almost-boyfriend. He told me he had been listening in when Gail uttered the cursed words "Don't tell Don." I was mortified. He wanted to know why I hadn't invited him, why I hadn't "considered" him. He thought our relationship had been more important than a rock concert, and now he couldn't trust me *anymore*, didn't want to look at my face ANYMORE. Woe was me. How long was *anymore* anyway? Was *anymore* another word for forever? I was feeling "lesser than" again. I performed my chores by rote, and read *Where the Wild Things Are* one more time for two little munchkins who had no idea that their nanny was contemplating joining a nunnery. To my shaking, quaking relief, he showed up that night after I was huddled in my bed and gave me another tongue-lashing, and then we fucked and made up. At least I thought we did. Sometime in the night he crawled out of my bed and went home.

Even though I was a pathetic, remorseful jackass, I was still thrilled and honored to have spent a few moments with Pete Townsend. He was one of The Ones, I believed, who had been sent from On High to more than entertain us mere mortals. "From you I see the glory, from you I get opinions . . . From you I climb the mountains, I get excitement at your feet."

Five long days went by and I didn't hear from Donnie. I was thinking about ending it all when he pulled into the driveway and the breath was yanked from my body long enough to suspend my heart in midair. He buzzed the intercom and announced his divine presence, and I met him on the porch, pretending not to be petrified. Did he have a change of heart? Did he miss me? Did he want to slap me in the face? Did he want to pull my panties off? Please-pleaseplease. What Donnie and I went through that day was what I used to call "heavy changes." When I saw him coming up the stairs, I figured he must really care about me, but when I saw the look in his eyes, I started stuttering. He came right out and asked me if I had slept with anyone else, and I was stunned when he intimated that he had received an intimate infection from me. Being the world's worst liar, I blathered the tear-stained truth, leaving out the part about the kitty-cat underpants and the fact that I had just returned from Dr. Birnbaum's office for "just-in-case" shots (Gail's idea). Donnie flipped. I was trapped like a cheating rat in front of *that face*. While I whimpered he told me I wasn't worth the trouble, the whole thing was bullshit, and I had better find out who I was and why I fucked with people's heads. I stood there with streaming tears, feeling wrung out and ruined, and watched him leave.

December 11 . . . I totally freaked, thinking how I had *truly* blown the best thing in my life, so I was throwing the I Ching when he called and told me to forget the entire day and how we would never sort out our problems by leaving each other. I thought for a few seconds that I might go nutty, dealing with so many emotions in such a short space of time. The I Ching said, "Reunion; two souls separate but return to each other in harmony."

Donnie accepted me back into his arms, but he had the upper hand from that day forward. Neither one of us needed shots either; I think he made it all up to see if I would confess to something. He always did have good intuition.

Mr. Zappa got knocked offstage in London by a crazed guy because his girlfriend adored Frank, and this loon wanted him completely out of the picture. He almost got his wish. Gail got the call at the crack of dawn and was winging her way to England to tend to her broken husband before I could wipe the sleep from my eyes. I bustled Moon and Dweezil off to Hawaii to stay with Gail's mom, and I had a paid vacation. On December 18, three days after his twenty-second birthday, Donnie told me he loved me. I told him I loved him too, and after the big announcement had been made, he started the creative process of molding me to meet his specifications. He was completely cock-of-the-walk sure of himself, and doled out heaping tablespoonfuls of praise, sprinkled liberally with suggestions on how to make me a "better person." I sopped it all up like I did Aunt Edna's gravy, and tried to smooth out all my edges so he would continue to adore me. I wanted to be what he wanted me to be: perfect.

December 28 . . . Well, here it is, 1971 coming to a close. I feel like I've learned more about what's going down in the last two months than all time put together. With the help of my Donnie, I've been figuring it out, seeing how and why it led me to where I am today. Our relationship is so high. I didn't know two people could be so closely related; feeling the same things, seeking the truth and looking for it in the same way. He really makes me look at myself. He says I'm the most aware chick he's ever known, and then he'll show me (helping to make me *see*) the

hang-ups in my way; my main hang-up is that I don't realize I have all the answers within myself. It's incredible.

The Christmas season was full of tidings complete with comfort, joy, and hot sex. Donnie bought me exquisite little trinkets of love, and even spent the day with me at my parents' house. The aunties, nieces, and cousins were smitten with his country-boy charm and down-home good manners. He shot the shit with Uncle Carl, trading information about the complexities of fishing poles, and wowed my mom with gracious praise about her oyster stuffing. He wore the shirt I made him for Christmas, and held my hand during grace. After stuffing our faces full of scalloped potatoes and fresh cranberry sauce, we went back to his house and fucked by the firelight for hours. I gazed in wonder at his Adam in Eden nakedness, his aquiline Elvis nose, and sweet red lips. I cradled him to my bosom, and my love for him transcended space and time.

We kissed the New Year in at John Phillips's house, spinning and reeling on a ton of holiday cheer. I swore to "put down," and felt guilty for "bringing in the new" stoned out of my mind. Donnie agreed, and we made our resolutions while the rest of the party animals carried on, oblivious to the transcendental occurrence in our little corner of the wacked-out world. "Pay Attention. Push away my ego. Get rid of all selfishness. Tame my jealousy. Don't inflict my downtimes on those around me. Don't waste precious time. Continue The Search INTENSELY."

The Zappas came home, and I soon realized my freedom was the number-one priority. I *HAD* to be with Donnie, so I gave the best boss on earth, Gail Z., two weeks nanny notice, and she was kind enough to understand my desire for unceasing endless hours with Mr. Johnson. It was too soon to move in with him, so the few nights we weren't together I crashed around at my girlfriends' pads until the commitment began to take on shape and form.

Donnie got depressed. He needed to work. I felt like he took it out on me. I cried. I wrung my hands and moaned. I felt impotent. I was trapped in a demanding, total love affair, neglecting any creative urge that cropped up in favor of kissing Donnie's perfectly shaped royal ass. I enjoyed it. Despite his lack of acting jobs, we talked constantly about bettering ourselves and the world and how we would accomplish this.

> January 21 . . . Seeking, seeking . . . dispelling of the ego, learning to be unselfish, giving, giving. Donnie shows me parts of myself that have no value; I hide a lot, I fear too much. . . . We have gone through so many traumas, he's so hot-tempered, but the traumas always amount to us learning something about ourselves and each other. We have come up with an idea of incredible proportions: a TV series, young married couple in love, opening a little health-food store in Hollywood. An old health man (Johnny Weissmuller) flips out for us, and helps us to open health-food stores ALL OVER THE WORLD!!!

Chuck had three thousand dollars stolen from him, and all fingers pointed to a little blond vagrant whom Chuck called "Supersonic." The Wizard had an open-door policy on a cosmic level, and all kinds of weird, needy walks of life paraded in and out of his wide-open door, which was painted with a third eye. Supersonic was a spaced-out teenager from Seattle with a would-be Beatle-do, and he seemed needier than most. He found the dough and raced off into the wicked night and bought a little green Triumph. We know this because he drove up in it the next day, wracked with guilt, and handed Chuck two thousand dollars and the keys to the car. Chuck was feeling benevolent; besides, he owed Donnie some dough, so he handed the keys to him. We had instant transportation! He told Supersonic that his penance was to work for me and Donnie, doing anything we asked of him. He bowed and scraped, humbling himself, begging for a task to undertake. We had an instant houseboy! The first thing we asked of Supersonic was to drive us to the movies, and to watch a double-bill of *Zacharia* and *200 Motels* with us. Donnie and I thought this was an interstellar occurrence. Supersonic fell asleep.

I continued my acting, doing scenes in workshops for agents and

casting people to no avail. I did a scene from *Royal Gambit* with
TV's *The Millionaire*, Marvin Miller. He played a big, fat old king
with a booming voice, and I was a very young devotee who adored
him, with a fair to middling English accent. Donnie came to see
it, and gave me pointers afterward, which I humbly lapped up,
panting and thankful. I was in awe of his talent, and desperate for
him to think I could ACT. He was with the William Morris Agency,
and went out on interviews all the time. Each one he didn't get
made him more pissed off, and he would become silent upon his
bed of thorns, switching channels on the TV and eating my cauli-
flower-pineapple surprise without so much as a "yum." I tended to
him quietly, offering bits of praise and back massages to alleviate his
actor's angst. He read for a particularly lame Patty Duke TV movie
and lost the part to someone nobody ever heard of, so I tiptoed
around in the semigloom hoping one of his rowdy boyfriends would
come by with a barrel of pot and get us high. I had to scurry Supersonic out of Donnie's way on these occasions, and get him to run
some silly errand until the storm subsided and that drop-dead grin
reappeared.

Donnie was broke, and even though I had started making more
shirts, I couldn't make a dent in his Hollywood Hills rent. The big
bachelor pad was about to slide out from under us and we had to
find a quick replacement. I was perusing notices posted at Hughes'
market, and one of them seemed to call me by name. A house was
for rent on Franklin Avenue, and the person renting it was named
"Chief Red Cloud." I called him, and as soon as he heard my voice,
he said, "*You* are the *one*. I'm telling all the other applicants to
forget it." He wanted to meet Donnie and me immediately, and
Donnie was intrigued, so we went to the Chief's pad for a cup of
herb tea.

He looked like an Indian all right, complete with two long black
braids, a feathered headband, and a beaded vest. After introducing
us to his eighty-six-year-old silent bewigged mother (who also wore
a Minnehaha halo on her pitch-black wig), he told us his story,
sitting cross-legged amid every kind of tacky Indian knick-knack never
sold outside a reservation. He had gone through a windshield a

mediocre businessman, and had come out the other side a self-realized Indian. Unfortunately, his taste had remained behind. His house was tepee kitsch, covered with paintings of scowling, toothy braves clutching bows and arrows done in Tijuana on black velvet, little plastic Indian dolls in Naugahyde fringe, and twin tepee-shaped lamps with red bulbs inside. He had obviously searched high and low for these genuine artifacts. He tenderly fondled his arrowhead collection, pointing out the ones that he, personally, had carved in previous lifetimes. Donnie was rolling his eyes, trying not to crack up, and I suggested that we look at the house he had for rent. We trudged up Franklin—a curly blond giggling girl-woman in leopard-skin spikes, hanging on to an amazingly handsome hunk wearing a poorly made velvet shirt, who was trying to keep up with a six-foot-five lumbering guy in Man-Tan and dyed braids. What a world. We couldn't afford the house, and for a while we looked around for roommates to share it with, but no one was available. The last time we saw the Chief, he was unhappy because his vision had not come to pass. We apologized like crazy for not being the right people, and he lifted his right hand in a weary, bedraggled "how"-type gesture. In his left hand he held a worn copy of *Bury My Heart at Wounded Knee*.

After some serious struggling, coupled with unflagging determination (and sixteen tons of talent!), Donnie got the lead in a movie. He was going to play Stanley in *The Harrad Experiment*, a tawdry, pretentious piece based on the best-selling novel about co-ed college dorms. His co-stars were James Whitmore and Tippi Hedren, as the crusty but benign pipe-smoking headmaster and his understanding, comely wife. The rest of the co-eds were pretty much unknown. (Most of them remained that way.) Donnie got an advance, and we began to search in earnest for our very own love nest.

February 22 . . . We're looking for this place with nothing being said like, "Oh, look! We're moving IN together!!" He is some-what of a stranger to me tonight, he's put on a different face. I can almost see where it's coming from, and then all of a sudden, he gets melancholy. God, it's so involved. How bizarre to truly entwine yourself with another part of the whole . . . To

be groping around in untraveled space. Donnie certainly does
make me challenge myself, that's what keeps me from flipping
out; it all has to work this way to complete the whole; we are
what each other make us. WO! I can see the UNITY, The I AM!!
He is in a "Hare Krishna, you Motherfucker" mood. But if I look
at it in another way, it's like taking a test, knowing you didn't
finish your homework.

The barrel he had me over was full to the brim. But if I look at
it in another way . . .

While Donnie slaved away under the hot lights in a massive
mansion in Pasadena, tantalizing his demure, doe-eyed co-star, I
scoured Hollywood for an inexpensive cuddle-cave. To my joy and
relief, I found a delightful old furnished single on Las Palmas, half
a block from Sunset Boulevard, and we moved in the next morning.
My daddy loaned us his '62 Cadillac limousine to drag all our
overpacked boxes to the tiny hole in the wall, and Donnie dashed
off to work, leaving me sitting among the stacks of things. I sobbed
with sheer joy. This was the first time I had ever moved in with a
man, and what a man! I had lived with Marty in London, but he
didn't even know I was coming, and I wound up staying way too
long. This was the real thing, a momentous, awesome occasion, and
I accepted it gratefully and silently, not wanting to throw an emotional monkey wrench into the works. When Donnie came home
from the set that evening, I had turned the hovel into a haven, and
after he looked around at my handiwork, he hurled me onto our
new single bed and we had at it. In fact, not one single day went
by when we didn't have at it. I was in continuous orgasmic bliss.
The one scary thing in my way was his humongous bad temper,
which came out of nowhere like a clap of thunder and created dark,
threatening clouds that hung around on our ceiling. I would slide
along the walls and cower while thinking very positive thoughts until
the storm subsided, but I could stand the fighting, just as long as
we could always fuck and make up.

I desperately wanted a part in *The Harrad Experiment*, so Donnie
coached me on the weekend, and I went in to read for the part of

Jeannie, an older girl that Stanley straps on in the backseat of a car on his way to Harrad. I thought I was very well qualified for the part, but I didn't get it because I didn't look old enough. Kind of a mixed blessing.

> **February 28 ... Donnie just took me to the director's house to read for the part of "Jeannie." Alas, I was actually too young, but Donnie says I'm a good actress and all I need is "more colors." Wo! I'm really getting there. I value his creative opinion with my life.**

Donnie's creative opinion reigned supreme on Las Palmas Avenue, and that's the way I wanted it. I got up before the sun every morning and made his breakfast, washed his hair, and ran his lines with him. When he was gone, I sat and thought about him, tidied up the little pad, and planned our precious evening meals. My creativity was spent adoring him, and I started to feel like a weed in the garden of life. The last thing Donnie wanted was Betty Crocker in the kitchen, but since that was what he was getting, he expected picture perfection. I set all his vitamins out in a row on the shelf, I ran his bubble bath and scrubbed his back. Sometimes it wasn't enough, and sometimes it was too much. The happy medium seemed to elude me.

> **March 14 ... After a rather frustrating week of too much domesticity, Don let me have it. Nothing about me pleases him; I'm letting myself go, I'm annoying him. Sometimes I just don't feel domestic, even though I really want to be, and if I forget something or make a little boo-boo, it's hell. He forgets the things I remember and remembers the things I forget.**

And then he would apologize, fork over that delicious smile, kiss me, cuddle me, and compliment my carrot-corn casserole. Serenity regained, I would gaze upon my love object, take ten deep breaths, and thank All That Was Holy for his presence in my luckyluckylucky life. My love object was starting to miss me, so he got me some extra work on *Harrad* so we could be together when he wasn't emoting. I sat around in a human circle, tits exposed, holding hands with the star-studded cast and a bunch of underpaid extras, playing a ludicrous game called "zoom" while the nutty professor observed the proceedings from a scholarly plateau, the lady from *The Birds* behind him, nodding her head and taking mental notes.

Even though Donnie wanted me on the set, I was jealous of everybody. I should have stayed home, cooking the royal repast, peering out the window for his regal return, instead of quizzing every female under forty about her marital/romantic status. If she had a husband or boyfriend, I relaxed. If she didn't, I made sure to spew off about *my* living arrangements with the sex-god star of stage and screen. One afternoon I lost Donnie in the lunch line, and I spent every second that I should have been using to replenish my body wandering through the mansion, opening all the closed doors, petrified I might peek in on an indiscretion. My heart resounded with relief when I spotted Donnie coming around the corner with a little freckle-nosed girl wearing a Hawaiian shirt and a pair of bell-bottom jeans. He waved good-bye to her and saw me standing there, gaping like a besotted bonehead. I laughingly told him I was worried that he had been bedding down his co-star, a voluptuous peep-voiced bleach-out, and he replied, "I've been talking with sweet young Melanie." Hmmmm.

Sweet young Melanie turned out to be Tippi Hedren's beautiful, barely bleeding, budding baby daughter. She was fourteen. I was nine years older than she was, and I always would be. From that day forward, I watched her every minuscule move. She was tagging along with Mommy, but her brand-new tingle was for *my* boyfriend. She was too innocent to pretend otherwise. She giggled when he looked her way, which was far too often for me to stand it, and she took to lingering around me so she could be near him. She told me she was ready to have sex, and I didn't want to hear it. I told her I had been nineteen, and even *that* had been waywayway too early. She wanted to be my friend, she wanted to be *our* friend. I dreaded going to the set, but I thanked God that I could, because I didn't want Donnie to be alone with her. We all ate lunch together, and Donnie was enthralled with her dumb girlish anecdotes. I wanted to be cosmic about it, but I just couldn't; I wished she would catch a cold and have to sit home and watch *Mister Rogers*, I wished she would drop off the face of the earth. Luckily, she went to visit her dad in the Virgin Islands (*virgin* islands?? ouch!), which was far enough away for me to pretend that she might never come back. She promised she would take us to her mom's lion ranch upon her return. I couldn't fucking wait.

When the movie was over I had Donnie all to myself again, and we got up every day determined to churn out something unprecedented. His creativity was surging and we wrote a country song called "I Don't Think That I Can Persevere" and started working on a screenplay with Chuck about a male prostitute on Hollywood Boulevard. On top of stretching our imaginations, we intended to become immortal and bought gallons and gallons of Puro spring water and started Arnold Ehret's mucusless diet, which consisted of raw fruits and vegetables ONLY. We planted wheatgrass in flats, put it through a meat grinder, and had to hold our noses to swallow it. I truly believed we were in on the early stages of reconstructing the planet. Of course, when two bodies merged into one planet, earth elevated a notch.

March 25 ... We went OUT THERE on love, we made love all night and the air was heavy and sweet. Everything was sticky and wet and hot. We were SO HIGH. Heavy Business. Sometimes I love Don so much I can't see straight, things get cloudy and my surroundings become blurry; all that matters is Donnie Wayne Johnson.

We ran into beauteous Beverly at a party Miss Lucy threw for Vito and "the old gang," and I reverted to sloppy-kissy all over her. Donnie got insanely jealous and burned a hole into me before storming out in disgust. Beverly didn't notice because she was a total bombed addict by this time, but I was tortured by his behavior. I went home, hoping he would be there and I could explain my innocent adoration for my ex–teen queen. I waited until three A.M., when the phone rang and he accused me of wanting to cheat on him.

> **April 3 . . . He went nuts 'cause he swore I wasn't being honest with him. We all have our own personal thoughts that we don't tell the world, right? He actually said I was lying. So untrue. Honesty has always been the best policy in my life, and I'm crunched that Donnie would think otherwise. It's really unfair if you ask me.**

The Triumph died, and as we were hitching to a friend's house one night, we got picked up by a famous local DJ, whose name I won't mention because he went on to make a paranoid asshole out of himself. He took us to dinner and got more and more drunk, swigging away at the gin until he was rabid. He pontificated about the world's greatest pot, which just happened to be in his kitchen drawer at home, so we careened through the canyon at breakneck speed, taking the risk of getting squashed against a telephone pole for a piddling toke on a reefer. We sat around in his darkened den, camouflaging the dire need to escape until we killed a few more brain cells stone-cold dead with the cuckoo bird's killer weed. We were delving into the subject of music, and I was in the middle of a delightful Beatle anecdote, when the combination of substances swirling through the DJ's mind must have pulled up eerie memories, because he picked up his precious framed gold Beatle album, personally given to him by Paul McCartney, and cracked it over his own head. Gold-plated Beatle remnants splintered into a billion tinkling fragments, falling all over his shoulders and into the deep pile of his rust-colored rug. Donnie, being a concerned, loving soul, attempted to assuage the disc jockey's grief, but he wasn't having any of it. We were afraid he might damage himself with the little bits of glass he was crawling around on, but he was sobbing and yelled for us to leave. I carefully avoided his time slot on my favorite station until he disappeared from the airwaves forever.

We got a postcard from Melanie (which I momentarily thought about ripping to shreds), squeaking in ball point about how she couldn't wait to get home so she could hang out with us. Donnie acted like it meant nothing to him, and I was thoroughly relieved. Short-lived. Short-lived. Short-lived relief. She called the day she got back; I was home alone, and could have been so rude that she might have crawled back to her arithmetic homework on her perfect, flat teenage belly, forgetting all about my boyfriend. I couldn't do it. It wasn't in me. I was sweet and nice to the innocent infiltrator, and told Donnie, like a dutiful concubine, that the Little Miss had called, and oh, I was *so* looking forward to seeing her again! Her big brother dropped her off the next day, and we went out to lunch and cruised around Hollywood in my dad's limo. She sat in the middle and it was all very chummy.

April 18 . . . The day with Melanie wasn't so bad. My head was out of control, but the situation, in actuality, was cool. He was extremely lovey and affectionate to her, and I felt grandma-ish and klutzy, but that was to be expected. Donnie told me he has no designs on her, and I believe him.

I also believed that for every drop of rain that fell, a flower grew.

Even though I got a job as a cashier at the new hotspot, the Rainbow Bar and Grill, Donnie continued to reprimand me for my incompetence. He said I didn't pay attention to anything and I needed to work on observing, and remembering what I've observed. He said that with my caliber of mind, it made him crazy to see me so unobservant. I reveled in the fact that he thought my caliber of mind was worth reprimanding. He had me in a swirling state of turmoil at all times, trying to mend my magnified flaws. He was absolutely right about most of his "constructive criticism," and I believed he was being selfless for my sake, so I smiled and stood it. A week later I lost my job at the Rainbow, because I was reading an Alice Bailey book when I should have been gazing out into space like a numskull. Donnie was not amused. We had no money, and the rent had been due for three days, my dad's limo kept conking out, and neither one of us was working. All of these horrendous circumstances led to a knock-down drag-out in which we slapped each other in the face with tremendous force. Needless to say, he went first. I stunned myself by slapping him back, and it was orgasmic. He had just told me he had cheated on me when he went to visit a friend in Santa Barbara, and my infantile lovey-dovey illusions trickled down my betrayed, slapped cheeks like burning rain. Me oh my. We fucked like fools after the madness, but paradise was lost.

I did some shots for *Playboy*, but my tits were too small. I read for a couple of movies, but didn't get a call-back. It was dismal. The rent was so overdue that we had to move out, and I was petrified that we would break up.

May 6 . . . We moved O-U-T of the Las Palmas tent. Lots of tears, but a great understanding of the reality that is going down. I have no idea what will happen, but we're still very much in love. Don keeps saying it will be good for us, but who knows? We came dragging my things back to mom's. I don't know how she copes with it all.

Donnie stayed with a friend, and I was back at my parents' house. We kept our relationship afloat against a stormy sea of odds. We went to see my old friend Brandon de Wilde in the play *Butterflies Are Free* in San Diego. I was hoping they would hit it off on an actor-to-actor level. Brandon was brilliant as the blind guy, and we all went out for a drink afterward and had a laugh, promising to get back together after Brandon toured around the States with the play. It was so great to see him again, and I intended to stay in touch with him for all time. I always retained a stunning friendship with most of my *amores*, which made me feel like life was worth living. All the hours of lunacy and love had actually amounted to Something.

I was visiting Donnie in his temporary apartment when the phone rang, and the *infant terrible*, Melanie, was on the line. I listened for a few minutes, and went out on the balcony to clench the railing hard, turning my knuckles white and my face red. It was blatant that they had been in constant communication. In my heart I knew what was going to happen, and I needed to get out of town, because I just couldn't be in the same city with the two of them thinking those thoughts.

My traveling friend Renee came to the rescue, inviting me to drive with her to the wide-open spaces of Wyoming to meditate and eat a lot of home-grown vegetables. I grabbed at the opportunity to escape my obsessive, ulcerous ache for monogamy. I told Donnie my head needed fresh air, and I left the town of Lost Angels to seek some solitude. We stopped off at the Grand Canyon, a truly wondrous wonder of the world, and I tried to convince myself of how grand the real scheme of things was in comparison to my itty-bitty problems with Donnie. I gasped at the splendor of Mother Nature, and cried because Donnie wasn't there to share it with me. I drove for eight hours straight, merging with the highway, and did a lot of "behind the wheel" thinking. I desperately wanted to be able to accept anything that might happen, to be on such a spiritual high that any kind of indiscretion would roll off my back like so much wheatgrass juice. I bitched at myself for conjuring up naked images, and tried to replace them with huge and holy thoughts. I got a ticket for going ninety-four miles an hour. When we finally got to the ranch in Wyoming, I found out I had to sleep in a small bed with a hippie farmer because there was limited room in the inn. I flopped down, trying to avoid the large bony man already under the covers, and found myself staring up at a poster of Donnie in *Zacharia*. It figured.

I sat on a hill every day and attempted to quiet my babbling brain by taking deep breaths, in one nostril and out the other. I became temporarily serene. I ate thick barley-vegetable stew out of cumbersome crockery, learned how to create alfalfa sprouts overnight out of a handful of seeds, and was taught the fine art of making sun tea. I read *Siddhartha* and thought I was ready to face facts. I got on a Greyhound back to L.A., ready to make good on some of my new insights.

May 25 . . . I think too hard, I break everything down into tiny bits, and distort the reality. My concentration level is nil, I cannot escape my body and "go out there" because my mind is all

cluttered up with bullshit. I'm going to create a strainer inside my head to clean out some of the conditioned crud that has piled up there, and that continues to enter every second. I'm obsessed with Donnie, I've gotta work on it. It's a low energy DRAG!

Donnie seemed happy to see me, and didn't seem to notice the newly implanted strainer in my head. The first twenty-four hours were so perfect, I let myself relax and adore him. We had wild, sloppy sex for hours and then went to the movies, where I cuddled into the crick of his arm and watched Liza Minnelli become a legend. I cooked his dinner, employing my newfound vegie knowledge, and he ate every last bite. Life was a cabaret, old chum.

The twenty-fifth hour brought reality skulking down around my shoulders. He went to the Renaisance Pleasure Faire with Melanie and Tippi, and even though I made an immense attempt at being cool, I guess the truth seeped into my voice, and the truth was, I felt like I was gargling with insecticide. He said he couldn't stand the pressure of my jealousy, the look on my face, or the desperation in my voice. I felt like a used up, wrung-out old dishcloth, and "sweet young" Melanie was an unopened, spanking-clean, brand-new sponge, ready to soak up all of Donnie's perfect pearls of sweat and/or wisdom.

June 1 . . . No matter how many stars I wish on, how many eyelashes I blow into the wind, or how many dandelion fluffs I scatter, I feel him slipping away.

It was at the screening of *The Harrad Experiment* that I caught the clandestine look that little Melanie threw across the room at Donnie. She didn't really know how to give a clandestine look yet, and that's how I spotted it. He had probably given her one already, but since he was such a pro, I didn't pick up on it. I knew then and there that something damp had gone on while I was *om*ing in Wyoming. I shuddered so hard that I could feel icicles forming on my vertebrae. I put on my best Sunday School smile, and applauded my boyfriend's brilliance when the lights came on.

The Stones came to town and I went to the show and to the bash afterward. I would have invited Donnie if he hadn't already called that morning to cancel our dinner that night. The tickets came up at the last minute, and I split for the scene a complete mockery of forced high spirits, determined to forget Donnie for at least fifteen fucking minutes. I rocked out, I got wantonly drunk and wicked, and when I saw His Satanic Majesty, he called out across the room, "Miss Pamela, the girl of my dreams," and I'm afraid I made a fool out of myself, once again. I ran through the trendy mass, half out of my skull, knocking him down onto a flock of pillows, where I plunged my hand down his pants and into the crack of his sweet famous ass. That's the last thing I remember.

I woke up in my old bed at the Zappas', and had no idea how I got there. My head felt like it had been screwed onto the neck of some skid-row derelict, and I pitied myself for being a pathetic, groveling pissant in a world full of heroes and heroines. An old friend had seen me crawling around on my hands and knees at the Stones' party, called Gail, and she suggested that this kind soul deposit me in my old bed for safekeeping. I had several cups of tea with the teapot queen and tried to recall what on earth had happened. All I could remember was poking around in Mick's pants.

When I spoke to Donnie that evening, he wanted to know what I had been up to, so I told him about the concert and party. He was irate.

June 16, 1 AM . . . With wine all over my dress, I write . . . All dreaded thoughts have proven to come true. DJ is having quite a romantic involvement with Melanie. He told me about it because he was *so* pissed off about me going to Mick's house without inviting him. He had the nerve to say I was selfish not to call his fucking service and leave the address of the party after he was too busy to see me. I'm supposed to be understanding while he's out informing Miss Innocent about the facts of life, HA! Forgive me, I'm drunk. I just saw "Mary, Queen of Scots," and I think I have problems.

Donnie still wanted to see me while he dated little Melanie, but I wasn't evolved enough to share my boyfriend with this budding baby girl. When he told me that *she* was willing to accept that he would still be seeing *me*, I sobbed, "How swell of her." I couldn't hate her, she was too young and sweet, and hardly existed yet. I couldn't hate him because I loved him. I bowed out ungracefully. I crawled off into the dismal evening with my tail between my thighs, but I knew I was standing up for myself, and it made me feel like staying alive. I just couldn't see myself saying, "Have a good time with Melanie tonight, honey. See you tomorrow."

"There goes my baby with someone new. He sure looks happy, I sure am blue. He was my baby 'til she stepped in. Good-bye to romance that might have been. Bye-bye love. Bye-bye happiness. Hello loneliness. I think I'm gonna die. Bye-bye my love, good-bye."

I wandered around in a blue fog for the first few days, and luckily Led Zeppelin charged into town and I drowned my sorrows in Jimmy's big available bed. He was getting real high by then, and I happily joined him in never-never land. I spent two whole weeks in blotto city, and I was just about ready to whisper some sense into myself when Brandon died. I had gone to Joe Woo's to get Chinese takeout for my parents, and when I came back in with the steaming junk, a weird pall had fallen on the living room, my little mom's face was ashen and stunned. I could tell she was dreading something. I said, "Who died?" ha ha. It had just been announced on the news that Brandon de Wilde had suffered fatal injuries in an automobile accident in Colorado where he had been starring in the play *Butterflies Are Free*. I threw myself on my old twin bed and mourned the joyous life that had been torn from my dear, sweet triple Aries madman. At eleven o'clock they showed his handsome smiling face and told how he had hung on for twenty-four hours even though his back and neck had been broken. It was pouring rain, he didn't see the CAUTION—FREEWAY NARROWS sign, and his van went *under* a flatbed truck, squashing it flat. I found this out when I went to the memorial service at a big, bright Buddhist temple, where all his friends got together and chanted for him to have an easy lift-off from the earthly plane. He had just started chanting and had been off drugs for three months. His timing was awesome. I had never lost a loved one before, and when I remembered all the real important stuff, the stuff that Really Mattered, it helped me start the slow repair process on my ripped-up heart. I found I could stand it after all. Bidding farewell to Donnie wasn't going to kill me. Maybe we could even be friends.

I loved Brandon a lot, and I missed him like crazy. He was so wildly alive, you could hear his heart beating from across the room. His departure left a big fat hole in my world, and I thought about him all the time. Sometimes I even spoke to him, and I could hear his mad laughter out in the big blue sky. The silliest things cracked him up; he always thought it was pretty funny that I forgot my name in the back of his van. I still say hi to him once in a while, and I'm pretty sure he hears me.

Chris Hillman had a new band with Stephen Stills called Manassas, and they were playing the Hollywood Bowl. I called the Bowl and asked for the backstage (you could do things like that then) and Frankie, the Manassas roadie, put Chris on the line. He told me to get my ass over there because he wanted to attack me.

> July 17 . . . Needless to say, I became hysterical and flew down there with wings on my tootsies. Frankie got me a seat down front by saying, "She's with Chris Hillman, he's up there on the stage." I rolled. God knows.

I spent a few days with him, and lived out all my teenage dreams. He and his third wife, Jeannie, weren't getting along. I could hear them arguing on the phone, and I got a nasty thrill of satisfaction. We stayed at the Beverly Hills Hotel, drank champagne, ordered room service, and made love. I looked into those blue eyes and raptured out. When he played me all his new songs, I knew he thought of me as a real person, and I felt blissed out and blessed.

Because I had lived with Donnie, I had grown up a lot since my last encounter with Mr. Hillman, and could finally carry on a decent conversation with him, listen to his problems, and sympathize without foaming and stuttering. I even recounted my tragic tale of woe with Donnie, and he was all ears. When he went back to Colorado, I felt like we were friends. "Fairy tales can come true, it can happen to you . . ."

When Chris left town, I got back on the circuit, went to a lot of parties, and hopped onto a merry-go-round of men. I would have preferred to march down the aisle with someone and forget the endless search for Prince Charming, but the need to be in love was always my first priority. With each man who entered my sphere, I put another notch in the handle of my love gun:

1. I began a fling with my Sassoon hairdresser, Fernando, and we made out in the closet amid rows and rows of bottles of hair spray and conditioner. I did hair shows, walking down the runway with purple streaks, winking at Fernando in a salacious way. He invited me to rendezvous with him in Acapulco, which I did, enjoying many shrimps and lobsters squirted with lime in between lolling around under the baking sun and frolicking with the scissor king in the stone shower.

2. I went to the movies to see *Harold and Maude*, and I *knew*, without any doubt, that I would know the star, Bud Cort, in a very real way. In fact, I got up in the middle of the movie, announced to the audience that I had just seen a future friend, and to the sound of "sssssh" I ran to call my mother so I could tell her I had just seen someone on the screen that would loom large in my legend . . . "Mark my words, Mom." She was used to this kind of outburst and said, "I'm so happy for you, honey."

3. One of my ABSOLUTE heroes toddled into town, with his group, the Kinks, and I would have walked the plank to please this guy. Ray Davies was Mr. Sensitive, Mr. Elegant, Mr. Mystery. He made me swoon with his delicate dimples and gentle gap-toothed smile, and those lyrics! He truly understood the Hollywood addiction: "You can see all the stars as you walk down Hollywood Boulevard,

some that you recognize, some that you've hardly even heard of. People who worked and suffered and struggled for fame, some who succeeded and some who struggled in vain." He got it, he recognized the narcissistic need for recognition, the cloying, gasping, clammy desire for all heads to turn in the I-I-me-me direction. He was a sorrowful, exquisite rock and roll Emmett Kelly, and I wanted to show him how much I appreciated his selfless contribution to rock and roll. He found me enchanting, despite the fact that I was clamoring for attention from idols. To tell you the truth, I think he appreciated me for this very reason, so after a party one night, he invited me to his hotel for a visit. I brought two bottles of cheapo Boone's Farm apple-raspberry wine because I was very nervous about being alone in his divine dapper presence. He sweetly picked my brain and gallantly sipped the $1.29 wine, while I guzzled it to stupefy myself into relaxed nonchalance. After he found out what made my Mickey Mouse watch tick, I sat on his bottom and massaged his thin white shoulders while he told me sad tales of his childhood. We got to third base, but no further because he was a married chap and I was an adoring devotee who passed out before I could break my married-man rule. When I woke up, very embarrassed, dribbling apple-tinted sleep-drip down my chin, he wanted to take a walk down Sunset Boulevard in the middle of the night. We held hands up and down the Strip, discussing plaster-casting, the fall of the GTO's, Rodney Bingenheimer, and Hollywood in general. He made me feel like a celebrity, and his place on my honor roll was fixed for life.

4. I lost my mind for Marlon Brando after a friend of mine had a screening of *One-Eyed Jacks*. I wanted his large talented body pressing on top of my very own. When I told Mom about my newest addiction, she told me *Viva Zapata!* had been on TV the night before. I fell on the floor and screamed. Michele Myer worked at his answering service, so I got his home phone number and started leaving semipornographic/spiritual messages on his answering machine. His very own "I could have been *some*body" voice chimed in my ears every time I called, but no return calls were forthcoming. I didn't give up hope. I got his address from the very same source,

and sent up a dozen partially clad candids of myself with enticing messages written on the back. He didn't write back. Hmmm. Was this man out of town?

5. On September 9 I was twenty-four, and Don Johnson took me out for a birthday dinner and fucked my brains out. Enough time had passed so that my heart didn't shred into useless lumps when he came to the door to fetch me. He was, as usual, a shining vision with a wicked grin and randy hands. I was careful not to latch onto him and covet too much, so we had a hilarious time. He had been living all over the place, but was still very much involved with "sweet young Melanie." When he told me that he and Melanie were getting engaged, I pretended I hadn't heard this scorching bit of info and climbed onto his golden body to come buckets. I knew we could never get back together on any kind of permanent basis, but we stayed intimately chummy for a long time (one night we did it on the bathroom floor at Wolfman Jack's house), and plain old chummy from then on. When time had done its work on my wounds, I went crazy for Melanie. She was genuinely sweet and so in love with Donnie that I warmed right up to her. However, I still felt awkward, intimidated, and short around her. She had grown several inches in a mere few months, and I, of course, had remained the same size. Sigh. If I hadn't been trying real hard to maintain some thread of spirituality about the whole incident, I might have frozen-shouldered both of them. Bravo, bravo for me that I could grimace and bear it.

6. Keith Moon came to Hollywood to castrate a few TV sets by tossing them out of the Beverly Hilton's sliding glass doors. I don't know how he conned that particular hotel into allowing him entry; he probably told them he was the Prince of Bavaria. I stayed there with him for five of the most perverse, bewildering days of my life. To think that he lived his life in this fashion EVERY DAY sends shudders through my tailbone. He came to emcee a huge outdoor rock show for a local radio station, KROQ, starring the Bee Gees and Stevie Wonder. He wasn't satisfied just to announce each act, he wanted to be a different person for each introduction, and I was his assistant. We shared a dressing room with the Bee Gees, and

they watched in transfixed amazement while Keith donned his several outfits, hurling his paraphernalia all over the room as he became each character. He was an old, old man, I became an old, old woman. He was a drunken lion trainer, I was an insecure tightrope walker. We carried on conversations as if we were new people every fifteen minutes. His last character, the sleazy blond hooker, got into an intense argument with my character, the missionary out to save his/her hopelessly damned soul. He was happy being anybody but himself. At night he would wake up ten times, bathed in medicine-smelling sweat, jabbering about running over his roadie and burning for eternity. He couldn't wait to pay for that horrible mistake. We took handfuls of pills, and he drank vodka like he was dying of thirst. There was no way in the world I could have kept up with him, unless I swallowed every capsule he bestowed upon me until the Quaaludes came out. Please, I didn't need downers to conk me out after a full day in his presence, but he would gobble reds and Quaa-ludes to escape himself and still wake up every couple of hours in terror. He would screech and sit bolt upright, switch on the light, gasping for breath, and try to calm his wild racing heart. Sometimes I feigned sleep because I was so totally exhausted, but other times I would hold him and promise eternal life, eternal love, or anything that might induce oblivion. One night he woke up in hysterical laughter and shouted, "Hurtling elephants of a sort!" The next day he bought me a gorgeous stuffed elephant at the airport and kissed me good-bye. He gave me all his costumes from the show, and paid for me to join SAG. I gave the spangly silver dress and blond hooker wig to Mercy. She was thrilled.

9

♥

TAKE MY HAND,
TAKE MY WHOLE LIFE TOO

*M*iss Christine, GTO, the Dr. Suess character of the group, died a tragic death alone in a hotel room in Boston. She spent eleven months in a full body cast to correct her horrendous crookedness, and her proud back had only two measly weeks of perfection before a killing combo of prescription drugs did her in. I was a homeless wonder, hanging out at Chuck's Cosmo Manor, when Mercy slashed her way through the sandlewood and found me in the den, writing to Marlon Brando. "Miss Christine is dead," she somberly announced through her blackened tears. Her mascara had coursed down her cheeks in a splendid design, and I fixated on this while she gave me what little details she had been able to get out of Cynderella. We never found out what really happened, Cynderella being a confirmed and habitual liar; we don't know if she meant to take a lethal leave of absence, or if some big fat chemical accident took place without her ever being aware of it. I just know that I never saw her again. I thank God in all His many forms that I had bumped into Christine at the Whiskey two months earlier, and that she had put her scrawny arms around me and told me she deep down cared about me. It was actually an ancient apology that had been struggling to get out for a few years, and I got all misty-eyed and held her skinny white hand while her large old boyfriend, Albert Grossman, looked absently past us. After her loving little announcement, she said, "You know I'm just a frigid housekeeper at heart."

With one fifth of the GTO's in another dimension, any hidden hopes for a GTO revival were dashed onto deadly rocks. What was I going to do with my life? Could I continue to spend six-day stretches with some pop star who belonged in a loony bin? How long could I daydream about becoming the fourth or fifth Mrs. Hillman? Did I really want to live in Colorado anyway?? How long could I take guitar lessons, hitchhiking to the Valley to get a bargain-basement teacher? How many theaters could I clean in exchange for some half-assed acting lessons that were getting me nowhere? How long could I crash at my pals' pads, cooking my vegetarian specialties, wishing I could serve them to Marlon Brando wearing nothing but an apron?? I was seeking a higher, more devotional way of life, but still wanted to drag my brightly painted toes in the sludge. I vowed to scrub my third-eye area with a scouring pad to get rid of all the layers of gooey negative substances. I started yoga classes. I went on a four-day papaya fast and dropped a foul-tasting peyote button. The universe rolled out in front of me like one of those magic carpets made of flower seeds that cost $9.95 in the *Gardening Made Easy* catalogs my mom gets in the mail. And the big Answer to my big Question was "Stop trying." I floated down from my trip and felt like a lizard shedding old see-through skin.

I stepped out of my fuzzy cocoon and into the light, and had to tell Marlon all about it.

Dear Marlon,
I just realized something, and I wanted to share it with you: TRYING IS NOTHING. You can't say, "Well, I'm going to try to do it." You do it or you don't. If you're not doing it, you're doing something else. Trying is a limbo state of nothingness. My mind is such a clutter. I must just let myself be. Meditation is the emptying of the mind so that one can see clearly. I don't see things the way they really are because they go through a process of distortion first, dodging the crap in my cluttered mind. It's like an obstacle course. I've been telling myself, "Time to take out the garbage, Pamela!"

My journal had turned into an ongoing letter to Marlon Brando. Every few days I would send him a ream or two. When Chris Hillman came to town, I told Marlon how I had waited for seven and a half years to hear him say, "I think you really know who I am." It was a milestone; it made me appreciate myself because he knew that I knew who he was. Oh, brother. It helped me scrape up a kind of sideways self-acceptance, because Mr. Hillman had always epitomized manhood to me. He invited me to Boulder, but I would have had to hover in the background while he fought with his wife and sought solace in some local hotel room with me. Uh-uh. At least I had come far enough not to subject myself to being a plate of steaming leftovers . . . even if the man of my dreams would have been the one holding the knife and fork.

While I made shirts for dough, and studied acting with a motley assortment of out-of-work actors who made a living bleeding innocent fame-seekers by hurling *est*-type "constructive criticism" at them, I also made the rounds. Looking for Mr. Right became a full-time occupation. He eluded me. I wasn't getting any younger. I kept changing the color of my hair, hoping for a little excitement. I begged Marlon Brando to invite me over so I could sponge him down in his Japanese bath.

I realized how desperate for attention and affection I was when good old Led Zep came to town and I flopped around with Jimmy again. The first night was wonderful, even though he had started to imbibe many harmful substances, but the second night he left me stranded in front of the Whiskey like a floundering, faded Jezebel while he sleazed off with a thirteen-year-old nymphet called Lori Lightning. I sat around all night with the rest of the group, getting pissed, and they all agreed that I was too good for that sort of treatment. Oh, well.

The rock and roll girls were getting younger, and I was no good at competing. They hated me because I had been there first, and they called me awful names at Rodney Bingenheimer's English Disco, "old" being the most popular odious declaration of loathing. I let them get to me; they told me I was over the hill, and I looked in the mirror, inspecting my twenty-five-year-old face for early stages of decrepitness. The most hideous of these tartlets was Sable Starr. She thought she invented nipples and pubic hair. At an Elton John party on the lot at Universal, she shouted out to me, "Give it up, you old bag." I flipped her the bird right in front of the newest piano-playing wunderkind. This behavior conflicted with my holy rose-colored thinking, but I believed the GTO's had paved the way for these infant upstarts, and I thought they should show me some kind of respect, or at least recognition for my groundbreaking Strip-walking efforts. Needless to say, they didn't show me jack-shit.

Robert Plant did an interview in *Rolling Stone* that put these puppies in their place: "It's a shame to see these young chicks bungle their lives away in a flurry—to rush to compete with what was in the good old days, the good-time relationships we had with the GTO's . . . when it came to looning they could give us as much of a looning as we could give them."

I moved back into the Zappas', and took care of Moon and Dweezil in exchange for my cozy old pad. Gail was always helping me out with my self-respect, and made me laugh my ass off about being called "old" by a bunch of upstart pip-squeaks. She also convinced me to take the tattered Jo-Rei "focal point" from around my neck.

February 23 ... Great conversation with Gail—love her so—discussing how the "focal point" can be any form of energy release, like Frank's guitar. It makes sense!

We started writing a children's book inspired by her offspring, and attended many Ruben and the Jets rehearsals. Ruben was a hunky hot Chicano with satin-smooth olive skin and coal-colored eyes; the Jets were his back-up group, and Mr. Zappa was producing their first album. Within days Ruben and I were holed up in a four-dollar hotel in downtown L.A. on a squeaky, creaky, saggy old bed, sharing huevos rancheros and jalapeño-flavored kisses.

I pulled "Angel Baby" out of the trunk and sang it onstage at the Whiskey, wearing a black push-up bra, garter belt, and black-seamed stockings. I lived out the Ronettes' fantasy, looking slant-eyed over at Ruben in his black skin-tight slacks. "Oooh-hooo, I love you, Oooh-hooo I do . . ." Alas, the attraction was almost purely physical, even though I made an attempt to hike up my skirt and wade into his intense Chicano heritage. He regaled me with stories about down-trodden swarthy heroes, and what I really wanted to do was pry open his belt buckle. When the relationship came to an end a few weeks later, it was the first time I was able to say *adios* without so much as a trickling tear. I didn't even try to force out a few. It was pretty much undramatic and amiable. Could it be that I was growing up? God forbid.

I put on the same bra and garters and hightailed it to the Troubador, where Waylon Jennings had decided to do something about "all this long ha'r and everthang." He was considerably shaggier, hipper, and hornier than the last time I had seen him. He growled, he squinted, he itched his crotch area while he eyed mine. My partner in crime, Michele Myer, worked next to the Troubador at Conroy's flower shop, and supplied me with several dozen yellow roses which I tossed onto the stage at regular intervals, squirming and wriggling, begging for another audience with his hot-shotness. In between shows I met one of my heroines, Patti Boyd, in the loo. I was numb with respect and went about powdering my nose, wondering if her Beatle husband was in the building. She said, "George and I think *you* are the star of *this* show! Keep it up!" Not only did this answer my silent breathless question, but it made my night. It made my entire month. Glory halleluja, I was breathing the same air as George Harrison once again. I peered through the dim smoke, searching for those ears, but he must have been up in the balcony.

After the show, Waylon introduced me to his friend Willie Nelson and actual real-live Bob Dylan. Willie was gracious as he ogled my outfit, but Bob put out a limp, damp, world-weary fish hand for me to shake, and I said, "I've waited ten years for this?" I was raging drunk and regretted it royally later. I went home a steaming urn of burning funk, and thank heavens Waylon called at three-thirty and sent a cab for me. He told me to wear my garter belt, and I obliged. I had been there half an hour when I saw the little pile of uppers on the nightstand, and he had obviously taken a million of them, because he just couldn't get enough. Halfway through the sweaty ordeal, he said, "You better watch out or I'll shove you through the wall." I wouldn't have put it past him. Before he finally collapsed in a soggy heap, he played me his newest favorite song, "Amanda, light of my life, fate should have made you a gentleman's wife . . ." and kissed me on the forehead. I left him a little note as he snored away, and tiptoed out of the room. Halfway down the stairs, I realized I had left my favorite jacket in his room. Oh, God. I had to wake him up to get it, and he once again made a big attempt at shoving me through the wall. I got home a bedraggled wreck, with the sun beating down on my seamed fishnets, but this incident removed the only one-night stand from my record. I was thrilled and relieved.

Ray Davies came to town, and I escorted him to the Santa Monica Civic where he enthralled his adoring fans, singing solo under the blue light. "Don't step on Bette Davis, 'cause hers is such a lonely life . . ." Then we went back to the hotel where we discussed Rudolph Valentino and John Barrymore. I rubbed his back again, and sent him off to dreamland.

Keith Moon arrived and I escorted him through his eternal internal madness, trying not to let it get under my skin. "Dear Marlon, I've just spent another week with Keith Moon, and I pray daily for his soul. He is so drug-ridden and tormented, but such a sweet guy, and generous to a fault. He has to totally ego out to help himself feel worth something. Poor baby. It's such a circus ride!" He disappeared for twenty minutes one night, and reappeared, breathless and gleeful. "Come, darling, I have something to show you." He pulled me to the sliding glass door and pointed down twelve stories to the bubbling fountain, and I do mean bubbling! He had dumped several boxes of suds into the water, and bubbles frothed out of the fountain and down the street like an *I Love Lucy* sketch. He cracked open another bottle of hundred-year-old cognac, donned his royal-purple floor-length robe, and sat back to enjoy the spectacle.

And then Chris Hillman woke me out of a deep sleep to tell me he would be in town on the twenty-third. Where was it all getting me? I made out with Howard Kaylan in a broom closet after an Alice Cooper show, I had a clandestine few hours rolling around with Donnie under his satin comforter, I spent thirty hours in bed after drinking several bottles of Dom Perignon with Led Zeppelin. Who needed it? I called Marlon and poured out my long-winded heart to his floating voice, begging for immediate entrance into his life. He didn't respond. I wondered why he didn't change his phone number.

I sat in the pool house that had become my home behind the bustling Zappa manor and pondered my fate. I stared holes into the olive-green carpeting, trying to make sense out of my wacky life. After a quarter century on earth, I didn't even have my own apartment, job, or fiancé. I wondered how many children my Beatle-friends had between them. Did they play bridge like Beaver Cleaver's perfect parents, Barbara Billingsley and Hugh Beaumont? Did they attend PTA meetings? Had they driven a Ford lately? I didn't want to return to that kind of normalcy, but I had to do something quick or I might turn out like Wild Man Fischer or Vito and Szou, who were on the lam for inciting lewdness in minors. The values my parents had instilled in me were clambering for acknowledgment; sharp little voices needled my hangover like pointy fingernails. As much as I loved Gail and all the Zs, I needed my own place. I had never lived alone before, and now was the time. I borrowed three hundred dollars from my mom and dad and went on a search for the perfect private retreat. While I was in the office at the Screen Actors Guild, looking on the corkboard for some kind of show-biz part-time job, I spotted a sign for an apartment for rent in Charlie Chaplin's old castle on Hampton Avenue. I said a prayer and went to check it out. After many promises to pay the rent on time, I moved into the most exquisite little fairy-tale pad on the planet. In the courtyard there was a wishing well overgrown with itty-bitty roses, the windows still had the original stained glass from the twenties, and each miniature apartment had its own turret. I sat in front of the window, multicolored light streaming in, and made cowboy shirts, determined to start a new stage in my life, full of satisfaction, success, and maybe even a husband. I wouldn't take any more drugs, and only have an occasional glass of wine with meals. Yessiree.

I tried dating a few of what I considered "normal" people, including the British director Michael Winner, in an attempt to see how the saner half lived. He was veddy proper and hoity-toity, and on our first date he took me to dinner with Burt Lancaster and his ladyfriend. I had been reading palms at the Renaissance Faire, and doing very well, thank you, so I asked Mr. Lancaster if I might read his big giant palm and he obliged. Michael Winner rolled his eyes. I told Burt he was warm and bull-headed and horny. He had been living in sin with the very sweet ladyfriend and he was obviously proud of it. She nodded in agreement that he was indeed warm and bull-headed and (blushing) horny. Michael promptly changed the subject. I also had dinner with Lee J. Cobb and Charles Bronson, but during an outing at Disneyland (he called it "a slice of Middle America"), Michael announced to his kiss-butt male slave and I that he was the only person in the whole park who was wearing a pure-silk shirt. The slave solemnly nodded, and I said, "You're probably right. Ha ha." But after that, I sort of slid away. I made him his dozen shirts (polyester-cotton blend) and split the scene. He hadn't given me a part in his newest Charles Bronson killing spree anyway, even though I had flashed my SAG card at him several times.

I also went out with a certain French actor because he lived at Marlon Brando's house, and drove his big four-wheel drive around Beverly Hills while Marlon basked his burgeoning belly in the Tahiti sun. He took me to movie-star parties where I sipped champagne and wore normal clothes, my legs crossed at the ankles, nodding and smiling. We went to a bash at Roman Polanski's pad once, and I gave him my phone number. He was definitely *not* normal. He called several times and I finally told him he scared the shit out of me. He laughed like a hyena and never called again. I eventually slept with the French actor in Marlon's king-size bed, and when he fell asleep I went through Marlon's drawers and closets, sniffing articles of clothing and rubbing them against my cheek. This relationship didn't blossom either, and I had to say farewell to Marlon's friend. Sigh.

July 10 . . . Saw the actor again and he took me to an art opening full of "the beautiful people," and the image I got was of everyone padded with cotton. I feel as if I'm forcing a relationship. I don't want to fake something with him just so I can meet Marlon. I'm seeing my soul take a turn to the right.

My soul may have taken a turn to the right, but I still wanted to be a famous actress in this particular lifetime. (I believed that I had been a blossoming chorus girl in the thirties, who, aching too long for stardom and unable to bear it anymore, either climbed up on the big *H* on the Hollywood sign and plunged into the lights, or maybe took a fatal overdose after being thwarted by Ramon Novarro or some other lifted-eyebrow personality. I even spotted myself in the chorus line in an old Busby Berkeley book.) I put my pictures in the Academy Directory, sent a zillion résumés to casting people, slogged myself around Hollywood, and finally had a major career breakthrough! I was going to be featured in the Richard Roundtree blockbuster *Slaughter's Big Rip-off*!! My acting career was finally in lift-off position! I reported to work at six A.M. having memorized my four lines, and was lined up in a row with three other girls. We were told to remove our tops, which we did, and then the charming director, who had copious amounts of gold chains swinging almost to his belly button, snatched the piece of paper with my four lines on it and handed it to the girl with the buck teeth and pendulous breasts. My little titties paled in comparison, and I was put out to pasture behind the pool and told to dangle my legs so the water would ripple around and look nice.

I should have quit show business right then and there, but I didn't. I needed some more humiliation, so I read for a part in a brilliant work of art called *The Carhops*. I went to a crumbling mansion in Los Feliz, and after a three-minute reading I had to disrobe and parade around in a field wearing only my high heels, striking beauty-queen poses while some geek filmed the whole process. He called it a screen test. While I was gathering my clothing out of the brambles, scratching bug bites on my ass, trying to appear dignified in a truly undignified situation, the cheap replica of a producer told me I got the part. My reading must have been earth-shattering. I played the part of a naughty, shameless carhop in heat, who taunted the male customers with padded pushed-up cleavage and a mini-mini-mini neon-orange carhop skirt. It played at the World Theater, east of Vine on Hollywood Boulevard, with three other equally degrading disasters. The poster had me leaning on a pickup truck, holding a tray up in the air, shoving my falsies proudly into the pickup driver's leering face. You might be able to find the tempting *Carhops* poster peeling and fading in the window at one of those Hollywood memorabilia shops on Las Palmas or Cherokee. Grab it, it might be collectible by the turn of the twenty-second century.

I was making a shirt for some record producer when the phone shook me from my buttonhole stitch. It was Michele Myer with the news that Gram Parsons had been found dead in Joshua Tree. I felt a dull thud somewhere inside myself and started to bawl. A song that he did on his first solo album came into my head and stayed there all day: "In my hour of darkness . . . In my time of need . . . Oh, Lord, grant me vision . . . Oh, Lord, grant me speed." And I

Mini-mama in platforms

♥

SAM EMERSON

*P*latinum blonde on Alice Cooper's lap, with Rodney Bingenheimer in the background as usual (to my right)

RICHARD CREAMER

RICHARD CREAMER

The night Jimmy Page sleazed off with a giggling pubescent

GOLDMAN

On my high horse with Nudie, the famous rodeo tailor

RICHARD CREAMER   Robert Plant and I at The Riot House. Sigh.

RD CREAMER

Clutching on to Michael
in my corset backstage
at the Whiskey-a-Go-Go

RICHARD CREAMER

My decadent Marquis, Michael Des Barres

Tickling Andy Taylor and making him scream

MICHAEL DES BARRES

Old friends

MICHAEL DES BARRES

Moon and Dweezil Zappa, all grown up

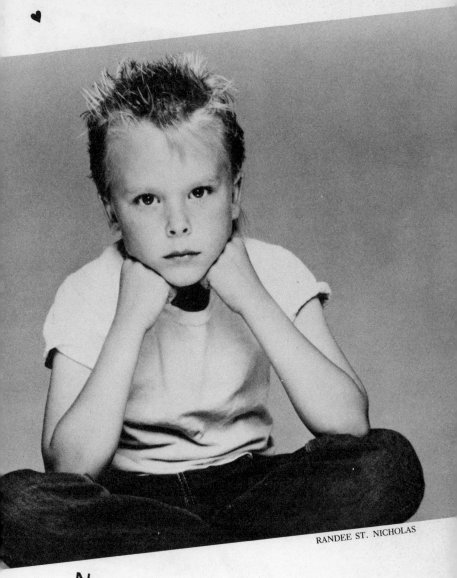

RANDEE ST. NICHOLAS

Nicholas Dean Des Barres—carrying
on the family name

JACKIE SALLOV

Thirteen years later   ♥ ♥

prayed real hard that He did. Even though he had started to sing with a chime-voiced girl, Emmylou Harris, Gram had gotten thick and clumsy, like a puffy old man, way before his time. He wasn't quite twenty-seven when he OD'd in his favorite spot in the desert at the Joshua Tree Inn. I put together the sketchy reports that filtered in during the next few days, and came up with this sad scene: Gram was with a few friends in room 10, getting higher than several kites, when the friends went to get something to eat. During this half hour, Gram supposedly ingested deadly amounts of coke and heroin, and died in the turquoise Naugahyde chair looking out the window at the desert. When the people came back with the pizza or whatever it was, they called an ambulance, but it was way too late.

Gram had always wept easily; he was so fucking sensitive, he could barely stand himself. I'll never forget him cracking up and sobbing while listening to George Jones on the little record player in his bedroom in the Valley, wrapped up in his sky-blue leather jacket, rocking back and forth and saying, "Listen to that pain, man." I listened to Gram's pain every time he sang, and I felt it cut into me like a sliver of sharp ice, making me feel stuff that I didn't know was down in there. The last time I saw him blundering around, he was wearing a spangly cape in the lobby of the Troubador, his beautiful hands dangling at his sides like forgotton flowers. He looked like a shabby, misshapen Keith Richards, but when he saw me, he smiled his sad smile and gave me a big sloppy hug.

In death, Gram became more famous for a few days than at any time in his whole life. His manager, Phil Kauffman, wanted to respect Gram's wish to be cremated, even though his family in Florida wanted the remains sent home for burial, so Phil and a friend removed Gram's body from the Florida-bound train, took the casket out to the desert, and set fire to it. The papers called it a ritual sacrifice and poor old Phil got called a body-snatching grave-robber and then got arrested. The pathetic thing was, the casket hardly smoldered and was sent back to the family anyway. Phil had a tasteless benefit for himself in his own backyard, called it a "wake," and charged ten dollars a head to see Bobby "Boris" Pickett sing "The

Monster Mash" amid a bunch of paper-mache tombstones and crabgrass. He sold Gram Parsons T-shirts and bottles of Gram Pilsner beer. I bought everything, and still use the beer bottle as a candle holder, even though I thought the dingy event was a dismal finale for the world's most underrated country soulman.

I wanted to use some of my spiritual revelations to aid Gram on his way to never-never land, so I had a meeting with the head of the Jo-Rei church to find out how I could expedite his trip. I put my focal point back on, got in my '67 VW (*Carhops* dough) and drove to Joshua Tree, checked into room 10, and settled down to channel the light so that Gram could see it and go in the right direction. I chanted away into the night, sitting in the Naugahyde chair where he drew his last breath, telling him he was on his way to bigger and better things, envisioning him thin and happy with a smile on his face.

> November 3 . . . Dear Marlon, I finally made it to Joshua Tree to help out my old pal, GP. I want to reach him so badly, my sweet Gram, I feel such a link with him. I'm spending the night here in the room he went out in, looking around at the last things he saw, hoping he knows I'm here, adoring him. There's a ceramic horse-head on the lamp here and it has *such* a sweet look on its face.

Contemplating the happy horse head, I fell asleep and had a dream about James Dean. I was in a fifties juke joint, crowded into a big booth with a bunch of fifties-looking teenagers. James Dean and I were the only people in color. He gave me a piercing stare and I slid down in my seat, crawled through the bobby socks and saddle shoes, and squeezed in next to him. He said, "Help me." I figure he picked up on the good vibe I was tossing through the spiritual airwaves and glommed onto it.

I went to see *Last Tango in Paris* by myself. Me and a bottle of Kahlúa. It was better than any of my wet dreams ever were and I massaged my pubic area while Marlon unwrapped the butter. I ached to have it melt in my underpants and puddle under my thighs while he pulled his polyester pants down just far enough so I could feel the crack of his ass. His thin graying hair and slight sexy paunch incited me to a private riot in the theater, and I went home a blubbering basket case to call him and tell him just what I thought. I was raving on into his tapemachine, telling him what I wanted him to do to me, when *that voice* said, "Pamela . . . ?" I was so stunned, I was choked into silence, and then Marlon Brando said, "Pamela, don't hang up." He must have known I would do just that, and I did. I sat staring at the phone, unable to breathe. After a couple of minutes of hyperventilating, I took a long swig of stinging coffee-flavored confidence and redialed the number. He picked up immediately and I launched into a preposterous plea of lust, followed by many flowing drunken reasons why our nonexistent relationship should be consummated. After a lot of haggling, he told me to *look* to *myself* for the *answers.* He said the answers were all there for me, and I didn't need to look for them outside myself. A certain side of him was probably interested in meeting the girl in the nude photos, but the upstanding side came forward. There were actually a few seconds when he considered the proposition. AAAAGGGHHH!!! Instead of taking the butter out of the fridge, he told me heavy anecdotes about instances in his life when he searched for the damned stupid answers somewhere else and found them right there inside himself!!! He said it would be better for me spiritually if we never met. The convincing fight I had been putting up disintegrated, and before he said good-bye, he gently reminded me, "Remember, look to yourself!" I didn't know whether to throw the phone across the room or pick up the Bhagavad-Gita. I cried for two solid hours, and slept for twelve more.

Ooooooh, my eyes were roaming around for somebody to love. The old Paul Anka forty-five played over and over again in the remnants of my teenage jukebox mind:

"I've got everything that you can think of, but all I need is someone to love. Somebody somebody somebody somebody please . . ."

I did have just about everything you could think of, including incredible new spiritual wisdom, my SAG card, a couple of silly acting jobs, and a Polaroid commercial where I got to prance around and wear a chichi showgirl outfit and feathers on my head. Chuck was in the process of writing a film script called *Arizonaslim* for me and one of Donnie's best friends, Sean Walsh, who was an amazing pool hustler, and his nickname was, guess what? "Arizonaslim." I was supposed to play myself, a sweet, adorable groupie on the verge of becoming a sweet, adorable aging groupie who latches onto Sean in an attempt to fall in love. Drug deals, a British rock star, and ego problems get in our way. Meanwhile, I was seriously lonely for romance.

A new pop band popped up under the direction of Kim Fowley, called the Hollywood Stars, and for desperate need of somebody to love, I got a crush on the cutie-pie lead-guitar player and set my snare. Michele Myer agreed to help me throw a spaghetti party at her pad so it wouldn't look like a blatant bear trap. We invited about a dozen people, and cooked up a sloppy pot of red goo and dumped it over plates of rubbery pasta. I flirted with the man of the moment wildly, while I poured tumblers full of Ernest & Julio to the thrown-together groovers. I was just about to make my move when the doorbell rang. Who else was coming? Michele looked up from her plate and said, "Oops, I forgot to tell you. I invited Ron Scott and he's bringing one of his new clients." I was always ready to meet a new client, so I pried myself away from my crush and flung open the door dramatically to reveal a smiling blond publicist and a world-class hunk. The publicist pumped my hand up and down, and Mr. Hunk stood there in his bib overalls creating a perfect dimple in his left cheek. The two of them lingered in the hall, waiting to be invited in, but I felt like I had been struck dumb by a dimpled hammer in skin-tight overalls. Michele appeared behind me and ushered them in, served them spaghetti, and started the small talk before I had even shut the front door. It was one of those deals where no one else existed after he walked in, and the poor guy I had been salivating onto probably had neon question marks bouncing around on top of his head. I wouldn't know because I never took my eyes off Lane

Caudell. He was six feet four in his cowboy boots, and as he made his way to the table, he kept his hands in his pockets and his dreamy hazel eyes on the floor in this perfect "aw shucks" manuever. I saw stars. I saw the rings around Saturn. Ron introduced him to everyone and he mumbled hello in his Southern accent, dimpling up as he did so. I thought, "The only way I'll be able to reach this hunk is to get tipsy," so I proceeded to trample my stunned nerves into Gallo submission so I could appear cool, calm, and collected. The reverse occurred and I was climbing onto his lap within thirty minutes. Since I never looked at anyone else after Lane arrived, I have no idea how my brazen-faced behavior affected the rest of the room. I think I actually started disrobing before the last of the guests had the presence of mind to scuttle out the door.

What resulted was a night of bliss followed by many more until my toes touched back down to planet earth one day and I noticed Lane and I didn't have one single thing in common. It was too late to do anything about this realization because rolling around in the hay with him was magic. His body was a majestic work of art and I was the one caught in the bear snare. He spent Christmas with me and my parents, and since he and Daddy were both from North Carolina, they got along like a hotel on fire. Right in the middle of Christmas dinner Chuck called to tell me I had to leave for New York on December 30 to film the New Year's Eve scene in Times Square. Wow!! It was really going to happen! I wasn't just starring in my own movie, I was going to play Pamela Miller from Reseda, California!! During pumpkin pie, Lane said, "Gee, why don't you come with me to North Carolina on your way?" We left the next morning and I entered a foreign land full of stuffed deer heads, trailer courts, and tap beer.

December 28 . . . Actual bliss and Hell all rolled into one. I wish I could stop feeling so UN. His beauty overwhelms me. I get boiling hot every time I look at him, every time he breathes. December 30 . . . Man, I've been through so many brain changes with Lane in such a short period of time. His smile is enough to flatten you, and so many times instead of saying what I felt,

I held it in. Though a couple of times I've showed him the real me and he pretended not to notice. He pulled a Chris Hillman one night and totally cut me off; silences and aloofness until I nearly blew my brains out. This is the first time I've rolled for somebody who loves red meat, hunting and beating people up. He actually looks for a fight.

He would lean against the sink, eating a balogna sandwich smeared with Miracle Whip on white Wonder bread, and it took my breath away. I went to rowdy bars, said grace with his huge family at suppertime, hung out with his dad in his wood-paneled trailer, and watched with dumbfounded silence while he polished his honey-colored rifle handle. Lane and I walked hand in hand around Ashborough, where all the women knew his name, we visited his pretty mom where she worked in the local drugstore, and I looked up at him with some of the fiercest old-fashioned pride I had ever conjured up. I wore my jeans, tied my hair in pigtails, and blended into his realm, wishing I were one of the locals so Lane and I could run the Laundromat or gas station and never have to go back to the real world. Ha ha. Who was I fooling? This *was* the real world! We held hands in the Ashborough cafeteria, and he took a pink plastic rose out of the nubby white vase and handed it to me with a look of unabashed, wholesome cleanliness mixed with drop-down-dead hot, horny sexiness. After he gathered me up off the linoleum, we went back to his sister's bedroom and stirred up the silent afternoon air, collapsing in a sweaty bundle just as his mom got home from work.

When Lane got drunk, he started in with a little mush (he said his feelin's for me were amazin'), but it was gone the next morning. I wanted to blurt out many words of love, but I held them in check, hidden under the folds of my checkered shirt, buried down under there somewhere with the real me. He was a singer/songwriter searching for a record deal, and he would sing real sweet to me while I held my swoon in abeyance. He was all over the teen magazines already because of his extravagantly gorgeous *face*. When I saw him sing with one of the local bands, I swore the whole world would be swooning real soon.

I took all of my *16* and *Tiger Beat* pictures of Lane to New York and stuck them on the wall of my hotel room at the Beekman Tower. One of them was a life-size poster, which I goo-gooed at while I learned my lines. It was important to have somebody to pine over. I was so overjoyed about starring in a movie, and determined not to be a nervous shambles, but it was really weird having to memorize all my own catchphrases out of context: "Face it, Sean, either I roll for somebody, or I have NO time!" Working with Sean was a bit of a nightmare because he had never acted before. He was playing himself and he had started getting real high. Chuck told him right from the start that pinned eyes were a no-no, but Arizonaslim was irreplaceable.

One late night I was trying to memorize chunks of myself when Chuck called and asked me to meet him up in the bar. When my eyes adjusted to the barblack I saw Chuck in a huddle with my newest, favest rave, Robert De Niro, and my bladder almost burst. When I sat down, Chuck introduced me and kept on attempting to convince Bobby that the part of Sean's sidekick was a coveted one. One of his lines was, "A stiff dick has no brains." I was reeling. Bobby said, "I'm just about to start rehearsals for *Godfather II*, but I might consider the lead." I held my breath. Chuck wanted him to play the sidekick. I was mortified. I said, "It was great meeting you, but I have to go study my lines." I never saw him again. Damn. Double damn.

I brought my new friend, Bud Cort (told you–told you–told you) to meet Chuck, hoping he would offer *him* the lead. Har de har. Chuck wanted the realism that the *real* Arizonaslim would bring to the production. It turned out all Sean could do was play pool, and there weren't any pool-playing scenes.

Poor old Yvonne De Carlo, the B-feature queen, was playing the contessa and had to work with Sean, who was in a grotesque, hapless condition. I'll bet Mrs. Munster never dreamed the day would come when she would have to prop up some glassy-eyed guy who didn't even have a SAG card while some flunkie whispered lines into his ear. Sheesh.

It was a very low-budget movie, financed by a famous New York hairdresser, Paul MacGregor (the executive producer), who was wooed by Chuck Wein (the writer/director) with promises of fame, fortune, and eternal life. He hovered around the set, a suntanned specimen, constantly working on our hairstyles, hoping hysterically for a hit. Keith Moon was supposed to show up to play the pop star, and the day before his big scene we realized he was missing. No one seemed to know what country he was in, and due to set rentals and lack of funds, we couldn't wait for him to be discovered driving one of his cars into one of his pools. We scoured New York for an English rock star who might be able to act.

On January 24, 1974, I flounced onto the set on MacDougal street in the Village wearing my Betsey Johnson hot pants, looking for the pop-star replacement. My scanning eyes ranged over the room, and there he was, curled up on the couch, wearing silver lamé and ragtag leopard, his gnawed fingernails painted lots of different peeling colors, last night's makeup flaking down his angular English cheekbones. His long, matted, blondish hair had been haphazardly sprayed silver and he was wearing girl's white patent flats with ankle straps. When he looked up and caught my entrance, I could see the lurking story in those deep, dark, wacked-out blue eyes—little or no sleep for many moons. He had the classic look of the loony pop star on the road. There was some kind of upper-crust elegance hidden beneath the costume jewelry and kohl, however, and I thought the scene in the elevator would prove to be a memorable one. He hadn't taken his eyes off me, or should I say my hot pants, since I stopped in my tracks a few feet from him, pretending to search intently for Chuck. The co-writer, A.D., and resident tarot-card reader, Geraldine, slinked up beside me and said, "Come meet Michael Des Barres from Silverhead. It's his birthday today. Aquarius with a cancer moon." Okay. Fine. If some little creature had appeared on my shoulder at that moment and told me, "Hey, you're about to meet Prince Charming in the flesh, the guy who is going to be your one and only, your husband, the father of your child!" I would have said to him, "That's a real humdinger, tell me another lulu while

you're at it." Michael, this is Pamela. Pamela, Michael. What are
you doing on this movie, Pamela? I'm the fucking star of this movie,
thank you very fucking much, Michael.

That first day with Michael Des Barres was full of hard work, a
lot of drugs, and some inspired conversation regarding James Dean,
Elvis Presley, and Krishnamurti. We had the same heroes. It helped.
Just as I suspected, he had had little or no sleep the night before,
and together we consumed enough cocaine to wreak internal turmoil.
By the end of the working day, thirteen hours later, one of my co-
stars, who was playing the psychiatrist, had slapped my face real hard
twice (it wasn't in the script) and Chuck had gotten mad at me for
not "going with it." Michael had slammed Sean in the face with a
gooey pie (it wasn't in the script either) and Sean had to be held
back from punching the slack-shouldered 124-pound poncing, pos-
ing pop star. I was scouring people's pockets for Valiums, trying not
to chew my own lips off. A tall handsome guy, Ted Danson, was
playing one of the party-goers, and I had him asking the girls for
downers to no avail. Finally, Michael came to my rescue, producing
two Valiums he had sweet-talked from an extra, and then he disappeared. Hmmm. I was suprised he hadn't asked me to do *something*
with him, but I was also relieved because I had unspent jitters and
was hoping to unwind and get some good sleep. In the taxi on the
way back to the hotel, I thought about this ephemeral tidbit. He had
surprised everyone by being a wonderful actor; we all cheered after
his big speech. He had studied acting for years before deciding to
sing, and had even played the kid wearing sunglasses in *To Sir with
Love*. The persona he created for himself typified the English rock
star to a tee. He was a degenerate drug-taking sex-dog toting two
bottles of Southern Comfort, wearing two dozen silver bracelets on
each arm. The change in his pockets annoyed him, so he threw it
away. He even wore his sunglasses at night.

Silverhead was one of the first glitter bands and were playing to
a packed glittery house in New York, where Chuck decided to film
backstage to show how the aging Miss Pamela hung out in the inner
sanctum. I sat on Michael's lap while the band tuned up and he

yelled "Yeah yeah." I could tell he was impressed with me, and I turned up the heat. Lane Caudell was in North Carolina and Michael Des Barres was rubbing my left thigh right here in New York City. He encouraged me to effervesce and show off, which was something Lane had discouraged in a big way. I never told Lane about the GTO's, but Michael adored our album, and even said that he had had a big crush on me in 1970. He came back to my hotel that night and gave me head for two hours, but couldn't consummate anything because his dick was about to fall off from some unutterable thing he had caught in Japan.

> January 31 . . . I had such a *glorious* time with Michael. He even took me out shopping and bought me things, then we went to Luchow's and had an incredible dinner; violins and romance, gooey eyes and posing. God what fun we had. He makes me want to OPEN UP! He'll be in L.A. when I'm there but will probably bring his "sort of" old lady. He asked me to marry him, even. What's going on? Crazy witty poseur.

He had already been married to his "sort of" old lady for a mere three weeks. Of course I didn't get this little bit of info for quite a little while. Oh well, our shopping spree was a lot of fun. He bought me a bunch of pretty clothes, and when the heel fell off one of his brand-new red-velvet pumps, he threw them in the gutter along with the leftover coins. He bought a bottle of Southern Comfort and told the shocked salesclerk to keep the change. It seemed he had money to burn, but I found out later that he had spent two weeks' per diem that day to show me he was falling in love with me. He went back on the road and I put my pictures of Lane back up on the wall and finished my movie.

Lane sent me a few little notes and called once in a while, but remained noncommittal and aloof, with the occasional "baby" and "sweetheart" tossed in. One night he called up drunk and told me he really missed me and had been doin' a lot of thinkin' 'bout me. I sighed and moaned and wanted his symmetrical rock-hard chest pressing me into the box spring. Michael called me from the road constantly with hilarious anecdotes. He was a well-bred lunatic with an abundant vocabulary who drank like a school of fish; he popped, dropped, and slopped up any and all mind-altering substances without even asking what they were. He didn't take many showers, and his teeth were all chipped from banging them into the microphone, but I found myself wanting to see him again. Maybe he would even be finished taking his Japanese medication by the time we got together.

I was trending it up at Elaine's to celebrate the end of shooting, and I felt someone staring at me from across the room. Being a bit near-sighted, I asked the person to my left about the balding miniman in glasses who was staring in my direction, and she said, "That's Woody Allen! Are you blind or something?" Well, yes, actually. By the end of the evening we had exchanged pleasantries and phone numbers, and the following night I found myself sitting at his dining-room table, eating duck jubilee and spinach salad.

February 7 . . . Had a swell time with Woody last night (full moon in Aquarius). His cook had an exquisite dinner for us. We then shot off to see "The Exorcist," which was full of sensationalist bullshit, but he made it hilarious. He called this morning, rolling, wanting to see me again. Such a brilliant little fella. Yay yay.

When Linda Blair peed on the floor, Woody said, "You can't take kids anywhere" real loud and sunk down in his seat, pulling his fishing hat over his face. When she growled, "Your mother sucks cocks in hell, Karras," Woody yelled, "You raise 'em, you try to bring 'em up right, and look what happens." He took me to the Continental Baths to see Judith Cohen, the girl who played my best friend, Michele Myer, in *Arizonaslim*. When people noticed him, he became even more noticeable by slouching, yanking his hat down over his ears, and turning red. The first bar we went to, the bartender cried out, "Well, if it isn't Woody Allen. Take a bow, Woody." Woody told the bartender to take a bow and we rushed down the street. We sat in the bar at the Beekman and he got me to tell him my whole life story, all the way back to the Rainbow Rockers, and he seemed thrilled, just like in *Annie Hall*. It felt great to be mesmerizing. He sat there in a trance and I felt power way down in my panties. He invited me to Sardi's with Dick Cavett, and when he had to go to the bathroom, he asked me if I saw anyone watching him. He studied every table, making sure all the patrons were involved in their conversations or plates of food before he put his fishing hat on and scuttled through, so conspicuously inconspicuous that all heads turned. Heads always turned when he was around and you could tell he felt like pulling his thin red hair out in frustration.

> **February 9 . . . I really like Woody, he's so cuddleable and kind and sweet. I can't imagine having an argument with him. He says he'll come to L.A. and we'll go to Disneyland, tho' he's so insecure, it'll probably take a lot of coaxing. 82 people came up to him tonight despite his disguise and came up to ask for autographs, and every time it happened, he looked like the world was coming to an end.**

I got back to Hollywood and began a wild roller-coaster ride between the Hyatt House, where Michael Des Barres was staying, and Lane's apartment in North Hollywood. I was so confused! Here was Lane, teetering, on the verge of telling me something romantic, but was I ready to cook pork chops and spend the holidays in Ashborough? Could I give up the identity I had so carefully cultivated in favor of kowtowing to this big, gorgeous country boy, blending into his wallpaper, tiptoeing around his silences, keeping his home fire burning??? OR . . . was I even *slightly* interested in following Michael's group, Silverhead, around the country, sleeping in the same room with Rod "the rook" Davies? Was there any way on earth I would be able to keep this boy clean? Did he even own a single pair of underpants? How do you wash silver lamé anyway? And what about the "old lady" in London? With these weighty questions tumbling around my cluttered mind like Michael's spare change, I knocked on Lane's front door.

We were making out fervently—hearts beating fast, heavy breathing, the whole bit—when the phone shrieked and stopped my trembling hand in mid zip-down. When Lane said, "It's for you," my mind raced out of slobber consciousness and somehow my salivating mouth was able to form the word *hello*. It was Michele, and I was blind with anger because she was interrupting my cataclysmic rendezvous with Mr. Universe. Before I could bawl her out, she told me she was with Michael Des Barres at the Hyatt House and he was threatening to jump seven stories if I wasn't knocking on his hotel-room door within thirty minutes. The nerve of this guy! I told her to tell him to forget about it, and went back to Lane with renewed fervor. When the phone rang again, I begged Lane not to answer it, but once again he handed it to me. I was deaf and dumb with rage. Michael himself was daring to call me at my boyfriend's house!! I couldn't believe it! How was I going to explain any of this to Lane? What kind of balls did Michael have anyway? They must have been the size of cymbals because he insisted I tell Lane to fuck off and rush over to him instantly. He chose this moment to tell me he was titled, his father was a marquis, and I could be a marquise one day if I got tired of being a commoner. After a lot of pleading and haggling, I begged off and sheepishly told Lane that some wigged-out British count had gotten a crush on me in New York, and, hey, it wasn't my fault!

I woke Michael up at two the next afternoon, and after he wiped the glutinous goo out of his eyes and took several mighty swigs on his Southern Comfort, he seemed ecstatic to see me. He had broken his arm falling off the stage, and his cast was sprayed silver to match the sparkly mats in his hair. He staggered around his messy room, stepping over broken glass, poking through the remnants of his luggage for something to wear that was vaguely clean. I gave him a bath, washed his hair, and tried to clean his fingernails before we went down to the coffee shop for something to eat. He wanted apple pie and 7-Up for breakfast, but I convinced him to try an egg. He said all he ever ate for breakfast was apple pie, and pulled the Southern Comfort bottle out of the pocket of his fake leopard coat and dumped the remains into his bubbling soda pop. He took a couple of bites of scrambled egg and ordered apple pie. All the while I wondered, should I tell him now or later about the disadvantages of eating sugar?? I spent the day with Michael and the night with Lane.

> **February 15 . . . I** dropped Michael off at MCA to rehearse and went to see Lane. He was finishing a great song and was in a fabulous mood because he just signed with Snuff Garrett. We went to bed and proceeded to have a very heavy conversation. He wanted to know what I wanted out of *A* relationship, what I wanted out of *our* relationship, very long and drawn out, coming to no conclusions. He still doesn't want to fall in love. He's more mixed up than I am! On the other hand, Michael keeps asking me to marry him and have his baby.
>
> **February 18 . . .** Taking turns with Lane and Michael . . . I must say, Michael is growing on me daily. He totally rolls, and it's been an age since I've been rolled over and appreciated on this heavy level.

Lane wouldn't come near me when I had my period, and Michael turned into Dracula. The difference between Lane and Michael was like night and Des Barres.

After I saw Michael perform, any reservations about sliding into love and romance came to a screeching halt. He came out on stage shirtless and got supersweaty, shiny, and slippery, snapping his suspenders, yanking a little plastic hammer out of his back pocket and bopping the squirming girls over the head with it while they screamed. "I'll bang you, baby, with my heavy, heavy hammer." His voice was ear-splitting and raunchy, and he sang songs about long-legged girls, getting his rock and roll band financed, and being more than your mouth could hold. I got to know him before I saw him at work, and seeing him perform was like steamy, sloppy icing dribbling down the sides of the cake. I couldn't take my hands off him. His waist was smaller than mine, his ears were pierced and mine weren't. I wanted to wear him around my neck like some blatant bauble, and shove him down the throats of the teenage girls who thought I was over the hill. When he came to see me at my mom's house with not one, but two bottles of Southern Comfort clanking around in his pockets, she was kind and polite, but her eyes were darting around like they wanted to rest anywhere but on his blushed and dusted cheekbones. She took me into the kitchen, held my hand gently but firmly, and said, "You're not serious about this one, are you?" Her concerned mom's eyes were pleading with me to be reasonable. She was happy to know I was still pretty confused about the subject of *lasting* love, because he already had a girlfriend and was a resident of England.

> February 25 . . . (George Harrison's birthday) Michael left this morning amidst tears and I love yous. Ah, the drama of it all. Together constantly the last few days, minute to minute rolling. I've spoken to Lane a couple of times. God, do I ever delusion myself. He's a swell guy, but not my type, and I just cannot be myself with him. I'm sure I'll see him again, but I feel a bit of tapering off.

The love bug bit me in the ass and he wasn't about to back off. I didn't see Lane anymore. Michael wangled some money off his bass player's L.A. girlfriend, and I met him in Atlanta for some filthy, upside-down, inside-out baying at the moon. We rented a six-dollar hole at the Kingsmen Motel so we wouldn't have to room with "the rook," and it turned out to be a totally black neighborhood. I loved it; people were singing blues in the street and dancing on all four corners. I ate sweet-potato pie at Henry's Grill while Michael sound-checked, and got stared at as though I were the only white person on the planet. The old guy sitting to my left offered me twenty dollars to eat *him*. I politely refused.

Michael was the first man who let me be me; in fact, he let me *become* me. He adored me more than anybody ever had, and since he adored me first, I got to shine like a pornographic stained-glass window instead of groveling at his feet. The very reason I was un-acceptable in normal-formal circles was the very reason Michael fell in love with me. He loved the idea that Jimmy Page carted me across the country, he was thrilled I had a ticky-tacky titillating past, and I knew I would never have to hide anything from him. I could let my gaudy guard down and hold my head up high. It was a heavenly relief. He gave me scabies and I didn't care, even though my family doctor wagged his head in sorrow that I could have sunk so low. Michael and I rubbed the smelly kill-cream into each other and took the infected sheets to the Laundromat with hysterical glee. I knew I was in love, but there was still one thing that drove me to distraction—the girl back home.

> March 12 . . . I sink into Michael on *all* levels, drown, drool, and COME forever! We stay up for hours all night, every night, fucking and sucking beyond my wildest dreams. I'm getting hot just thinking about it. Sometimes I think I want him with me FOR LIFE, but he's such a street rat; two separate life-styles, but the same point of reference. Madly in love, rolling and foaming, fangs hanging out. I'm jealous to death of the old lady back home, Wendy. Oh well, she saw him first, and that's a fact. We'll see what happens, but I get so damn crazy and I hate to feel jealous.

Since Michael had only finagled a one-way ticket for me, I sold the little velvet number that Mick Jagger had given me to Ben Edmonds, the cute blond editor of *Creem* magazine, so I could get a ticket back home. Ben was going to have a contest so that some obsessive fan could slide into Mick's garment and do some panting and heaving in the middle of the dark and sweaty night. "Now I need it more than ever, let's spend the night together now."

Michael went back to England to dispose of his "girlfriend," and I began the process of telling all my old flings that I was out of commission forever. Keith Moon was the most pissed-off. He sent his personal, Dougal, to pick me up, and I met him at the Record Plant, where he was hanging out with John Lennon (Beatle number three for me). Mr. Moon was in his formal elegant mode, and greeted me with unusual pomp and circumstance, getting on one knee and kissing my hand. He escorted me into the studio, where Harry Nilsson, Ringo, and John were sitting on the floor, listening to some backup vocals. May Pang was a passive silent observer. When the big moment came, and I was introduced to the guy who was more popular than Jesus, Keith very gallantly said, "Pamela, John. John, Pamela." John scowled at me and started a little chant—"Pamela, John. John, Pamela. Pamela, John. John, Pamela"—until the words turned into mush. I guess he met one too many people that day. He was right in the middle of his hideous Kotex phase, so thank goodness I didn't expect too much.

April 3 . . . It's great being around those high energy people, but just hanging around (same old story) won't get me anywhere; tho' it is very high levels. I had some neat talks with Ringo, he's such a regular guy. He kept flipping out, saying, "Where are the new groups to take our place?" I agree. Not much happening in rock and roll except the oldie-moldies. It was a drag to see how zongoed they all got. They kept asking each other why they had to get so high to have fun. Keith and I went through ninety thousand trips about how I can't grease him because of Michael. It's all so sad. He is so in need of a good friend; greasing is secondary, but I can't be around him with limitations, so I guess I shan't see him again. Sigh.

April 19 . . . Mr. Moon finally left town. I heard about his local appearances everywhere, and I felt his pull the whole time he was here.

One by one I told my former *amores* that I was taken, and most of them were happy for me. Waylon wanted to shake the hand of the lucky hoss who won his angel. He kissed me good-bye on the forehead.

I got myself a little dump with the *Arizonaslim* money and a newer VW I called "Piddle" after her license plate, PDL. I bought some forties bamboo furniture, a four-poster bed, and a TV, and sat in my doll house, playing the old waiting game. I waited days and weeks, putting big X's across my calendar just like when Elvis was in the army. England was six-forever-thousand miles away, and sometimes it felt like Michael was a figment of my madhouse imagination. I would lie in my bed at night and try to remember what it felt like to see true love in those dark-blue eyes. I relived the moment when Rodney Bingenheimer announced our engagement over the loudspeaker at his club, Rodney's English Disco, and I was validated in front of the teenies. I had the permanent, quick-drying, waterproof rock and roll seal of approval. Ha ha! We got a hold of some mogul's credit-card number and spoke on the phone for hours, our crackling long-distance voices heating up the wires. I moaned obscenities to him and he came into his sheets on another continent.

Michael conned his record company into one more tour of the U.S. and I met him at the airport, nearly faint with anticipation. I had on my yellow sunsuit and leopard panties to match the new leopard sheets on the four-poster. I couldn't wait to christen it. My throat was constricting and my heart was stammering; being apart so often made us insane with nerves, lust, and tactile neglect. The smell of him made me want to shove his bandmembers Nigel and "Tommo" Thompson into next week, shed every stitch of clothing right there in baggage claims, and rip into him with obscene abandon. I had to hold myself back and I ached all over for at least fifteen minutes. Michael was in town for a mere three days, but after flaunting my fiancé a little bit, I kept him all to myself and tried to set the night on fire. Girl, we couldn't get much higher. I was out of money, and Michael owed his soul to Purple records, so I couldn't follow him into the back doors of rock and roll clubs around the country like I desperately wanted to. I worried about the groupies when he was on the road, but when he went back to England, I could feel my love-sodden heart sinking into my left heel. I couldn't reach him half the time because he was crashing all over London, having moved out of the house he shared with Wendy. He told me they had broken up totally, and she knew all about me. I almost believed him.

May 15 . . . I *will* ease out of my jealousy. I almost wrote "combat" my jealousy, which is double bad-rap. Just thinking about Wendy gives me high blood pressure. What's going on in that section? I haven't spoken to Michael in 5 days. The clue tonight after seeing "Magical Mystery Tour," was "Let it be." *Let things be.* I know Michael and Wendy had/have a heavy trip, and why

should I interfere? They have to clear it up one way or another,
and me being crazy jealous with negative energy could only
have an ill effect.

I was about to find out just how heavy the trip was. Wendy read
about Michael and me in the English rock press, and found a way
to let me know she was the one and only Mrs. Michael Des Barres.
A photographer friend of hers was coming to L.A., and he knew
someone who knew someone who had met a friend of mine a couple
of times. I was writing a stack of mush to Michael when the phone
rang and the girl I didn't know told me I was engaged to a married
man. I was ready to say "I don't believe it," when this bearer of
black tidings came forth with the date, time, and place. "I'm sorry
to be the one who had to tell you this." Yeah, *sure* you are, pal o'
mine. I sat in a stupor with *Father Knows Best* blaring the innocuous
mealy-mouthed fifties into my stunned brain; "Kitten, Princess, Bud
. . . this way!" Michael was unreachable, so I had a couple of days
to ponder all the possibilities before confronting his ass. I knew for
a fact that he loved me. I also knew he wasn't living with Wendy
anymore, because I'd been calling him at different numbers all over
London at all hours of the day and night. I figured he was afraid I
wouldn't marry him if he was already married. Yeah, that made
sense.

July 26 . . . (Mick Jagger's birthday) So, Michael is married. I'm
proud of myself for such a slight wig-out. He's obviously been
fibbing and deleting facts galore, but somehow this has made
me love him and miss him more. I'm still going to kick his ass
hard all over the room for telling me lies, but I was right, he
didn't want me to know because he thought I'd leave him.

He told me they had gotten married right before Silverhead left
for Japan in a last-ditch effort to save the seven-year relationship.
He threw in the important fact that it was Wendy's idea. But of
course. He said they had been together since they were teenagers,
and had grown very far apart. He even admitted to being an irre-
sponsible aristocrat for not giving her the big heave-ho long before

now. He said she was an unhappy, miserable drug puppy and he was guilt-ridden and agonized, but their relationship had turned into a debauched, stormy, drugged-out mess. He could finally admit all this to himself, because the minute he saw me, he knew I was The One. He said the moment he turned his head and saw me standing in the doorway in my short shorts was a slow-motion miracle, and it had been his birthday to top it all off! He told me everything I wanted to hear, and I curled up in the fetal position and slept like a baby, knowing I was cherished and adored beyond my wildest dreams.

After Michael had been gone eleven weeks, he called to tell me he had gotten some ill-gotten gains together and was coming back to me for good. He was leaving his mother country to come live with me and be my boyfriend. I hardly knew how to react. I was used to waiting. I was used to pining. Had I gone through the endless stream of pop stars, rock stars, actors, and salesmen, drummers, dance-hall clowns, Indian chiefs, and lunatic-asylum candidates to reach *this* moment??? With my ear pressed tight to the receiver, listening to words of love being crooned through thousands of miles of telephone wire by a titled, married glam-rock Aquarius with a Cancer moon, the answer was a big, fat, swoony yes!!!

Three days before Michael was supposed to arrive, I got a call from Michele. She told me that Larry Geller was looking for me because (get THIS) *Elvis* was having a few friends over to watch TV and He didn't have a date. Larry was Elvis's hairdresser and spiritual confidant. I guess he was appointed official date-finder on this particular night, so he described me to Elvis and the King said, "Get her over here." MY name was spoken in the presence of Elvis Aaron Presley. Larry wanted to come over and pick me up right away. He wanted to take me up to Elvis's house so I could sit next to Him on His humongous couch and watch His king-size TV.

I said no. I said no because I was in love with Michael Des Barres. I heard myself say no and I knew I was totally in love with Michael Des Barres. I could have sat beside the King, but I wanted to sit on the face of my prince. And he *was* COMING!

He arrived with five dollars in his pocket and his hair dryer in a paper bag. He didn't even bring a toothbrush or a pair of socks, much less a pair of trousers to put on the next day. He left everything behind, including his address book, intending to forget his former life and create a new one with Pamela Miller from Reseda, California.

♥

EPILOGUE

*T*he wedding bells rang for Michael and me four and a half years later. The happy event would have taken place sooner, but it took Michael that long to get a transAtlantic divorce. We had a lovely ceremony in Catherine James's backyard in Laurel Canyon. (She and I made chummy long before this blessed occasion.) Michael showed up at the wedding ten minutes before the appointed hour, wearing a crumpled white tux, bombed out of his mind. He said he had spent the night reminiscing with his bass player. Oh, yeah. A tall, skinny guy who had gotten his minister's diploma in the mail married us, and eleven months later our son, Nicky Dean Des Barres (after *James* Dean, of course), was born after a mere four and a half hours of hard labor. All the yoga I did finally came in handy. I started dribbling baby water at Moon Zappa's birthday party while she was opening her gifts, and Gail had to drive me to Hollywood Presbyterian in her Rolls-Royce. All the way there she chanted, "You're going to have a baby today." She was pregnant with her fourth. After Moon and Dweezil came Ahmet Rodan, and finally, sweet little Diva.

Most of the first year of my relationship with my would-be husband was spent without him. He had been in L.A. less than a month, and we were still getting used to each other, when I landed a part in a soap opera that shot in New York. I was thrilled to be working, but crazed about leaving Michael behind. All the money I made on the show was spent on airplane tickets. It was a really dumb role—a Polish premed student named Amy Kaslo who was in love with her best friend's fiancé. They kept changing my hairdo and my character until I was just reporting plot lines and consoling everybody. John Heard played my bespectacled boyfriend, Michael Nouri played my brother, and Morgan Fairchild was a bad-girl neighbor who kept winding up behind bars. All I cared about was my darling Michael, who was getting a new group together and crashing on his manager's couch in the Hollywood Hills. The aforementioned manager was also a big bad coke dealer, so I chewed my fingernails worrying about the white powder eating away at Michael's membranes. I became obsessed with his addiction, always listening for the telltale sniffle. I wanted to believe him so much when he said he had a bad cold. He always had a bad cold. I couldn't concentrate on my lines, and I worried all the time. My prince was a fucking drug addict. This unsavory fact became the bane of my life. I hadn't taken any drugs for two ages and I swore off chemicals for eternity so that I could be a shining example to my loony lover. I wouldn't even go near an aspirin.

Woody Allen and I had become pen pals, so when I came back to New York we got together. He had his limo driver park two blocks away and he huddled, crouched, and covered up for the little walk to and from my pad. I had learned a lot of stuff from Woody, and I wanted to tell him in person I was engaged to Michael. He wasn't amused. We had dinner and I never saw him again, except in the movies.

Search for Tomorrow and I didn't agree, so after six months I was cut loose and slammed back into Michael's life. I was just in time too, because he was getting used to taking the old solo flight. Dangerous. I got another car and an apartment with soap money, and we started our life together in Hollywood with no holds Des Barred. There was nothing in the way, except for drugs and booze. He formed a new band, Detective, and signed with Jimmy Page's label, Swansong. We saw a lot of Zeppelin, and they were not aging gracefully, except for Robert, who still had his shoulders thrown back. Jimmy wore a Third Reich costume, made the *Heil Hitler!* gesture, and had to be propped up by two flunkies at all times. I saw him take twenty minutes to crawl across the room to get to a black bag full of pills. He kept toppling over, and everyone else in the room pretended not to notice. Or maybe they really didn't notice. Maybe he was doing it for effect, who knows? I saw Robert not too long ago, and he's clean and sober and gorgeous. Bonzo died a drunken horrible death and Jimmy and Charlotte broke up. I hear their daughter, Scarlet, wants to join a convent. I don't know what John Paul Jones is up to. I know all his redheaded daughters are teenagers now.

Detective put a couple of albums out and went on lots of tours. I kept trying to get acting jobs, finally getting a part in *Paradise Alley*, a Sylvester Stallone bomb. I played a hooker and I had a big scene with Armand Assante, which got cut out. It killed me. I also played a hooker in a Jack Lemmon movie. It also got cut out. I died another death, but I took the Nestea plunge and made a lot of dough. I also did lots of plays in cruddy little theaters. Even after Nicky was born, I dragged him to rehearsals and he gurgled through all my big scenes. When I decided to quit acting a couple of years ago, I thought I would feel like an arm or a leg had been hacked off. Instead, all I felt was a glorious relief. I dumped all my pictures and résumés into the garbage and waited for the tears to flow. I couldn't even push them out. Still, whenever I pick up *Hollywood Reporter* I find myself looking at "What's Casting." I still pay my SAG dues—I guess The Dream never dies.

I lost a lot of friends the way I lost Gram and Miss Christine. The last time I saw my beauteous Beverly, she was tumbling down the stairs at the Rainbow, her golden hair flying. Even though she landed with a precious thud, she was feeling no pain. She looked up at me from her cockeyed position on the stairs and whispered, "I love you." She gave herself a fatal injection a couple of weeks later in her gray frog palace on Honey Lane. It wrenched my heart, but I wasn't surprised. Speaking of heroin, my *Granny Takes a Trip* boyfriend, Marty, was found dead of an overdose in his dad's bathroom in Brooklyn not too long ago. I heard rumors the last time I was in London that he had started getting high with his idol, Keith Richards, and *nobody* could have kept up with *him*. Lowell George, the marijuana smoking Mother, wore his big body out and had a drug-induced heart attack. Keith Moon might as well have stuck a lance through his own heart. He didn't think he deserved to be alive, so he died in the same shitty way that Jimi Hendrix, John "Bonzo" Bonham, and Mama Cass did. He mixed too many drugs and booze, passed out, and choked on his own vomit.

For years I worried that my darling Michael would wind up one of these pathetic statistics. He used to say that all great artists got high and died—F. Scott Fitzgerald, John Barrymore, Monty Clift, even James Dean had a self-destructive bent. He said ALL great rock and roll artists got high and I couldn't think of a single example to toss in his face—except Frank Zappa. When the King kicked the bucket, he said, "See what I mean?" I told him all these people were miserable and pointed out that Woody Allen was a genius and he didn't get high. You should have seen the look I got. I tried to make up for the abuse his body was forced to take by loading him up with vitamins and lots of fresh fruit and vegetables. I told him he had a son now and should become a shining example. When I almost ruined *my* health by worrying about *his* health, I kind of closed off and gave up on the idea of cleaning him up. There was nothing I could do. Sometimes he stayed out for three days, and then I didn't speak to him for another three. One morning after I hadn't seen him for a few days I woke up and saw him looking out the window. He looked wasted and resigned. That night, he went to an AA meeting with a friend he used to get high as a kite with, and, miracle of miracles, he hasn't had a drink or any kind of drug since. He goes to drug rehabilitation joints and talks to the kids, and has even formed an organization called RAD (Rock Against Drugs). He has actually become the shining example I dreamed about. He's the best daddy in the world and the funniest guy alive; we still laugh our asses off about the lunacy of life.

Whatever happened to the GTO's? Mercy married the young mulatto guitar player Sugie Otis, the son of Johnny Otis, who is now a frenzied downtown preacher. Johnny had a hit with "Willie and the Hand Jive" when Sugie was a toddler. Mercy and Sugie had a son, Lucky. (She called him Jinx at birth, but decided Lucky was a luckier name. I couldn't have agreed more.) She had a stint as a punkabilly haircutter, calling herself "Ravee Rave-on," but people complained that they couldn't sit under the scissors for eight hours at a time. She and Sugie broke up, and she went through a rough drug-crazed phase. Somehow she and her son survived; in fact, Lucky gets straight A's. She managed a couple of breakdancers for a while, and you could see her on the Santa Monica Pier, her magenta hair shining in the sunlight, passing the big plastic bucket around while Turbo and Puppet gyrated for the astonished onlookers. She and Lucky are living in Lake County now, where she is trying to start a blues society to enlighten the locals. If you ask her where she lives, she'll say, "In a silver aluminum trailer right next to the lake where Johnny Burnett drowned."

The last time I saw Sandra, she was having lunch at Canter's Deli on Fairfax with her carpenter husband and *three* children. After much hugging, she told me they had been saving their money and were finally going to Italy.

I haven't seen Cynderella for years. When she and her husband,

John Cale, broke up, I heard a rumor that she sold his piano and he was irate. I spoke to her mother on the phone when I was trying to find her, and she told me her darling daughter Cindy was living in Las Vegas, looking for a job in "communications." Hmmm. I saw her once, many years ago, hanging on to a rotund old guy in Westwood. We pretended we didn't see each other. Herb Cohen tells me she came into his office a few months ago wearing bib overalls, looking like a clean-cut farmer's daughter. She was always full of surprises.

Sparky married an actor from *Hair* and they had a son, Santo, who goes to the same junior high that we used to go to. Can you believe it? The marriage didn't last too long, and after years of waitressing she decided to become a cartoonist and was an overnight success.

I heard a rumor a few months back that Miss Lucy had gone the way of Miss Christine, and I called her number immediately, expecting the worst. I heaved the old sigh of relief when she answered the phone. When I told her the nasty rumor that she had OD'd, she said, "Good evening, honey!" She has two sons and lives in Reno with her third husband, who is exactly half her age.

I wish I knew what happened to all my boyfriends. As far as I know, all the Rainbow Rockers are still alive. Dino went into the service, but I think the other guys play Top 40 bars in low-rent neighborhoods. I caught a glimpse of Bobby Martine in *Saturday Night Fever*. His hair was back in a pompadour, and he looked reeeeeal coooooool. Victor Haydon dropped out of the world (or into it) and lives among the redwoods with no electricity. The last time I heard from him, I was doing the soap in New York. I got a beautiful letter from him telling me to join the Vedanta Society. I wrote and told him I was into Krishnamurti. His cousin, Captain Beefheart, continues to thrill me. He lives in the desert in his trailer and had an art show in New York. I read about it in *Newsweek*. I'm waiting for him to become a famous painter because I have a painting he did in 1962 called "Rocketship to the Moon." Vito is still up North in Cotati, giving dance lessons to unsuspecting pupils who want to free their bodies and souls. He's got to be seventy-five by now. He and Szou have broken up, and she is working for a lawyer. Unbelievable. I'm sure she's reverted to plain old "Sue." Karl Franzoni is still Captain Fuck, and Rickaewy Applebaum has a group called the Tattooed Vegetables. My old flame Chris Hillman has been married for seven years to a girl named Connie who wanted him almost as long as I did. I really give her credit for hanging in there. They have a cute little redheaded daughter, and live on the beach. He's recording a country album for MCA. We've stayed friends for all these years, and I'm proud to be his pal. Nick St. Nicholas lives somewhere in the Midwest and owns his own record shop. I'm sure he's the hippest resident of Somewhere, U.S.A. He's had a couple of wives since Randy Jo, and has a couple of sons to carry on the grand St. Nicholas name. I heard Noel Redding is straight as a die and residing in Scotland, living a farmy life. (I'm glad he has one to live!) I also heard he's writing a book. I'd like to read it. Howard Kaylan is married yet again, and he and his partner, Mark Volman, are the highest paid session singers on the planet. They sang on Bruce Springsteen's "Hungry Heart," and Howard took me to see Bruce in concert, where I got to stand onstage and receive little pellets of sweat from The Boss. I became senseless. Oooooh, I still have my idols. Howie and I are still friends and share tacos once in a while. Tony Sales has two exquisite children with Taryn Power, and Lane Caudell gave up show biz after playing a caveman in a TV movie and a brief stint on *Days of Our Lives*. He's probably back home, driving the resident females of Ashborough to distraction.

We all know what happened to Don Johnson. After years of pilots, miniseries, and low-budget cult films, he's become mega-mega-mega man. I called him every six months or so through the years, because he was The Man I Loved Most until I met Michael. When I heard he became a father, I was mightily intrigued about the mother. His ex-wife, Melanie, who had married again and finally gotten into her twenties, threw a big bash, and Donnie brought the mother of his child, Patti D'Arbanville. I made every effort to look stunning, to show my ex-love I hadn't let myself get flubbery or wrinkled. The sight of his handsome grinning face turned me into a jellyfish. He had been sober for three weeks, so he and Michael hit it off in a big way. Kind of a soul-brother thing. After Patti realized I was very married and not out to snatch DJ, she and I hit it off in a big way. Kind of a soul-sister thing. To cut down this absurdly long story, we all became best friends and lived happily ever after.

Melanie and I have come a long way. I can't believe she's almost thirty. I never thought I would see the fucking day. She has a little boy, Alexander, and I was at the hospital with her the night he was born. I also cut his first birthday cake, which was shaped like a fire engine. When she and Donnie broke up, as the old fates would have it, I was the one who drove her to her new apartment off Hollywood Boulevard. Any minute now she'll be winning that Oscar I always wanted so bad.

Moon and Dweezil Zappa are tall people now, and I love them so much. Gail continues to offer assistance whenever Nicky gets some weird rash or talks back to me in a particularly hideous fashion. Mr. Zappa is still Mr. Enigmatic, and I still find it difficult to call him Frank.

My big gorgeous daddy died three years ago, leaving a big empty space, but I can still hear him laughing when I fall asleep at night, and guess what? My mom still loves me, and I know she always will. There is nothing more powerful than a mother's love. Now that I'm a mom, I know this for sure. Nicky bumped his head on the third day of school, and a knot the size of a baseball sprang up out of nowhere on his precious little skull. I had to smile reassuringly and pretend I wasn't about to faint dead away, while Michael administered unto him.

All those high ideals I had as a flower child, the Bob Dylan lyrics imprinted on my soul, the freefreefree feeling of spinning in the sunlight at the Human-Be-In, the united oneness sitting cross-legged on the Sunset Strip, the spiritual torture I put myself through in Kentucky, have made me what I am today: one happy chick. Every morning I wake up and say "Yay!"

Two summers ago, Michael was visiting with Donnie on the set of *Long Hot Summer* when he got a call from John Taylor asking him to join the Power Station. Robert Palmer didn't want to tour, and Michael took his place, fulfilling every private-plane fantasy. He did Live Aid and winked intimately into the camera at two billion people. We became chummy with John and Andy Taylor, and there I was, in the middle of the rock and roll whirlwind once again. Andy Taylor has now become "Malibu" Taylor, and one of our best friends. We call him "the rat."

Something truly glorious happened not too long ago. Michael's producer, Bob Rose, called from the recording studio and said, "I'm here with George Harrison, would you guys like to come over and say hello?" I'd be quite prepared for that eventuality, thank you very much. Now, many things had happened to me since that day I turned into a damp spot on the A & M blacktop; I was in my thirties, I had gone through labor pains, I had been married for many years, and I had matured into a fairly sensible woman. I would probably be able to handle a handshake with history. Correct? Yeah, sure. That face! Those ears! That voice! I had to sit down and take several deep breaths while Michael had a musical chat with the man who had called his hairstyle "Arthur." He was so sweet and regular, however, that I soon regained my composure, and when he said, "We've met before, haven't we?" I was able to say yes. Bob Rose told me later that George had admired my legs, and I felt like it had all been worth it.

Our little boy, Nicky, is living a very different kind of life than I did. The phone rings and he calls out, "Daddy, it's Ozzy Osbourne!" In 1956, if the phone rang and Jerry Lee Lewis said, "Hi, Pam, can I speak to O.C.," I would have fainted dead away.

Michael and I have one of the longest running relationships in rock and roll. We're still in love. He still leaves me little mush notes when he goes on the road, and seems very happy to get back home again. I accept the fact that girls want to pull his pants off. I have seen this happen more than once onstage. When I'm around, at least, it doesn't happen *off*stage. (I don't think about what might go on while he's in Milwaukee.) He accepts that I would like to lift a few weights with Bruce Springsteen and dance the night away with Prince. I guess I was just born that way.

I'm dying for some action.
I'm sick of sitting around here, tryin' to write this book.
I need a love reaction.
Come on, baby, give me just one look.

♥

APPENDIX:
LAST WILL AND
TESTAMENT, 1965

I, Pamela Ann Miller, a resident of Reseda, state of California, declare this to be my last will and testament, and revoke all former wills.

First: I direct that my just debts (I owe Linda sixty-eight cents. I owe my mother three dollars for the purse, I owe Knit Togs eleven dollars and fifty-six cents. I owe the public library a dollar fifty-seven) and funeral expenses be paid.

Second: I declare that I am not married, but I am going steady with Robert Jasper Martine, a resident of Farmingdale, Long Island, New York.

Third: I give, devise, and bequeath my rollers, my Beatle albums, scrapbooks, magazines, pictures, cards, my Hollywood Bowl pictures, souvenirs, my pictures of Jesus and the big one in my room, My bible and one third of my clothes to Linda Lee Oaks, a resident of Reseda, California.

I give all my other records (except Rolling Stones) to Iva L. Turner, one third of my clothes, my bras, my bed, and all furniture in my room, my phonograph-radio combination, my jewelry, all books, papers, notebooks, and everything having to do with school, my stuffed animals and my dolls, my hair bows, ribbons and makeup, and for her to tell my boyfriend, Bob, of my death.

I give my Rolling Stones records, one third of my clothes, the possesion of one William Hall, British pen pal, paints, charcoals, art paper and brushes, all information, pamphlets, maps, and booklets on Great Britain, my nylons, my Ten-O-Six lotion, my Phisohex, my shampoos and hair rinses to Linda of Northridge, California.

Above all, I give Robert Martine anything of mine that he wants, plus my never-dying love and my car (a 1959 Chevy Impala convertible).

I give Victor Haydon anything having to do with the Stones, any information on them that I've acquired, plus a lot of love that he never knew about.

I also leave my parents anything of mine they want to keep plus the love and respect they deserve. I appoint as exutrix of my will my mother, Margaret Ruth Miller. In the event she is unable to serve, my father, Oren Coy Miller, shall be appointed as executor. This will and testament is subscribed by me on the twenty-fifth day of May in Reseda, California.

♥

PERMISSIONS

Grateful acknowledgment is made for permission to reprint from the following:
Lyrics and liner notes from the GTO's album *Permanent Damage*, © 1969
Bizarre Productions.

UNCHAINED MELODY by Alex North and Hy Karet
© 1955 FRANK MUSIC CORP. © Renewed 1983 FRANK MUSIC CORP.
International copyright secured. All rights reserved. Used by permission.

THE TIMES THEY ARE A-CHANGIN'
(Bob Dylan)
© 1963 Warner Bros. Inc.
All rights reserved.
Used by permission.

LIGHT MY FIRE
Written and composed by Jim Morrison, Ray Manzarek, John Densmore, and Robby Krieger
© 1967 Doors Music Company

"For What It's Worth" Written by Stephen Stills
Copyright © 1966 Cotillion Music, Inc., Ten East Music & Springalo Toones
Used by permission. All rights reserved.

MR. TAMBOURINE MAN
(Bob Dylan)
© 1964 Warner Bros. Inc.
All rights reserved.
Used by permission.

YOU CAN'T ALWAYS GET WHAT YOU WANT
Written by Mick Jagger and Keith Richards
Copyright © 1969 ABKCO Music Inc.
All rights reserved.
Reprinted by permission.

"Bye, Bye Love" by Boudleaux and Felice Bryant
© 1957 by House of Bryant Publications
Gatlinburg, Tennessee 37738

CELLULOID HEROES
Words and music by R. Davies
Copyright © 1970 by Davray Music Ltd.

DANCING IN THE DARK
© 1984 Bruce Springsteen ASCAP

"The GTOs" by John Burks, Jerry Hopkins, and Paul Nelson, from *Rolling Stone*, No. 27. Copyright © 1969 by Straight Arrow Publishers Inc. All Rights Reserved. Reprinted by Permission.

Glenview Public Library
1930 Glenview Road
Glenview, Illinois